THE
DEVIL
INSIDE

D THE

THE
DARK LEGACY
OF
THE EXORCIST

EVIL INSIDE

CARLOS ACEVEDO

HAMILCAR
PUBLICATIONS
BOSTON

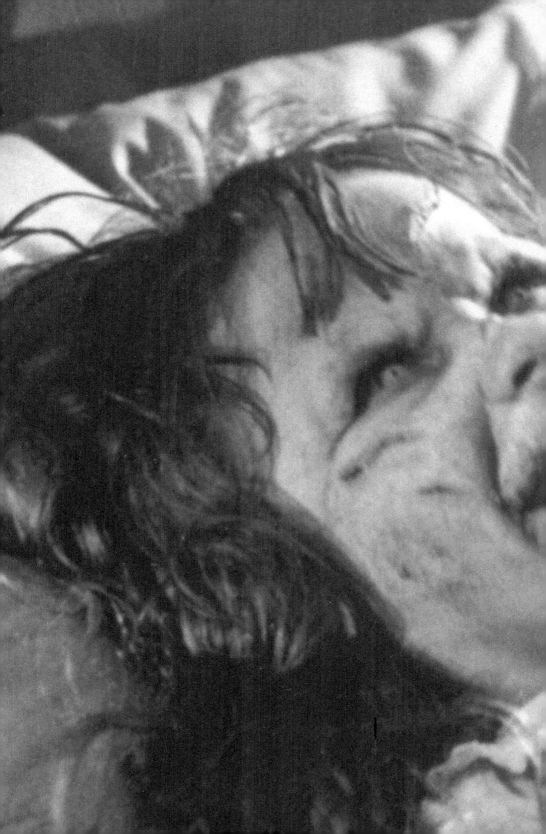

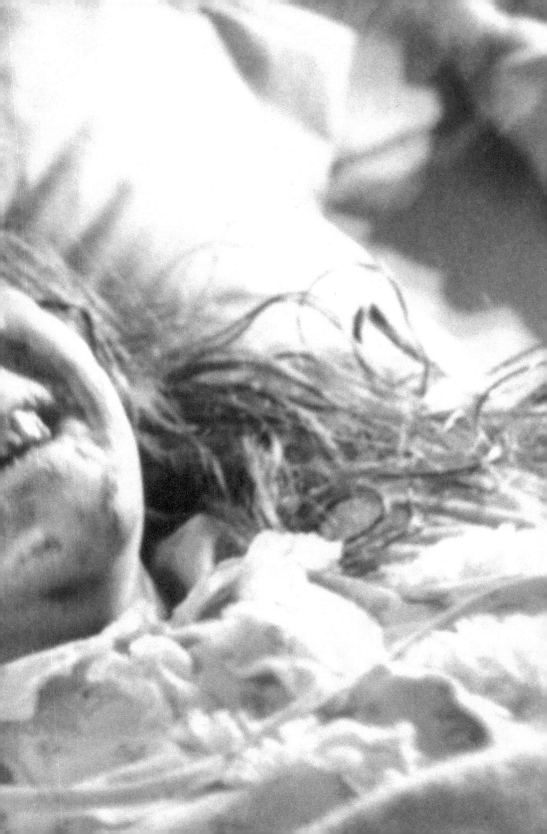

ISBN: 978-1-949590-65-4

hamilcarpubs.com

Aut viam inveniam aut faciam

In memory of Uroš Stojanović

I've always considered movies evil; the day that cinema was invented
was a black day for mankind.

—**Kenneth Anger**

CONTENTS

PART III
"What an excellent day for an exorcism"

PART IV
The Nightmare Continues

INTRODUCTION

In 1957, the gruesome film poster of *The Curse of Frankenstein*, a gory reboot of the Depression-era classic, featured two ominous taglines: "All new and never before dared" and "Try not to faint." Those catchphrases might have better fit *The Exorcist*, one of the most divisive, discordant, and disturbing films ever released.

Over time, *The Exorcist* has taken on a bewitched air, like the Winchester Mansion, or the Bennington Triangle, or the haunted battlefields of Gettysburg. When it opened, on December 26, 1973, *The Exorcist* was not just a hot ticket, it was radioactive. The initial reports of fainting, vomiting, and walkouts only made the film more alluring. Repeat viewings (sometimes from queasy filmgoers hoping to brave it to the end credits on their second attempt) meant that *The Exorcist*, despite an audience limited by its R rating, was on its way to becoming the highest-grossing film of all time.

Based on an overheated best-selling novel written by William Peter Blatty, *The Exorcist* is one of the rare film adaptations that improves on its source material, stripping the narrative of its worst excesses: cornball humor, trite dialogue, sentimentality, melodramatic subplots, and blunt, almost pedantic, messaging. Despite his protests about *The Exorcist* not being "horror," William Friedkin managed to produce an effective genre film, building tension, and adhering to elements that even by 1973 were already formulaic: candlelight in a dark room, jump scares, billowing window curtains, and occult mumbo jumbo. Still, *The Exorcist* is as exact as a machine, like the Harrow in the Kafka short story "In the Penal Colony" or like one of the grotesque torture devices of the Inquisition. The poor victim of *The Exorcist* in 1973 and 1974? It was the brittle spectator, whose endurance—both physical and psychical—withered under an unexpected visual, moral, and sonic assault.

Self-perpetuating hype propelled *The Exorcist* to box-office records and, even more astonishing, to a place in the national conversation, on radio programs, in op-ed pages, on television talk shows, in general-interest magazines—the dominant information platforms in an age when America was still a monoculture. Anton LaVey, founder of the Church of Satan, summed up half of the response to a film that generated nothing short of frenzy. "*The Exorcist* has become America's number-one cocktail party conversation opener," he said. "It's even passing astrology. Soon, comparing possessions will become the main topic of conversation at block parties."

The other half of the response included shock, outrage, revulsion, nightmares, and mental breakdowns. "I am afraid that such a phenomenon as mass hysteria could result, that teenage girls could identify with Linda Blair, the girl who is possessed in the movie," said Father John Nicola, who acted as one of the technical advisors for *The Exorcist*. "Indeed, psychiatrist friends tell me that they already have some cases because of the movie."

Behind the scandal and success of *The Exorcist* is a rich historical, sociological, and cultural context that doubled—or even tripled—its impact. These conditions have been the subject of several essays and books over the years, at times threatening to overshadow the film itself. William Peter Blatty, screenwriter and producer, and William Friedkin, director, practically demanded that *The Exorcist* be treated as sui generis, as something beyond a film, indeed, as a spiritual experience, and the popular press followed their self-regarding lead in lockstep. (*The Exorcist* also spawned books written by publicists who worked on the production, books and articles written by friends and superfans of the filmmakers, books written by access journalists for the express purpose of promoting the film when it was released, and books written, of course, by Blatty.) Not only did stories about a cursed set dominate the newswires, but numberless articles played up the "true story" behind *The Exorcist*: a case of possession that occurred in 1949 and had all the hallmarks of fraud and collective hysteria. (It was *The Exorcist* that made "Based on a true story" a selling point for future genre movies, with its remunerative formula duplicated to remarkable effect a few years later by *The Amityville Horror*.)

Most critical accountings of *The Exorcist* indiscriminately perpetu-ate its myths while at the same time overlooking the film industry and the filmgoing background of its production. In recounting the history of *The Exorcist* from a slightly different perspective—including a revealing look at the original possession case that inspired the novel—*The Devil Inside* aims at contextualizing the film as well as its riotous production and its stunning impact.

The Exorcist is not only rooted in its social moment—the unstable late 1960s and early 1970s—but also in its artistic moment, the specific circum-stances of tumultuous Hollywood, the contemporary state of the horror genre, and the uncertain expectations of the viewing public, exposed for the first time to the extremes of a flourishing permissive age.

The Exorcist also arrived during a new interest in horror films, spurred by *Rosemary's Baby* and, on a far more visceral level, *Night of the Living Dead*. When *Rosemary's Baby* opened in 1968, horror as a genre had lapsed into cheapie drive-in hooey. Even producer-director William Castle, who had made a living manufacturing low-grade chillers (with ludicrous pub-licity gimmicks as marketing bait), thought the genre had seen the end of its run. But *Rosemary's Baby*—which Castle produced—revitalized horror films, leading to pricey studio options on supernatural novels such as *The Mephisto Waltz* by Fred Mustard Stewart and *The Possession of Joel Delaney* by Ramona Stewart, with subsequent adaptations. It was *The Exorcist*, however, with its nightmare bombast, its unholy subject matter, its obscene excesses, and its cinematic verve that changed moviegoing—not just horror films—forever.

More than any other horror film, with the possible exception of *Psycho*, *The Exorcist* remains a cultural touchstone, its longevity partly due to the various myths surrounding it and partly due to its undeniable cine-matic qualities: a relentless pace, an atmosphere of dread, a first-rate cast, state-of-the-art special effects, and an air of taboo. That sense of taboo—graphic scenes involving a thirteen-year-old girl—would have been impos-sible to film just a few years earlier. Which underscores another point about background: *The Exorcist* began shooting at the height of what has come to be known as the New Hollywood.

During the chaotic last days of the studio system, the mid-1960s, when film lost its devoted audience to television and a youth movement that con-sidered Hollywood increasingly square, production heads turned to offbeat newbies (many of them graduates of the Roger Corman school of exploitation) and veteran filmmakers who had acquired reputations as arty washouts and malcontents (i.e., Robert Altman and Arthur Penn). With budgets kept under control, the studios gave some of these filmmakers carte blanche for six or seven years, beginning cautiously with *The Graduate* and *Bonnie and Clyde*, and then, incautiously after *Easy Rider* became a phenomenon in 1969. Only the biggest flops imaginable could fail to recoup a $2 million dollar investment, leading to an adventuresome run of films never seen before in Hollywood and rarely since.

And when Friedkin delivered on the modern studio protocols in 1971—turning the $1.5 million *The French Connection* into a box-office jackpot—he was on his way to becoming one of the New Hollywood rebels. Indeed, Friedkin was a featured scoundrel in *Easy Riders, Raging Bulls*, a 1998 book by Peter Biskind that chronicled the excesses of the New Hollywood and maverick visionaries such as Francis Ford Coppola, Martin Scorsese, Dennis Hopper, Peter Fonda, Roman Polanski, Bob Rafelson, Robert Altman, Arthur Penn, Terence Malick, Hal Ashby, and others. But Friedkin often seems out of place among that rowdy crew. Not only was Friedkin a teetotaler, for example, but his artistic philosophy contrasted violently with those of his peers. In fact, Friedkin openly disavowed the general ethos of the 1970s rebels—personal filmmaking—and his often-boorish admissions of pure commercial ambition sound no loftier now than they did then. "I'm not a thinker," he said in 1972. "I don't take a credit on my pictures, a film by so and so. If it's a film by somebody instead of for somebody, I smell art."

By 1973, when *The Exorcist* opened, Hollywood was still in flux, and films had never been more controversial. In 1971 alone, inflammatory productions such as *The Last Picture Show*, *Carnal Knowledge*, *Dirty Harry*, *A Clockwork Orange*, *Straw Dogs*, and *The Devils* all raised protests of varying degrees. But films had not yet pushed the limit of acceptability, and *The Exorcist* arrived primed to exploit the new moral laissez-faire of the post–Production Code era. Indeed, Friedkin seemed to acknowledge this approach: "It is very important to me to have made a film that is controversial and provocative," he said at the height of *Exorcist*-mania.

Finally, *The Exorcist* is the product of two men—William Peter Blatty and William Friedkin—whose ambitions drove the final, thrilling cut of *The Exorcist* but who also labored to create and control an often-cunning extracurricular narrative aimed to sell the film as both a religious experience and an existential rite.

On the surface, Blatty and Friedkin, from exceedingly divergent backgrounds, seemed to have little in common. As has been repeatedly pointed out, Blatty and Friedkin embodied the Irish proverb, "A man loves his sweetheart the most, his wife the best, but his mother the longest." Surprisingly, an intense adoration of their mother was not their only similarity. Both men had complicated personal lives; they were married eight times between them. They became rich at about the same time: Blatty after selling the film rights to *The Exorcist* in 1971, and Friedkin after scoring his first hit with *The French Connection* a few months later. Both men were raconteurs, each in a different key—Friedkin blunt, off-the-cuff, boorish; Blatty erudite, soft-spoken, euphemious. Whatever story they were telling, however, was sure to border on fabulism. That was another common denominator. Finally, they also shared a street-smart worldview, which might be surprising given that Blatty went from a prep school to Georgetown (BA in English) to an advanced degree from George Washington University (MA in English, his thesis on Shakespeare) while Friedkin graduated from Senn High School on the North Side of Chicago and often spoke of his days as a guttersnipe. But as a boy, Blatty lived a life of poverty-stricken instability and often accompanied his mother as she peddled quince jelly on the unforgiving sidewalks of Depression-era New York.

That wise-guy component highlights their major similarity: Friedkin and Blatty were both born hucksters. Although Friedkin was the far more distinguished of the two, a restless filmmaker with a tyrannical edge, he was obsessed with commercial success and, to that end, made film after film designed specifically with clamor and shock as their key elements. For *The Exorcist*, Friedkin also played the dual role of stage illusionist and carny barker, hyping the supernatural forces assailing the set and accentuating the "real" possession case that inspired the novel.

While Friedkin at least paid lip service to the populist audience he needed for box-office triumphs, Blatty routinely showed his contempt for the unwashed masses (as well as critics, other filmmakers, the Academy of Motion Picture Arts and Sciences, and even religious authorities who disagreed with his sensationalized theological beliefs). "I know how to do it," Blatty once said about his screenwriting method. "I just throw everything at the audience and give them a real thrill. That's what they want. They don't want to go into a theater and treat it like a book. They don't even read books!"

Blatty had a similar attitude about his readership, telling writer Douglas E. Winter: "I'm sure that many of the people who ran out and bought *Legion*, and who had been weaned on the more current crop of so-called horror novels, were probably bitterly disappointed that they had to start thinking on page two—that one of the characters had ideas."

The Exorcist represented a new approach to horror films, one rooted in big-budget shock tactics that would eventually inspire Hollywood to scale-up in the future, leaving the intimate works of Bob Rafelson, Robert Altman, Paul Mazursky, and others in the LA dust. Its reputation for terror, burnished by self-mythology, ballyhoo, disinformation, and the absurdities perpetuated about a curse, has never diminished. In fact, for fifty years, *The Exorcist* has been considered the zenith of horror films, a perennial hair-raiser despite the shifts in trends over the decades. The questions surrounding how and why *The Exorcist* appalled so many people are still debated a half-century later.

"The film has a power to move you and have a disturbing effect on the viewer," William Peter Blatty said, "which is greater than the sum of any of its parts."

And it is with Blatty that the remarkable story of *The Exorcist* begins.

PART
I

IF
THERE
WERE
DEMONS

CHAPTER 1

▲ ▲ ▲

Through the Crucible

Following widespread fame and success in the early 1970s, William Peter Blatty was never shy about admitting his ability to speak to the dead. Nor did he restrain himself from acknowledging that he had contacted spirits through a Ouija board, or that he had participated in the occasional séance, or that he had from time to time captured disembodied voices on a tape recorder. These supernatural exploits—which seemingly put Blatty closer to Spiritualism than to the Catholicism that he claimed was his guiding light—make it clear that *The Exorcist* was the work of a true believer.

Born in the Washington Heights neighborhood of New York City to Lebanese immigrants on January 7, 1928, Blatty had, on the surface at least, a nightmarish childhood that only seemed to make his future achievements resemble some of the miracles he so often invoked when he was older. "I have an intellectual awareness that I was, in fact, unhappy during those times," Blatty told Douglas E. Winter for the book *Faces of Fear*. "And yet, it's almost impossible for me to try to recreate the emotional sense of my misery. I reflect on those times as a blessing. If you can come through any sort of crucible intact, you're going to be steeled—but if you melt, you're sludge, and that's the end of it. I think it was a very beneficial formative period. I was miserable, but I would never undo it if I could. That's the childhood I want to have had."

If his ragtag youth held a nostalgic appeal to him decades later, it was because of the fierce love and appreciation he had for his mother, Mary. "You will love my mother," Blatty begins his memoir *I'll Tell Them I Remember You*. "An immigrant, destitute, suffering, loving, illiterate, defiant, a lion, a giant, she supported five children in New York, on Manhattan, on the heart-squeezing island where the sidewalks leap snarling, in the place where the kiss of the rich is indifference and the sleep of the poor is ice wounds that never knit and the fire-escape flame in August night without end; where they sleep without sleep."

This is the reverential tone Blatty adopts throughout the book, and while many of his reminiscences seem fanciful, his admiration for his mother is as reliable as a compass. His father abandoned the family when he was seven (some sources report a range of choices for how old Blatty was at the time: two, three, six, and eight years old) leaving him and his four brothers and sisters to fend for themselves during the depths of the Great Depression. With their resourceful mother, who sold quince jelly on the streets, the Blatty family managed to avoid living in a shantytown like Hoover Valley in Central Park or Tin City in Riverside Park. Like many impoverished families at that time, the Blattys were always just a step ahead of the landlord, fleeing one apartment after another when the back rent was due. According to Blatty, he had moved at least twenty-eight times growing up. "We never lived at the same address in New York for longer than two or three months at a time. Eviction was the order of the day," he said.

Somehow, Blatty excelled in school, receiving scholarships to Brooklyn Prep and to Georgetown University, and eventually earning a graduate degree from George Washington University. There was no guarantee that Blatty would rise above his background. That had been proven by his older brother, Maurice, who made headlines in 1934 when he was arrested for a series of burglaries as part of an organized B&E gang. When one of the gang members accidentally dropped a copy of the 1929 *Social Register* at a crime scene, Maurice Blatty was doomed: his name and address were scrawled in the flyleaf. (The *Social Register* had been used to target houses of the affluent, and the gang had left their incriminating copy behind in the home of John N. Willys, the automotive pioneer who manufactured Overlands and who had been US Ambassador to Poland as recently as 1932.)

A month after Maurice had been indicted, Mary Blatty appeared on the front page of the Elmira *Star-Gazette*, pleading for mercy on behalf of her son. This photo also hit the wire and materialized in newspapers in Oklahoma, Indiana, and Ohio. Her wit and charm, two attributes William

Peter Blatty always mentioned, were not enough to keep Maurice out of the Elmira Reformatory. Despite writing several autobiographical books, Blatty never mentioned that his brother had been incarcerated, although he did present Maurice as a World War II hero.

Rising above such a grim background—part Dickens, part Edward Dahlberg—was no easy feat, and Blatty credited his mother with his success. Her devout Catholicism (her uncle was a bishop) also instilled in Blatty an overriding belief in God.

After a stint in the Air Force, Blatty worked for the United States Information Agency in Lebanon, an experience that provided material for vignettes he eventually published in the *Saturday Evening Post* and, subsequently, his colorful first book, *Which Way to Mecca, Jack?* released in 1960. He also ghostwrote a book for Dear Abby, the advice columnist.

A year later, an appearance on a game show called *You Bet Your Life* netted him $5,000 and Blatty turned to writing full-time. Wearing sunglasses and pretending to be an Arab prince (a long-standing prank), Blatty showed comedic timing and a neat accent in the opening segment of the show. After announcing his real identity and plugging his book, *Which Way to Mecca, Jack?*, Blatty earned a twisted compliment from the host, Groucho Marx: "Well, if your book is half as shifty as you are, I'm sure it's going to be distributed by the Crook-of-the-Month Club."

Soon Blatty established himself as a journeyman comic novelist, a notch or two below someone like Peter De Vries (and several below Stanley Elkin, Joseph Heller, and Bruce Jay Friedman), and then as a scriptwriter who specialized in modern slapstick. His early screenplays (which included *A Shot in the Dark* and *Promise Her Anything*) seemed to augur a steady career in Hollywood. But as the 1960s advanced, the cultural atmosphere progressively darkened, and Blatty soon found himself out of work. "When I wrote *The Exorcist*," he told Winter, "the primary source of my livelihood— screenplay writing—was comedy. And comedy had dried up. I couldn't get a job, and no one would take me seriously as a writer of non-comedic material."

As early as 1963, Blatty had envisioned a book featuring an exorcism as its dark center. "But the problem was that no one else liked the idea," he recalled in *The Exorcist: From Novel to Film*. "Not my agent (then). Not Doubleday, my publisher (then). Even my dentist thought the notion was rotten. So I dropped the idea."

A few years passed. Blatty, now approaching forty, began thinking about reinventing himself now that comedy was on its way to extinction. To that end, he revisited a story that had captivated him twenty years before as a student at Georgetown: a reported exorcism in Mount Rainier, Maryland.

CHAPTER 2

The Hunkeler Possession

illiam Peter Blatty was a student at Georgetown in 1949 when he read an article in the *Washington Post* about a recent exorcism. Except for its understated style and its final phrase, the lede might have been something out of a future issue of the *National Enquirer*: "In what is perhaps one of the most remarkable experiences of its kind in recent religious history, a fourteen-year-old Mount Rainier boy has been freed by a Catholic priest of possession by the devil, it was reported yesterday."

At the time, an excited Blatty considered the report confirmation of his religious views. "And I thought, Oh, my God. At last, proof of transcendence, or at least the reality of spiritual forces," he told Douglas E. Winter. "I mean intelligent, disincarnated entities—demons, devils, whatever. It seemed a validation of what we were being taught as Catholics, and certainly the validation of our hopes for immortality. Because if there were evil spirits, why not good? Why not life everlasting?"

Blatty researched the case for years, including discussing it with Georgetown University faculty who knew about the strange happenings of 1949. But it would take nearly two decades for him to revisit this story with serious intentions and subsequently turn it into a cultural phenomenon.

On January 15, 1949, a home in Mount Rainier, Maryland, became the site of unexplained phenomenon centered around a fourteen-year-old boy named Ronald Hunkeler. (Over the years, several pseudonyms have been used to describe the participants in this case, and some books have confusingly intermingled these names in their accounts. For clarity, the real names will be used here throughout.) Scratchings, drippings, thumpings, and other aberrations eventually led to Hunkeler undergoing several exorcisms in Washington, DC, and Missouri over the span of a month.

Out of this basic scenario rose enough myths to power *The Exorcist* legend for more than half a century, with Blatty leading the charge in the early 1970s and refusing to acknowledge inconsistency after inconsistency in the story as the decades passed.

With few exceptions, the direct inspiration for *The Exorcist* has been cited with solemn gullibility by film reviewers, cultural critics, feature writers, and, naturally, those who stood to benefit economically from maintaining that what had happened in Maryland, Washington, DC, and Missouri was a clear-cut occurrence of the Devil Inside. But the deceptive elements behind the story have been systematically quelled by the self-interested.

To begin with, what happened in Mount Rainier did not happen in Mount Rainier. In 1998, a writer named Mark Opsasnick discovered that the afflicted teenager who had been freed from evil by Jesuit priests actually lived in Cottage City, Maryland, about a mile-and-a-half from Mount Rainier. The Mount Rainier headline in the *Washington Post* report was disinformation, possibly devised by the clergy to protect the identity of those involved. That would only be the first discrepancy made public about a mysterious event full of contradictions, fabrications, and confabulations.

Although Blatty certainly profited from fictionalizing the Hunkeler incident (he made tens of millions of dollars from *The Exorcist* franchise), he was a man of blind faith and may have had dueling motivations for his deceptions. "From the outset, I was biased by training and religion in favor of belief in genuine possession," Blatty admitted. And like many of the witnesses and participants in the case, Blatty was predisposed to believe in a literal Satan prowling among the earthbound, wreaking havoc and causing torment. And like so many of the others, he had supernatural beliefs that went far beyond traditional Catholic fire and brimstone. It seemed like a source of pride for Blatty to announce his multiple colloquies with the dead, his summoning spirits through Ouija boards and séances, and his ability to discern disembodied voices ever-present in the atmosphere.

According to Blatty, there were only three officially sanctioned exorcisms in US history. A 1928 case that took place in Earling, Iowa, which he dismissed as potentially bogus; an unspecified case that he considered just a rumor because of its lack of documentation; and, finally, there was the Hunkeler case.

Now ready to take his research to the next level, Blatty reached out to various Jesuit contacts and quickly hit pay dirt. After tracking down and exchanging letters with Father William S. Bowdern, one of the priests involved in the Hunkeler exorcisms, Blatty was convinced that he had found an instance of legitimate demonic possession. "I can assure you of one thing: the case in which I was involved was the real thing," Bowdern wrote to him. "I had no doubt about it then and I have no doubts about it now."

Citing a vow of secrecy, Bowdern declined to help Blatty with his book (which, at the time, was a nonfiction project), but he told Blatty about a diary written by another of the exorcists, Father Raymond S. Bishop, that would illuminate, in frightening detail, the events that took place in 1949.

Although Blatty claimed to have read the diary, he ignored its discrepancies and proclaimed it indisputable evidence of what he already believed. Unfortunately, the first entry in the diary is dated March 9, 1949, nearly two months into the Hunkeler ordeal, and most of the alleged manifestations that Father Bishop documented were reported retrospectively by family members of Ronald Hunkeler, sometimes at a distance. Father Bishop not only recorded secondhand testimony as fact, but he also accepted secondhand testimony from the Hunkeler family, who already believed in supernatural forces and who, by March 9, had already held a séance and contacted a medium to rid Ronald of the spirits controlling him.

None of the superstitious, occult backgrounds of the Hunkeler family ever made it into what Blatty wrote about the case. That Blatty accepted the diary at face value—without revealing to the public its shortcomings as a record of the unsubstantiated claims of a superstitious family undergoing distress—reflects his needs to have what occurred be "real."

Is it possible that Blatty truly believed in this possession despite evidence to the contrary? Yes. And are his omissions that much more egregious in hindsight? Yes. Blatty repeatedly publicized his novel and film as being based on the authenticity of the Hunkeler case, effectively tantalizing thrill-seekers and warning sensitive readers that such a perilous fate could conceivably afflict them. To that end, he misrepresented the facts of the Hunkeler case and positioned himself as an authority on its "truth," knowing that the particulars could not stand up to scrutiny.

▲ ▲ ▲

Born on June 1, 1935, Ronald Hunkeler was socially awkward and struggled in school with his peers. A friend of the family elaborated on his difficulties to Dr. Sergio A. Rueda, author of *Diabolical Possession and the Case Behind The Exorcist*: "While we were going to church, the mother told me that the boy was having problems with some of his classmates and a professor at school; also, he was not making good grades and some students were giving him a hard time."

There was also an air of dysfunction permeating the Hunkeler household. His mother was superstitious and demanding, and his father seemed mostly uninvolved. His grandmother, who lived with the family, was religious but not necessarily devout. More significant, Ronald Hunkeler had a favorite aunt who lived in St. Louis and suffered from multiple sclerosis.

Aunt Mathilda, who visited often, was a Spiritualist who taught her nephew that Ouija boards were portals to communicating with the dead and that restless souls could be reached via rappings and séances.

At one point, Mrs. Hunkeler explained that Aunt Mathilda was not only a Spiritualist but also had telekinetic energies. "The family claimed that the aunt of the boy . . . had some secret or psychic ability or power that she could reach porcelain saints on a shelf," recalled Reverend Luther Miles Schulze. "They were too high for her, and she had some way of getting these things down off a high shelf." (A Lutheran minister, Schulze was the first religious figure involved in the Hunkeler incident.)

At the time the Hunkeler house first began its mysterious scratchings and thumpings, on January 15, 1949, Aunt Mathilda was still alive, although seriously ill. In fact, she would die in less than two weeks. There is a possibility that Ronald desperately wanted to see her, and this hypothesis struck Reverend Schulze as the likeliest explanation for what was happening. "The boy had a favorite aunt and I thought initially that he was doing all these things to attract attention, avoid going to school, get the trip to St. Louis, visit his favorite aunt and obtain other multiple benefits," he told Dr. Rueda.

When Aunt Mathilda died on January 26, 1949, Ronald Hunkeler was despondent. In a sign that supernatural and abnormal notions dominated the atmosphere of the Hunkeler residence, a dejected Ronald, not yet fourteen years old, attempted to reach his dead Aunt via Ouija board. After that, the phenomena, which took place only when Ronald was present, began to worsen. His mother believed that a "phantom" was responsible for the disturbances.

Before Mrs. Hunkeler approached anyone for help, she demanded that the phantom—which she addressed as Aunt Mathilda—communicate with her through rappings, just as Spiritualist lore had outlined since the days of The Fox Sisters. Convinced that every gust of wind and every creaking floorboard demonstrated supernatural forces, Mrs. Hunkeler arranged a séance to determine whether or not her suspicions were true: that Aunt Mathilda, from beyond the grave, had a sinister hold on her son Ronald.

A séance, naturally, is a rational response from someone who has yet to consult a medical expert regarding the strange behavior exhibited by their troubled teenage son. According to a diary entry written by Father Bishop, the séance proved successful and the Hunkelers received a message from the dead. "It was from Aunt Mathilda: she was the spirit causing the unexplained phenomenon," wrote Thomas Allen in his book, *Possession*. "It was not the devil."

Alarmed by this development, the Hunkelers reached out to Reverend Schulze, who brought Ronald to his home for observation. There Schulze witnessed a few events that left him both suspicious and perplexed; although he ruled out demonic possession as a holdover from the Dark Ages, he considered the possibility that what Ronald was suffering from had its origins in the paranormal. To allay the Hunkelers, who still believed that the spirit of Aunt Mathilda possessed Ronald, Reverend Schulze organized prayer circles for the family at the local Evangelical Lutheran church.

One of the ironies of the Cottage City case is that an organized religious element emerged only because the Hunkelers refused to consult medical professionals. This is the exact opposite of what William Peter Blatty (and later William Friedkin) would claim and what *The Exorcist* fictionalized. "We had prayers because we thought we needed God to guide the family since they wanted no part of the hospital or doctors," Reverend Schulze said.

When Schulze implored Mrs. Hunkeler to take Ronald to a psychiatrist, she refused. Ruth Schulze, who knew the Hunkelers and took an interest in them while her husband Luther tried to help Ronald, confirmed that the Hunkelers fiercely resisted the possibility of science interfering with whatever was afflicting their son. "In the case, the family would never have the boy go to the doctor or the hospital, and even our own doctor, who wanted to be involved in it," she told Dr. Rueda. "They wanted the doctor to have no part in it."

In fact, according to Ruth Schulze, Mrs. Hunkeler was so far away from any notion of modern healthcare that she inquired about the possibility of arranging a powwow for Ronald. Powwow, or Braucherei, as it is known in the Pennsylvania Dutch dialect, is a folk religion with supernatural elements encompassing clairvoyance, precognition, healing, and the lifting of curses.

Geographically centered in Pennsylvania Dutch Country and the Mid-Atlantic, Braucherei (its American name, Powwow, is derived from the Algonquin word for "medicine man") was at one time fairly common among ancestors of the eighteenth-century German diaspora. And while the methods used during a powwow differ markedly from those of the Roman Ritual (for performing exorcisms), it should be noted that, as a folk culture partly derived from pre-Reformation days, Braucherei has links to Catholicism.

In trying to sell the narrative of a family so frustrated by the limitations of science that they turned to the power of the omnipotent Catholic Church for help, Blatty conveniently omitted the fact that the Hunkelers initially sought supernatural relief. Friedkin, of course, would echo the same rigamarole whenever possible. "They had exhausted all medical, pharmaceutical, and psychiatric treatments available at the time in an attempt to cure him, to no effect," he wrote in his 2013 memoir.

Reverend Schulze was present when the powwow healer arrived. "She was trying to prove to us that she had powers, and performed some magic tricks that I was able to replicate," Schulze told Dr. Rueda. "I remember now that this woman folded a piece of paper, and then it opened up. I did the same thing with a piece of paper, and it would open for anybody. I said, 'Look! I can do the same thing,' and she thought I had stolen some of her thunder." Even so, the powwow healer proceeded with her demon-cleansing ministrations.

Essentially—and this is not just another irony, but an important clue as to the dubiousness of what subsequently transpired—Ronald Hunkeler had already undergone an exorcism before any representatives of the Roman Catholic Church ever arrived on the scene. It was almost certainly this powwow session, along with the prayer circles organized by Reverend Schulze, that gave Ronald the religious framework for his troubles. With a bevy of feverish adults surrounding him, performing an arcane ritual to rid him of a spirit that had possessed him, Hunkeler now knew precisely what afflicted him and how best to conform to this informal but overpowering diagnosis. The idea of possession, advanced by the Hunkeler family, seemingly suggested and reinforced his behavior going forward.

While Blatty mentioned that Reverend Schulze (whom he calls "a Protestant Minister") had witnessed several "manifestations," he conveniently neglected to mention that Schulze did not believe that Ronald was possessed; Schulze thought that what he had seen might have been a case of psychokinesis or, possibly, poltergeists. Because his recommendation to consult psychiatrists was ignored by Mrs. Hunkeler (in favor of a powwow healer), Schulze was a key figure who could bring down the whole house of cards Blatty had constructed. There were no intensive, invasive medical procedures futilely performed on Ronald that drove the Hunkelers to believe that demons or spirits were involved. They already believed that some otherworldly power had possessed Ronald. And Reverend Schulze knew that, leading Blatty to understate his importance. Tellingly, Blatty never spoke to Schulze, who, unlike Father Bowdern, was not bound by vows of secrecy encouraged by an archbishop.

The Hunkelers were not just religious (they were part of a Lutheran congregation and regular churchgoers) but superstitiously religious, believing in Spiritualism and Braucherei. Aunt Mathilda, whom Ronald adored and the Hunkelers believed possessed strange abilities, regularly used a Ouija board and spoke about spirit rapping and contacting the dead. When Ronald began showing signs of serious disturbances, the Hunkelers arranged a séance to determine whether or not Aunt Mathilda was somehow involved from The Great Beyond. Then, because the Hunkelers were averse to medical intervention, Reverend Schulze organized prayer circles, without success. The next step for the Hunkelers? A powwow ritual performed by a healer determined to free Ronald Hunkeler of demonic forces. (Later, even with the Jesuits on the scene, the Hunkelers would hold a second séance, punctuating their fixation on unearthly powers.)

Mrs. Hunkeler finally took Ronald to the family doctor, who found nothing physically wrong with the boy and prescribed a barbiturate for him. Ronald Hunkeler also saw Dr. Mabel Ross, affiliated with the University of Maryland, at a county clinic. According to Dr. Rueda, psychiatrists there concluded that Ronald was normal but "somewhat high-strung."

At this point, the Hunkelers contacted Father Albert E. Hughes of St. James Catholic Parish in Mount Rainier at the suggestion of Reverend Schulze, who had determined that a Catholic priest would be of more use to the family than a skeptical Lutheran. That was when the Jesuits entered the picture. . . . And it was also when myth began overwhelming fact.

Among the many questionable incidents rehashed by Blatty and Co. was the long-unverified story of Ronald slashing a priest during an early exorcism at Georgetown University Hospital. This priest was eventually identified as Father Hughes, who reportedly needed more than one hundred stitches for his wound and withdrew from public view after the attack.

Father Hughes was one of the sketchiest figures involved in the Hunkeler exorcisms. Mark Opsasnick, who had published the first thoroughly investigative account of the Hunkeler case, shed light on Hughes by delving into his itinerary around the time of the supposed slashing when Hughes reportedly became something of a recluse. What Opsasnick revealed is that Hughes appeared at several public gatherings without signs of bodily injury. But Opsasnick reported something even more shocking: "Despite what is written in *Possessed* [by Thomas Allen], there is absolutely no written record of the alleged exorcism attempt by Father Hughes at Georgetown University Hospital."

Although Hughes was a bit player in the Hunkeler saga, his role has been dramatically exaggerated throughout the years. Again and again, the story of Hunkeler slashing a priest with a piece of mattress coil, often cited by Blatty, has been repeated with the certainty of an urban legend. The myth specified that Father Hughes was not only overpowered in his attempt to free Hunkeler of demons, but that he was also a victim of a vicious assault that seemingly proved the destructive power of the devil. Or did it? "Of further significance is that the St. Louis contingency, Father Bowdern and Father Bishop," Opsasnick wrote, "were never informed of the alleged first exorcism attempt, and their diary makes no mention of the event."

That diary is now available online and, indeed, makes no reference to the "first" exorcism performed on Hunkeler by Father Hughes. In fact, the diary makes it clear that Hughes did not perform an exorcism on Hunkeler at all: "Father Hughes was seeking permission from the Bishop for an exorcism about the same time when the [Hunkelers] were going to St. Louis. Consequently, he was unable to proceed with his plan."

Nor does the diary mention Father Hughes ever suffering a serious injury to his arm, which makes sense because if Hughes had never performed a failed exorcism, then he was in no position to be assaulted. Thomas Allen is stymied when Hughes, the only seriously injured participant in the

Hunkeler case, seems completely unaware of the slashing that supposedly left him with more than one hundred stitches and, for a while, a disabled limb. "In his account of the exorcism," Thomas Allen notes drily of a lecture Hughes once gave that mentioned the Hunkeler case, "Hughes does not mention this incident."

But Allen has more passive-aggressive formulations concerning Hughes. When Mr. and Mrs. Hunkeler first met Father Bishop, they mentioned what Hughes had done to help them in Washington, DC—and it did not include reading aloud from the Roman Ritual or sprinkling holy water hither and thither. "For some reason known only to themselves," Allen wrote, "they told Bishop that Hughes had not met Ronald in person. They also said that they understood that Hughes had taken steps toward performing an exorcism but had not done so."

By March, the Hunkelers were staying with relatives in a St. Louis suburb. Hunkeler wound up in Missouri by the request of the devil, who had burned the words "St. Louis" on his skin. In what seemed like something out of a future *Saturday Night Live* skit, the words NO SCHOOL apparently materialized as well.

These "dermal brandings" were also inconclusive. In a letter to parapsychologist J. B. Rhine, Reverend Schulze described what he saw when presented with the markings. "My physician and I saw no words," he wrote, "but we did see nerve reaction rashes which had the appearance of scratches."

Dr. Rueda also pointed out what few of the gullible or fanatical would ever admit: "Concerning the marks, it is important to note that most of the time they appeared when he was out of the sight of his family—moreover, in a place where sharp objects were kept."

On March 9, 1949, Father Raymond J. Bishop arrived and began keeping his diary, which also functioned as an official record for the Catholic Church. Two days later, Father Bowdern joined Bishop.

Even with the Jesuits on the scene in Missouri, the Hunkelers insisted on a decidedly non-Christian strategy to help Ronald. Somehow, they concluded that Aunt Mathilda was using Ronald as a conduit for an important message: She had hidden a large sum of money somewhere and hoped the Hunkelers would find it. With that in mind, the Hunkelers arranged a second séance in Missouri sometime between March 11 and March 16 in hopes of communicating with Aunt Mathilda and solving the riddle of the concealed money. The results of that séance have never been reported (although Father Bishop documented its occurrence in his diary), adding a buried-treasure angle to the list of oddities and loose ends.

On March 16, Father Bowdern, convinced after only a handful of days that he was in the presence of demonic evil, requested approval for an exorcism from Most Reverend Archbishop Joseph E. Ritter, of the Archdiocese of St. Louis. Although the Catholic Church has strict procedures and requirements before agreeing to an exorcism, it ignored them and assented to the ritual. "Evidently, the archbishop was aware that the case did not meet the standards established by the Roman Ritual for cases of demonic possession, except what had been reported to him verbally by Father William Bowdern," Dr. Rueda wrote. "Moreover, no medical, psychological or psychiatric evaluation had been presented to him, as the guidelines of the Vatican require for cases of demonic possession. Nevertheless, although the boy did not exhibit the conventional signs indicative of possession mentioned in the Ritual, Archbishop Ritter still granted the permission to Father Bowdern to proceed with an exorcism."

Even more perplexing, neither Bowdern nor his newly appointed partner Father Walter H. Halloran had any experience with exorcisms. They had been consulting Catholic manuals, so to speak, about demon possession as they went along. This on-the-fly diagnosis is likely why the Catholic Church never publicly acknowledged the Hunkeler case.

Ronald Hunkeler then underwent a confusing number of exorcisms in Missouri, possibly at St. Louis University College Church and then at Alexian Brothers Hospital. During the exorcisms, Hunkeler clawed, spit, slapped, growled, and cursed at the top of his lungs. Worse than anything ever reported in an exorcism case until that point, he also sang versions of "Blue Danube" (popularized by Deanna Durbin in *Spring Parade* in 1940), "That Old Rugged Cross" (often sung at funerals), and "Swanee" (a hit written by George Gershwin that had sold millions of copies). There were also reports of levitation and flying objects. Nearly all of these manifestations were witnessed by family members and priests already long convinced not only of supernatural forces but that these forces had latched onto Ronald, a troubled but largely nondescript teenager living in a quiet town with a population of 1,200.

It took roughly a month for Ronald to shed his demons. By the third week of April, it was all over. One night, Ronald intoned: "Satan! Satan! I am St. Michael, and I command you, Satan, and the other evil spirits, to leave the body in the name of Dominius, immediately—Now! NOW! NOW!"

The Hunkelers left Cottage City a few years after the last of the exorcisms, without speaking to the press. The *Washington Post* story published months later relied on unnamed Jesuit sources. What little is known of Ronald Hunkeler comes from the dogged Opsasnick. He spoke to childhood acquaintances of Hunkeler, including one man, whom Opsasnick referred to by the initials J.C., whose brother was best friends with Hunkeler. J.C. described his brother (given the pseudonym B.C.) and Hunkeler in an unflattering light. "They were loners who found each other and caused a lot of mischief," he told Opsasnick. "There was a close relationship there, a very close relationship. . . . You had these two mischief-makers that had a strong tendency to take advantage of people who were weaker than themselves. They were a pair of connivers and they had their act down."

Eventually, Opsasnick reached B.C., who gave Hunkeler, his childhood friend, the character reference of a lifetime: "People ask me what he was like back then, and I can tell you that he was never what you would call a normal child. He was an only child and kind of spoiled, and he was a mean bastard. We were together all the time, and we used to fight all the time."

In his final crucial scoop, Opsasnick interviewed one of the priests involved in the actual exorcism, William Halloran, and in the process, debunked several of the yarns surrounding the case:

> Opsasnick: Did the boy speak in any languages other than English?
> Halloran: Just Latin.
> Opsasnick: Did it appear he understood the Latin he was speaking?
> Halloran: I think he mimicked us.
> Opsasnick: Was there any change in the boy's voice?
> Halloran: Not really.
> Opsasnick: When the boy struck you in the nose, did he exhibit extraordinary strength?
> Halloran: I don't know; I never thought much about it. It certainly wasn't [Mike] Tyson hitting me in the nose or something like that.

A few years earlier, Halloran had spoken to Thomas Allen and sounded just as unconvinced. "I should never feel comfortable or capable of making an absolute statement," he told Allen. "You know, you have some things that are considered characteristics of exorcism. For instance, if this little kid exhibited prodigious strength. Well, he didn't. And the other thing is an ability to use foreign languages without having any experience in them. Say if a person were possessed, he might be able to speak Swahili. Another thing is feats of dexterity, walking up a wall, and things like that. These never happened. I don't have the faintest idea why the devil would need a possession. Satan would certainly have more effective means to spread evil than possessing someone."

In *Possession*, Allen also reported that the Jesuits themselves had doubts. "Archbishop Ritter, following Church procedure, appointed an examiner—a Jesuit professor of philosophy at St Louis University—to investigate the case," Allen wrote. "The examiner had the authority to interview participants under oath. According to a Jesuit who is familiar with the results of that investigation, the examiner concluded that Ronald was not the victim of a diabolical possession."

Like Reverend Schulze, Dr. Sergio A. Rueda believed that Hunkeler was initially motivated by an aversion to school and a longing to visit his sick aunt—both of these sentiments distorted through an emotionally disturbed personality. Eventually, the disturbances morphed into something darker with the arrangement of séances and prayer circles and the arrival of faith healers and priests.

Instinctually, Ronald Hunkeler seemed to read this audience well, realizing they had preexisting biases he could exploit for his obscure purposes. When the cavalry rode in, it was more of the same; the heroic Jesuits in their stoles and surplices were not surrounding Ronald in his torture rack of a bed to check his temperature. Had Ronald Hunkeler been scrutinized by Houdini or the Amazing Randi, two of the more famous twentieth-century debunkers of the paranormal, he might have changed his behavior. Indeed, when the parapsychologist J. B. Rhine drove up from North Carolina to observe Hunkeler, he reported that no manifestations took place at all. Rhine, too, was skeptical about what had been occurring.

Like the *Amityville Horror*, another remunerative franchise based on a hoax, the Hunkeler exorcism achieved its dubious status through the notoriety of its fictional versions and the efforts of those who were principally motivated by selling paperbacks and tickets. Then, every few years for decades, the Hunkeler exorcism was resurrected and perpetuated by unscrupulous newspapers, magazines, and television networks—all of them hoping for ratings, subscriptions, and, in the digital era, penny clicks.

But in a 2000 interview with the *Washington Times*, even Blatty seemed to back off from his certitude somewhat. The internet had made research a lot easier, and it brought to light much of what he had tried to keep hidden. Confronted by the reporting of Mark Opsansick, Blatty admitted, "Maybe the case wasn't genuine. I wasn't there."

A year after Hunkeler died in 2020, *Skeptical Inquirer* revealed his identity at last, sparking a final media mini-frenzy about the incidents that had inspired *The Exorcist*. Ronald Edward Hunkeler was eighty-six years old when he died. For forty years, he had worked as an engineer at NASA. In a feature story, the *New York Post* mistakenly printed the Blatty-approved version of how Hunkeler wound up surrounded by priests: "After Hunkeler underwent a series of medical and psychological tests, which failed to find anything abnormal, his family sought out religious leaders, beginning with a Protestant pastor."

But the *Post* also got a more telling quote about Ronald Hunkeler from a woman they called his "companion." "He said he wasn't possessed, it was all concocted," she told the *Post*. "He said, 'I was just a bad boy.'"

CHAPTER 3

Inspirations: Ira, Ray, and Mother Joan

As with so many of his claims post-fame, William Peter Blatty offered various reasons why he decided to write *The Exorcist*, his first serious novel. One particularly sentimental reason Blatty cited was his mother. When she died in 1967, Blatty underwent a religious crisis that forced him to confront spiritual matters in a new light. This included his faith, which had been flagging throughout the 1960s, and his vision of evil and its persistence.

Elsewhere Blatty claimed that he wanted to prove to the literary establishment that he was not a featherweight and could, if necessary, tackle solemn themes. Of course, the literary establishment of the 1960s took little notice of Blatty to begin with, undercutting the presumption that it anticipated any new material (serious or otherwise) from him. His last two novels, *Twinkle, Twinkle, "Killer" Kane* and *I, Billy Shakespeare!* received mixed reviews and, as he noted, coyly, "while they didn't sell fewer copies than *The Idylls of the King* in its Tibetan translation, certainly didn't sell any more."

Blatty was also fond of telling whoever would listen that *The Exorcist* was an altruistic pursuit. "It's an argument for God," he told the *Washingtonian* in 2015. "I intended it to be an apostolic work, to help people in their faith. Because I thoroughly believed in the authenticity and validity of that particular event."

Finally, Blatty cited economic necessity as the prime mover for writing *The Exorcist*. The market for zany screenplays had collapsed during the early, urgent days of New Hollywood productions. At the time Blatty was considering embarking on *The Exorcist*, he was in financial difficulties, a situation another obscure satirical novel would not resolve.

As a general rule, when trying to choose among claims from unreliable narrators (especially in motley subcultures such as boxing, professional wrestling, organized crime, and Hollywood), the best option is the account least flattering to the subject. In this case, the likeliest scenario is that Blatty saw his bank account dwindling while he saw *Rosemary's Baby* become an incredible commercial success as both a book and a film. With that in mind, Blatty decided to infuse a commercial novel in a suddenly popular genre (horror fiction) with his theological interests, interests that were also marked by a strange commitment to the occult—one of the cultural hot topics of the late 1960s.

In 1967, Ira Levin, a struggling playwright looking to pay a few bills after a pair of Broadway flops, published *Rosemary's Baby* to instant acclaim. While Levin had succeeded with a thriller called *A Kiss Before Dying* in 1953, the market for supernatural horror in the 1960s was mostly relegated to the pulp racks in drugstores. But Levin, with a gift for plotting to go along with his natural talent, made sure that *Rosemary's Baby* would not be an afterthought to a bottle of Tylenol or an egg cream.

What separated *Rosemary's Baby* from so many other run-of-the-mill ghoulish page-turners was its setting in a realistic milieu (no castles or Victorian mansions, no fog-shrouded moors or windswept cliff-sides) in 1965, with a deliberate topicality designed to give readers a sense of familiarity. This was before the twenty-four-hour cable news cycle, the internet, and social media created feverish micro-trends; events from two years earlier could still resonate to an audience participating in a monoculture. "I anchored my unbelievable story in the reality of Manhattan in that season—as much to make myself believe it as to win the belief of readers," Levin wrote. "I saved the daily newspapers, checking back through them on the transit strike, the incoming shows, the mayoral election, writing always a few months ahead of Rosemary and Guy's calendar."

Levin also focused on the domestic underpinnings of his narrative—marriage, city life, pregnancy—concerns to millions of Americans, and ripe for use as powerful subtexts. These elements—topicality, a social metaphor, and supernatural events intruding on a realistic setting—were direct inspirations to Blatty, who overloaded *The Exorcist* with social trends, contemporary themes, fads, and references. Some of the themes Blatty referenced included meditation, a drug-use subplot, allusions to occult books, and New Age activities. The Ouija board, for example, had been an object of suspicion for the god-fearing ever since it was first introduced commercially in 1891 by the Kennard Novelty Company; but in 1967, now manufactured by Parker Brothers, over two million Ouija boards were sold. By including it in *The Exorcist*, Blatty gave the Ouija board (after all, a mass-produced toy sold at Woolworth and Kay Bee Toys) the distinction of supernatural risk it has had in pop culture for the last fifty years.

To his credit, Levin kept the point of view limited to Rosemary, allowing for audience identification and also accentuating the overwhelming atmosphere of paranoia and encroaching doom. As the conspiracy threatens to subsume her, the reader suffers along with Rosemary, whose terror is made palpable. In *The Exorcist*, by contrast, Blatty works in the omniscient observer mode, giving nearly every character, minor or major, a subplot and reproducing, usually through italicized type, their thoughts throughout the text.

In 1968, a year after Levin had demonstrated that the occult novel could be a bankable commodity, the mass-market imitations arrived. Over the next few years, pulp paperbacks, which had slowly been diversifying from hard-boiled crime, sci-fi, and racy sex romps, began featuring Black Masses pentagrams, and demons on their lurid covers. While some of these novellas skirted the gothic romance genre (spearheaded by Virginia Coffman and Victoria Holt), they still featured villains with a noticeably devilish bent.

The spin-racks at Rexall, Eckerd, Woolworth, and Thrifty now carried titles such as *Mark of Satan*, *Witchfinder*, *The Ouija Board*, *To Play the Devil*, *Bury Him Darkly*, and *Spawn of Satan*. At the higher end were hardcovers by Fred Mustard Stewart (*The Mephisto Waltz*) and Ramona Stewart (*The Possession of Joel Delaney*) and reprints of the newly rediscovered H. P. Lovecraft. In 1971 alone, Richard Matheson published *Hell House*, and Thomas Tryon climbed the bestseller list with *The Other*, an eerie psychological novel with thirteen-year-old twins at its center. It was during this pop-culture occult resurgence that William Peter Blatty scored with *The Exorcist*, which, of course, would be the most successful horror novel ever published.

If Ira Levin and the occultish times were not enough of an inspiration to Blatty, in 1968 a night out with his wife would prove decisive. That was when Blatty saw *Rosemary's Baby*, the Roman Polanski adaptation sending shivers up and down the spines of moviegoers from coast to coast.

The importance of *Rosemary's Baby* to *The Exorcist* and to the entire horror genre (encompassing film and books) cannot be overstated. As Bryan Turnock noted in *Studying Horror Cinema*: "*Rosemary*, along with *Psycho* and *Night of the Living Dead*, is an example of 'modern horror.' All of these films bring the monstrous into the everyday here and now, the home and family."

Before *Rosemary's Baby*, American horror films were little more than low-budget kitsch fests destined for drive-in theaters in the hinterlands and sticky grindhouses in urban hot spots. Newspaper critics rarely reviewed such films; when they did, it was to eviscerate them in a mere paragraph or two.

While *Rosemary's Baby* had a black comedy edge, its nightmare scenario of a vulnerable woman (the fragile beauty Mia Farrow in one of her first starring roles) gaslit by a coven of Satanists steadily built tension until its shocking if low-key denouement: the devil wins. A blockbuster at a time when horror films seemed destined to remain B-status, *Rosemary's Baby* changed the way studios looked at the genre. "It opened the door for class-A productions of horror films," Paul Sylbert, production designer on *Rosemary*, told David Konow for his book *Reel Terror*. "The money spent on *The Exorcist* was pretty steep, but it paid off. *Rosemary's Baby* opened the door. It took it out of the schlock genre and put it up there with the other big successful movies."

Seeing *Rosemary's Baby* lit the spark in Blatty, who told his wife after emerging from the theater, "That's the kind of book I'd like to write. I could do something like this." In the future, Blatty would criticize *Rosemary's Baby* for its "moral compromise" of letting Satan triumph. He also mocked the final reveal of the baby: "All of a sudden the eyes turn into contact lenses," he told Jason Zinoman, author of *Shock Value*. "It was schlocky." Unfortunately, Blatty misremembered that scene—as have many over the years. The image Blatty alludes to is actually a brief flashback from the perspective of Rosemary, who recalls the demon that had raped her earlier in the film when she was in a drug-induced haze. Despite his concerns about the messaging in *Rosemary's Baby*, Blatty was determined to produce a similar work.

At a cocktail party thrown by novelist Burton Wohl, Blatty struck up a conversation with Marc Jaffe, editorial director of Bantam Books. At that time, Blatty was only a middling novelist (and as a screenwriter, he was no Robert Towne either) struggling with his finances, but Jaffe reacted enthusiastically at what he heard. "I had no story," Blatty told David Konow. "Only the theme of demonic possession, and whatever I told Marc took me no more than three minutes to do so."

They made a tentative deal after a few martinis, and soon Blatty received a check for an advance. From there, Blatty sequestered himself in an Encino Hills guesthouse owned by his ex-wife and banged out *The Exorcist* in less than a year, sometimes working fourteen hours a day, propelled by coffee and cigarettes. (In other, naturally conflicting accounts, Blatty said he rented a cabin in Lake Tahoe or finished the novel in Staten Island.)

Although most trace the roots of *The Exorcist* to *Rosemary's Baby*, Blatty probably had two other influences that shaped his novel. One was the Polish film *Mother Joan of the Angels*, based on the notorious Loudun possession case. The French equivalent of Salem, Loudun is a small town famous for a case of mass possession among nuns in an isolated convent during the 1630s. After years of the nuns suffering from seizures, undergoing psychological distress, striking hysterical poses, and spewing lewd provocations, a maverick priest named Urbain Grandier was accused of witchcraft. The nuns aligned against him, testifying that he had signed a pact with the devil (even producing such a parchment at the trial) and that he was the cause of their torments. Found guilty of sorcery, Grandier was tortured before finally being burned at the stake.

The story of the demoniac nuns and Father Grandier spawned *The Devils of Loudun*, a nonfiction book by Aldous Huxley in 1952, which, in turn, inspired a play by John Whiting, an opera by Krzysztof Penderecki, and, most infamously, *The Devils*, by maverick filmmaker Ken Russell, an outrageous Grand Guignol that raised the ire of polite society throughout the United Kingdom in 1971.

Mother Joan of the Angels, released in 1961 and directed by Jerzy Kawalerowicz, is notable for its stylized mass exorcism scene and its unrelenting gravitas. Although *Mother Joan* won a Special Jury Prize at Cannes, its status as a blasphemous provocation (as decreed by the Roman Catholic Church) prevented devout viewers in Poland from attending. The Associated Press reported: "Parish priests last Sunday forbade Catholics to see the film, which the episcopate in Warsaw denounced as 'slanderous, vulgar, unethical, uncultured, and disgusting.'"

In a 2001 interview with the journal *Kinoeye*, Kawalerowicz recalled the uproar *Mother Joan of the Angels* caused among the clergy. "At first, the Catholic Church was against the film. They forbade people from watching it. They put signs on church doors, saying that watching this film is a mortal sin." Years later, of course, *The Exorcist* would also spark disapproval from religious leaders. But *The Exorcist* and *Mother Joan of the Angels* have much more in common than ecclesiastical rebuke: there are themes found in *The Exorcist* seemingly plucked from *Mother Joan* that go beyond the general idea of exorcism.

During the mass exorcism scene, for example, which takes place in the abbey, a cluster of nuns, their white habits shroud-like, gather and perform various moves that suggest motor hysteria. They are seemingly inspired by Mother Joan, whose choreographed movements culminate in the same spider-walk position (a modified bridge) described by Blatty in his novel.

Another theme common to both films (and the novel) is the idea of actively transferring possession from an afflicted person to a priest. Two dialogue exchanges, in particular, suggest that Blatty paid close attention to *Mother Joan of the Angels* concerning transference. In a scene where Father Suryn urges Mother Joan to cooperate in releasing her demons, Mother Joan responds: "And what if Satan leaves me and possesses you?" In the finale of *The Exorcist*, Father Karras taunts or commands the demon to abandon Regan and, instead, inhabit his body, in what amounts to a kind of spiritual hostage exchange. With this gesture, Karras hopes to save Regan and, by then committing suicide, killing the demon outright. *Mother Joan of the Angels* features a similar conceit. A desperate priest, Father Suryn, in love with the possessed nun, draws her demons into him with physical contact.

Later, in an intense mirror scene, Father Suryn addresses himself and the demon in a desperate monologue. "The demon is in me," he whispers, hoarsely. "If you leave me, you will return to Mother Joan. Take me instead, and you will never go back to Mother Joan. You will never leave me. Now I am forever in the hands of Satan." (Here, both Kawalerowicz and Blatty might have been influenced by the Loudun case, where Father Suryn prayed for the demon possessing one of the nuns to abandon her and afflict him.)

A few years after its disastrous European release, *Mother Joan of the Angels* arrived, circuitously, in America, first in May of 1962, when Telepix Corporation released it for a limited run in New York City. Then, on

September 22, 1963, *Joan of the Angels* (as it had been retitled for its US pre-
miere) debuted in California, at the Surf Theater on Irving Street, just south
of Golden Gate Park in San Francisco. And while Blatty most likely never
made the nearly four-hundred-mile trip to San Francisco, it seems possible
that, as a true believer and a devotee of possession literature, he might have
traveled to the Los Feliz Theater at 1822 N. Vermont Avenue a few months
later. There, less than fifteen minutes away from the Warner Bros. Studio
building, *Joan of the Angels* had a short engagement, beginning on January
22, 1964. A week earlier, the *Los Angeles Times* had run an ad announc-
ing *Joan of the Angels*, possibly catching the eye of the young screenwriter
already thinking about producing a book that focused on an exorcism.

If Blatty missed the showings at the Loz Feliz Theater, he would have
a few more opportunities to indulge his curiosity. In January 1966, *Joan
of the Angels* played on a twin bill with The *Saragossa Manuscript* at the
Europa Theater. For two nights in April, the Chapman College Great Films
Guild presented *Joan* at the Orange Theater in Orange County. Finally, in
September 1968, when Satanism was already a full-throttle cultural movement in California, *Joan of the Angels* appeared at Royce Hall on the UCLA
campus.

More influential than *Mother Joan of the Angels*, however, was
The Case Against Satan, a novel published in 1962 and written by Ray
Russell, a fiction editor at *Playboy* and an all-around writer-for-hire, who
specialized in horror and science fiction. Not only did Russell publish a
demonic possession novel years before Blatty, but he was also a screen-
writer, based in Los Angeles, at the same time that Blatty was penning light
Hollywood fare such as *John Goldfarb, Please Come Home!* and *Promise
Her Anything*.

Just as William Friedkin would deny any kinship whatsoever with
horror films despite including a few stock genre moments in *The Exorcist*,
so Blatty rarely strayed from his claim that his main source for *The Exorcist*
was the Hunkeler case that he had read about in 1949. That makes works
such as *Mother Joan of the Angels* and *The Case Against Satan* even more
conspicuous.

Published by Obolensky, *The Case Against Satan* received universally
positive reviews from newspapers across the country, including praise from
the *Los Angeles Times* on July 1, 1962. (By then, Blatty was already working
on his first credit in Hollywood, the screenplay to *The Man from the Diners'*

Club, a Danny Kaye slapstick comedy that opened to poor reviews.) Unlike *The Exorcist*, with its extraneous murder mystery, various subplots, and cast of overstated characters, *The Case Against Satan* is a relatively stream-lined narrative. Susan Garth is a sixteen-year-old girl from a single-parent home and an unstable background. When she begins acting erratically (including stripping naked before a priest and then attacking him), Bishop Crimmins, convinced she is possessed, recruits a doubtful priest to perform an exorcism on her.

The two priests, one older and one younger, strap Susan to a bed located in the rectory of their church. Like Karras in *The Exorcist*, one priest, Father Gregory, is a skeptic whose faith seems to be at low ebb. Father Gregory is also interested in psychiatry, a secular pursuit that undermines pure Catholic notions about the devil and evil. In *The Exorcist*, Father Karras is a trained psychiatrist with similar doubts about his religious calling. (In another minor echo, Father Gregory, while not exactly a whiskey priest, drinks more than one would expect, the same way Karras does in *The Exorcist*.)

Among the behavioral similarities between Susan and Regan are: a dys-functional family background, a penchant for sexual obscenities, and the power of levitation. In addition, Susan, as inhabited by a demon (or psy-chosis), mocks and taunts her interlocutors with an erudition that most certainly did not appear in the Hunkeler episode. The theological sparring between Susan and Father Gregory prefigures that of Regan and Father Karras. (Unlike Russell, whose novel is less than 150 pages long, only Blatty uses this trait to indulge in extended moralizing and religious didacticism.)

The final parallel between the two possessed girls is definitive proof that Blatty had been taking notes from *The Case Against Satan*: Susan vomits, projectile-style, just as Regan does in both the novel and the film of *The Exorcist*. "There was a startling, gagging sound from the girl, and they turned to watch in pity and loathing," Russell wrote, "as she wretched vio-lently, her body curling in spasms, her fingers and toes clenched, her gaping mouth spewing jet after jet of reeking substance that covered her and splat-tered the wall and ran sluggishly in long viscous tendrils down to the floor."

Again and again, Blatty reiterated (and committed to print) his theolog-ical motivation for writing *The Exorcist*. "If there were demons," he wrote, "there were angels and probably a God and a life everlasting." This is only a semantic step or two away from what Russell posits in *The Case Against Satan*: "If God existed, logically his adversary existed."

The similarities between *The Case Against Satan* and *The Exorcist* are startling. While overlapping research might have accounted for a few commonalities in the ritual scenes, the resemblances between characters and their traits seem deliberate. In fact, Russell eventually filed a lawsuit against Blatty, claiming infringement. (The outcome of the lawsuit is unknown, but the lack of publicity it generated, at a time when any anecdote connected to *The Exorcist* would have prompted media coverage, suggests that a quick out-of-court settlement took place.)

Still, Blatty was the far-more-polished commercial writer, able to meet the melodramatic demands of popular fiction with gusto, tying together contemporary trends with an overheated style and a blunt message that made *The Exorcist* an immediate bestseller. Blatty also had the advantage of releasing his book during one of the most tumultuous eras in American history. Written in the early 1960s, when literature was still subject to potential legal ramifications (*Howl* by Allen Ginsberg and *Tropic of Cancer* by Henry Miller had both sparked recent obscenity trials), *The Case Against Satan* had little choice but to be the sanitized version of a demonic possession novel. In 1971, when *The Exorcist* was published, Blatty capitalized on the growing permissiveness of the arts. The sensational elements of *The Exorcist*—the sexual subtext involving a preteen girl, the unchecked vulgarity and obscenity, even the drug subplot involving Karl the butler and his daughter—gave the book a taboo appeal that Ray Russell could not have attempted less than a decade earlier.

CHAPTER 4

▲ ▲ ▲

Sympathy for the Devil

here was another unexpected development that benefited *The Exorcist*. By the late 1960s, the cultural zeitgeist produced not just rawer depictions of sex and violence in film and literature, but it also generated an occult mania centered on Satanism. Of all the sociological trends associated with the '60s—ESP, happenings, tie-dyed shirts and paisley, free love, sitars, communes, LSD, psychedelic rock music, hippies, Gestalt therapy, Transcendental Meditation, Hari Krishnas, astrology—none is as puzzling as the ascent of Satan, first as an antihero to the counterculture, then as a national bogeyman to the Silent Majority in the 1970s. As the country began its youthquake post-JFK, it fostered a rebellious pushback against not just establishment ideals but against traditional notions of reality. The Esalen Institute, the New Age movement, and what has been called the Occult Revival combined to challenge the facts as set forth by the "corporate state." This movement, more diverse and widespread today than ever, could be summed up by the title of a Paul Feyerabend memoir: *Farewell to Reason*.

Part of the occult revival, with its emphasis on paganism and mysticism, included the resurrection of Satan as a figure of reverence. In 1966, a circus veteran with the stage name of Anton LaVey founded the Church of Satan in San Francisco, securing overkill publicity and a lucrative new livelihood. LaVey, bald head, goatee, dark turtlenecks, and theatrical cape, was nothing more than a charlatan who read the cultural weather with the proficiency of a trained meteorologist. His Church of Satan, located on California Street and painted black for ominous effect, held hokey rituals and even the occasional "baptism," and while LaVey may have been an opportunist whose ostensible philosophy combined pinches of Nietzsche, Aleister Crowley, and Ayn Rand into a hedonist potpourri, his effect on those predisposed to twistedness was incalculable.

The diabolical floodgates burst open when Ira Levin published *Rosemary's Baby* in 1967. Aleister Crowley peeped out from the cover of *Sgt. Pepper*, Kenneth Anger had the word "Lucifer" tattooed on his chest, the Rolling Stones rocked out to "Sympathy for the Devil," and Arthur Brown, wearing a cultlike robe, demonic face paint, and a burning helmet, had an unlikely #2 Billboard smash with "Fire," a song whose roaring opening recitation suited the times: "I am the god of hellfire, and I bring you—."

Finally, Roman Polanski set the stage for the country—and for Blatty— with his disturbing adaptation of *Rosemary's Baby* (with LaVey falsely claiming to have been a technical advisor), crystallizing the paranoiac notion that Satanists had infiltrated America at every level. This outlandish plot point would spur conspiracy theorists for more than fifty years, gradually during the early 1970s and then, with alarming almost supernova-like power, in the 1980s and 1990s.

As much as Blatty (and later, William Friedkin) proclaimed that their collaboration was some sort of sui generis event only tangibly connected to film or even entertainment, the fact remains that *The Exorcist* was the tipping point of an increasing cultural trend that focused on Satanism and the supernatural. Blatty, for example, was not the only novelist inspired by Ira Levin. In fact, Blatty trailed Fred Mustard Stewart and Ramona Stewart (as well as dozens of paperback pulp meisters) in capitalizing on a remunerative literary fad. Similarly, the film was part of a wave of occult releases in steady production since *Rosemary*. Before *The Exorcist* opened in December 1973, there was enough diabolic schlock to keep moviegoers busy with pentagrams and spells until the Apocalypse. A small sample includes *Eye of the Devil* (1967), *The Devil Rides Out* (1968), *Witchfinder General*, *I Drink Your Blood*, *Demons of the Mind*, *Mark of the Devil* (all 1970), *The Devils*, *Simon King of the Witches*, *The Mephisto Waltz*, *Brotherhood of Satan*, *Blood on Satan's Claw* (all 1972), *The Possession of Joel Delaney* (1972), *Season of the Witch*, and *Child's Play* (1972).

But books and films were not the only pop mediums spellbound by the sinister. In the 1970s, one of the clearest measures of whether a trend had seeped into the cultural atmosphere—like smog in Los Angeles—was representation on television. Not just news reports or talk-show interviews but fictional productions: sitcoms, dramas, soap operas, movies-of-the-week. Before the appearance of *The Exorcist*, several made-for-TV films filled the airwaves with witches, hexes, demons, possessions, and maybe even Beelzebub himself.

At twenty-five, Steven Spielberg directed *Something Evil* for CBS, and Paul Wendkos, who would soon earn a satanic screen credit with *The Mephisto Waltz*, helmed a possession outing called *Fear Itself* (1969). Other supernatural-tinged television films included *Ritual of Evil*, *Crowhaven Farm*, *The House That Would Not Die*, *Black Noon*, *She Waits*, *The Devil's Daughter*, *Satan's School for Girls*, and *The Norliss Tapes*.

Even sitcoms reflected the growing interest in the otherworldly. Premiering in 1964, *Bewitched*, starring Elizabeth Montgomery, outlasted its direct competition for supernatural canned laughter (*The Munsters* and *The Addams Family*) by seven years, finally wrapping in 1972 only because of behind-the-scenes strife. One of the oddest shows produced during that era was *Dark Shadows*, a horror-themed soap opera about a family of vampires, which ran from 1966 to 1971. *Dark Shadows* produced a Canadian knockoff, *Strange Paradise*, which struggled in syndication from 1969 to 1970 before cancellation.

At no other time would Blatty have been able to turn a story of demonic possession into a money-spinning novel and a record-breaking film. He had arrived just as the Age of Aquarius was morphing slowly, inexplicably into the Age of Diabolus. This cultural trend of witchery, ghouls, diabolism, ghosts, and Satan (even reflected in a line of cereal products—Franken Berry, Count Chocula, and Fruity Yummy Mummy) allowed *The Exorcist* to fit right in, as the apotheosis of the ubiquitous paranormal entertainment movement.

CHAPTER 5

▲ ▲ ▲

"The Shocker of the Year"

Released on May 5, 1971, *The Exorcist* caused an immediate uproar and would go on to sell more than twelve million copies. (It remains in print, and in 2011 William Peter Blatty updated it to reflect an even more Catholic leaning.) Decades after *The Exorcist* had become one of the great publishing successes of the 1970s, Blatty claimed that it was dead on arrival until he made a last-minute appearance on *The Dick Cavett Show*. Most likely, this is another exaggeration from the self-mythologizing Blatty. First, *The Exorcist* earned stellar reviews from every major newspaper across the country, including a multipage write-up in the *Los Angeles Times*. (*Cosmopolitan* and *Life* also gave it favorable coverage. On the other hand, *Time* magazine vaporized it: "It is a pretentious, tasteless, abominably written, redundant pastiche of superficial theology, comic-book psychology, Grade B movie dialogue, and Grade Z scatology. In short, *The Exorcist* will be a bestseller and almost certainly a drive-in movie.") Second, Harper & Row launched a marketing campaign that blitzed print media and sent Blatty on a twenty-six-city tour. Finally, television listings reveal that Blatty appeared on *The Dick Cavett Show* on May 27, 1971, already scheduled as a featured guest, along with Keith Baxter and Ruth Gordon (an ironic link to *Rosemary's Baby*). He was not some lucky standby who popped up, at the last minute, to miraculously kick-start sales of his novel.

Howard Newman, a publicist for the film version of *The Exorcist*, summed up the appearance of the novel succinctly: "It was like the launching of a moonshot. With good reviews and incredible word-of-mouth publicity, the book zoomed up on the bestseller list and stayed there for 55 weeks."

Another headline-making aspect surrounding *The Exorcist* was the fact that the film rights had been sold to Warner Bros. months before the novel appeared. This exorbitant transaction—at the time reported to be $400,000 (equivalent to nearly $3,000,000 today)—gave *The Exorcist* a head start in buzz. When Harper & Row released its print ads in May 1971, they already included the tagline "To be a major motion picture from Warner Brothers." John Calley, executive vice president of production at Warners, openly acknowledged the zeitgeist in a wire report released in November 1970. "For the past year . . . we have been in search of a chilling, suspenseful and occult type of novel. We positively feel The *Exorcist* is the story we have been looking for."

In selling the film rights to *The Exorcist*, Blatty sought—and ultimately attained—as much control over the adaptation as possible. After years in Hollywood, Blatty had learned what William Goldman once said about the film industry: "The only one who gets screwed around with basically is the writer, because, as I say, everybody knows the alphabet." Blatty seized his opportunity for complete control when he found out that producer Paul Monash, who had purchased the rights, had misrepresented himself as a buyer when he was more of a broker, looking to sell *The Exorcist* to Warner Bros. at an immediate profit. After a brief industry skirmish, Blatty emerged not only as the screenwriter but also, remarkably, as the sole producer, guaranteeing him a fortune. More important, Blatty could now orchestrate the religious messaging that was so important to him.

CHAPTER 6

▲ ▲ ▲

Hurricane Billy

By 1970, William Friedkin was applying for unemployment benefits. Friedkin, in Hollywood only since 1965, expected a career intermission that might last longer than the average downtime between projects. His first four releases had been flops, including his critically lauded adaptation of *The Birthday Party*, a Harold Pinter comedy of menace as unfilmable as most Absurdist plays.

Even his last outing had been mostly well-received if not unanimously acclaimed. *The Boys in the Band*, which opened in March 1970, was another adaptation, this one of an Off-Broadway hit by Mart Crowley. Already saddled with a reputation as a live wire after essentially abandoning postproduction on the catastrophic *Night They Raided Minsky's* (1969), Friedkin hoped that an established property with a sociological hook might reverse his misfortune.

With *The Boys in the Band*, Friedkin produced a landmark film that depicted gay life without resorting to subtle (or overt) condescension or outright mockery, although its artificiality and its sentimentality has left it hopelessly dated. For Friedkin, *The Boys in the Band* has weathered the passing decades—with a bitter reminiscence. "I can still watch the film with pleasure," Friedkin wrote in his memoir, "but at the time, it was another box-office failure. Four in a row."

Neither *The Birthday Party* nor *The Boys in the Band* hinted at the future that awaited Friedkin in an industry where yesterday was all that mattered. Without a hit, without a prestigious award (such as a Golden

Globe), without a recognizable specialty, Friedkin was dangerously close to oblivion. He might have wound up returning to television, where he had started his career directing live programs and then documentaries, or he might have been forced into the thriving B-film market, where drive-in theaters and the urban grindhouse circuit would have allowed him to work on material far below his aspirations.

Instead, the dogged Friedkin teamed up with producer Phil D'Antoni (*Bullitt*) to shop *The French Connection*, a script based on Robin Moore's nonfiction account of an international drug ring waylaid by law enforcement in 1962. "After I had agreed to direct the film," Friedkin wrote in *Action* magazine, "D'Antoni and I spent the better part of a year working on what turned out to be two unimaginative, unsuccessful screenplays. The project was eventually dropped by National General Pictures, and lay dormant for about ten months. Every studio in the business turned the picture down, some twice."

With a revised script by Ernest Tidyman (whose novel, *Shaft*, would become a blaxploitation hit), *The French Connection* ultimately found a buyer in 20th Century Fox, a studio in turmoil, with a chairman, Richard Zanuck, months away from being fired. Zanuck offered D'Antoni a modest budget of $1.5 million—seventy percent less than Friedkin had worked with for *The Boys in the Band*.

But Friedkin had already decided on a new course, one that would make a smaller budget irrelevant. His measured approach in previous films would give way to a high-voltage style calculated to match the explosive popular material he now preferred over stage adaptations. "I would have embarked on a course of having made obscure Miramax type films before Miramax," Friedkin said in a 1999 interview. "But I had this epiphany that what we were doing wasn't making fucking films to hang in the Louvre. We were making films to entertain people and if they didn't do that first they didn't fulfill their primary purpose."

While Friedkin had once predicted that the future of American cinema could be found in the contemporary European art-house style, he also had a taste for the cynical suspense of Henri-Georges Clouzot, the askew pulp genius of Orson Welles, and, above all, perhaps, the pure cinema of Alfred Hitchcock. "I came back to clarity of presentation," Friedkin told writer Nat Segaloff about his approach to *The French Connection*. "Its impetus was in the thirties and forties films. American films of the thirties and forties had clear storylines and strong characters. Then the New Wave of European filmmakers took over, and we all went out and copied Godard and Fellini, forgetting where our roots were and trying to emulate something with which we had very little connection."

For Friedkin, this new philosophy was commercially motivated, but it was also far more compatible with his scrappy personality. Questions of aesthetics aside (Friedkin never hid his admiration for Truffaut, Godard, Antonioni, Kurosawa, and Bergman), a mainstream turn in the 1970s, when personal cinema was en vogue, was not exactly selling out artistically. Proof of this fact was that Friedkin found his biggest inspiration for *The French Connection* in *Z*, a frenetic political thriller that gave its director, Costa-Gavras, an Oscar and a global reputation in 1969. "Costa-Gavras's style was 'induced documentary.' The handheld cameras could go anywhere; the 'fourth wall' was shattered," Friedkin wrote in his memoir. "It was as though you were watching the story unfold rather than seeing something that happened in the past. I had never seen this style applied so effectively."

When *The French Connection* opened in 1971, its unglamorous depiction of grimy New York City street life left viewers exhilarated. Using his documentary background (and the influence of Costa-Gavras) to both pragmatic and aesthetic effect, Friedkin developed a raw, natural look that would influence dozens of films and television shows in the future. With stolen shots, handheld cameras, minimal rehearsal and blocking, improvised dialogue, and on-location shooting throughout, Friedkin created a spontaneous atmosphere that gave viewers the impression that they were watching the action from their windowsills.

At the heart of the film raged Gene Hackman as the foul-mouthed, racist, trigger-happy Popeye Doyle, an antihero in a porkpie hat, whose rancor and wrath seemed limitless. As the 1960s staggered along, cops in films became grungier and angrier. The precedents for Popeye Doyle can be glimpsed in *The Detective*, *Madigan*, *Coogan's Bluff*, and, to an extent, *Bullitt*, but nothing came close to *The French Connection* and its psychopathic narc, first seen in a Santa Claus suit, chasing down a suspect alongside his partner (played by Roy Scheider) and pummeling him in a rubble-strewn lot. (The air of verisimilitude Friedkin created included leaving a pair of bloopers in the final cut. Twice during the infamous "picking your feet in Poughkeepsie" scene, when Hackman befuddled a suspect with surreal questions, Scheider failed to keep a straight face and turned away, mirth-fully, from the action. Friedkin simply kept filming.)

The infamous chase sequence—where a car pursues an elevated train commandeered by a gun-wielding thug—was white-knuckle viewing and, incredibly, white-knuckle filmmaking as well. In fact, Friedkin adopted guerilla tactics for one of the most nerve-racking scenes in the history of Hollywood. A major part of this sequence was filmed without an official permit (meaning no safeguards) and with real traffic on the streets, imper-iling more than a mile of Brooklyn citizenry. "We put a police light and a siren on top of the car," Friedkin told Stephen Farber and Marc Green for *Outrageous Conduct: Art, Ego, and the Twilight Zone Case.* "We went twenty-six blocks through a lot of traffic, jumping lights. I handled the camera myself. I wouldn't let the cameraman do it because he had a family, and at that time I didn't. Anything could have happened. It was against every law. Thank God no one got hurt. I was very fortunate. I would never do that shot today."

Unimpressed by the work of stunt driver Bill Hickman (one-half of the memorable chase scene in *Bullitt*), Friedkin taunted him over drinks about his tame performances. "I said to him . . . I said, 'Hickman, you have no guts. You're chicken shit. You need a couple of drinks to drive good.' I kept getting under his goat. And he said, 'I'll tell you what. I'll show you some driving if you get in the car with me.'" Sitting in the back seat with an Arriflex camera, Friedkin, wrapped in a mattress for protection, waited for Hickman to hit the gas pedal on the '64 Pontiac and burn rubber into film history. "So I got in that car and he went for twenty-six blocks with just the siren on top of the car. We broke every stoplight. We went through everything. We went in and out of lanes. There was no control at all."

A breakout hit, *The French Connection* not only made Friedkin rich prac-tically overnight, but it also gave him carte blanche going forward. Friedkin saw his standing in Hollywood, nothing less than precarious a year earlier, rise even further when *The French Connection* dominated the Academy Awards in 1972, taking home Oscars for Best Picture, Best Director, Best Actor (Hackman), Best Adapted Screenplay, and Best Sound Editing.

Now the film studios, which had been forced to reconsider their rela-tionships with directors (previously considered little more than contractual employees with limited options) since the 1960s, had someone new with whom to reckon. In the handful of years Friedkin had been in Hollywood, he had already developed a reputation for being prickly, but it was *The French Connection* that solidified him as a renegade. He and Gene Hackman bickered throughout the film, with Hackman asking for walking papers at one point. Then there was the Bill Hickman incident and the subsequent impromptu car chase, which was not only risky but illegal. "There are times in the movie business," Friedkin once wrote, "when it pays to be thought of as a dangerously psychotic person."

But as far back as 1966, when Friedkin was fresh from LAX out of O'Hare, executives knew he was rambunctious. In the running to direct his first major Hollywood film—a full-length Peter Gunn feature—Friedkin sat down with producer Blake Edwards and offered a *brute* critique of the screenplay. A few minutes later, another man entered the office, and Friedkin repeated his savage appraisal of the script, ultimately costing himself the assignment. The second man who joined this meeting was the author of the screenplay. His name was William Peter Blatty.

▲ ▲ ▲

William Friedkin was born in Chicago, Illinois, on August 29, 1935. For years he had fudged his age, claiming that he had been born in 1939, a lie that led to him briefly having the erroneous distinction of being the youngest filmmaker ever to win an Academy Award for Best Director. As late as 1998, Mark Kermode, in a *Guardian* interview, lauded Friedkin for his "achievement," notwithstanding its fraudulence.

This fib not only reflected how competitive Friedkin could be, but it also underscored how much he enjoyed a good con. Friedkin ran the streets of the North Side as a teenager, where he avoided juvenile delinquency only because of the shame he felt when his mother discovered his lawless nature. "I didn't know right from wrong when I was a teenager," he told Alex Simon in an interview. "I had no particular education to speak of. I loved my mother and father and it was finally the fact that I was getting so much on their nerves that I just quit cold turkey and tried to be a human. This happened after I saw my mother crying when I'd been picked up for robbery at Goldblatt's department store as a teenager."

His mother was a nurse who quit her job to become a homemaker, and his father was a jack-of-all-trades who eventually lost his knack for picking up gigs, leaving the family on public assistance. After graduating from

Senn High School, Friedkin took a job in the mailroom of WGN-TV, where he quickly advanced into production. Like several of his eventual New Hollywood peers—Sidney Lumet, Robert Altman, John Frankenheimer, Arthur Penn, and Martin Ritt—Friedkin began his career in television, directing hundreds of live programs before switching to documentaries. (In fact, his development most closely resembles that of Robert Mulligan, who was a messenger for CBS in New York City and eventually worked himself up the ladder to A-list director.)

A viewing of *Citizen Kane* gave Friedkin an unexpected sense of destiny. Actually, it was several viewings. According to Friedkin, he was so mesmerized by what Orson Welles had wrought on the silver screen that he sat in the theater for several consecutive shows, finally exiting at midnight, stunned at possibilities he had never considered. With Welles as an example, Friedkin was now less interested in rote television: cinema became his lodestar.

In 1962, Friedkin created a stir when his first documentary, *The People vs. Paul Crump*, led to an inmate having his death sentence commuted. Although documentaries were often staged before the cinema vérité era, Friedkin used reenactments to dramatize historical events—an unusual approach in the early 1960s. "It was the first film I ever made," he recalled for the American Film Institute. "I learned how to make this film by doing it. I did it as a kind of court of last resort for this fellow [Paul Crump], who was on trial for murder and going to the chair and the film was instrumental in the governor of Illinois commuting his sentence to life imprisonment, but I knew nothing at that time about how to make a film at all."

Along with Bill Butler, a cameraman from WGN, Friedkin embarked on his first film, barely understanding the technical aspects of the equipment, much less narrative or editing. With an Arriflex 16 and a Nagra tape recorder, Friedkin and Butler hit the pavement to produce a documentary that would have real-world implications.

Even then, moonlighting on a $7,000 project for a local television station, Friedkin showed both his boldness and his barbarity. Indeed, his ends-justify-the-means philosophy seemed like a holdover from his days on the Chicago streets; as far as filmmaking went, it was there from the beginning. According to Butler, at one point, Friedkin slapped and berated Crump—an inmate in the Cook County Jail, that is, someone under municipal watch—to elicit tears for the camera. This may have been the first instance of Friedkin overseeing what would today be known as a toxic environment.

"So I'm a little away from Paul. Billy goes down to talk to Paul, and they're whispering, talking about a very touching intimate thing, I guess," Butler told author Thomas D. Clagett. "And suddenly Billy starts to slap him. Just started slapping the daylights out of him. It so shook Paul up. I mean, Billy's got Paul in a very intimate, trusting mood, and he just starts to slap the shit out of him. Paul could have killed him. There're no guards around. I mean, the guts to do this is beyond belief. I said to myself, 'What am I doing out here with this fool?' You can't believe it. He had me out on the South Side of Chicago at four a.m., and at that time, it was a totally black neighborhood, and I'm in black bars with a camera and light, taking pictures. I should be dead by now. Talk about living on the edge of disaster. You've got the man."

Despite being shelved by WBKB due to political pressure and never airing in Chicago, *The People vs. Paul Crump* won the Golden Gate Award for Film as Communication at the San Francisco International Film Festival, paving the way for Friedkin to work under David L. Wolper in Los Angeles. In the early 1960s, Wolper was a leading producer of documentaries for television and had built a reputation for quality programming. Tony Fantozzi, a local agent representing Friedkin, brought Wolper into the picture. Naturally, Friedkin had never heard of him. "I didn't give a fuck about network or worldwide or anything," Friedkin told writer Nat Segaloff. "The stories in Chicago interested me. I was very happy there. My memory is that the first time Wolper wanted me to go to work, I wasn't interested in leaving Chicago and didn't know who the fuck David L. Wolper was."

But when Sterling "Red" Quinlan, general manager of WBKB and a Friedkin supporter, resigned in 1964, Friedkin felt he had no choice but to leave the Windy City. Now Friedkin was on his way to Hollywood, the dream factory suddenly struggling to produce entertainment goods for an increasingly evolving market. He drove his Ford Fairlane to Alta Loma Road in West Hollywood, where he took a room at the Sunset Marquis, just south of Sunset Boulevard.

While Fantozzi hustled behind the scenes, Friedkin worked on several documentaries for Wolper, who characterized him in terse grammar for Nat Segaloff. "He was a wild young man," Wolper said. "Cocky and wild. Wild and super-hyper." One complete sentence, two fragments, and three "wilds"—a sketch portrait of the artist as an unruly young man.

Within two years, Friedkin got his first break: directing the final episode ("Off Season") of the *Alfred Hitchcock Hour*. On the Burbank set, he met one of his heroes, Hitchcock, who admonished him for not wearing a tie during the shoot. To Friedkin, it was an absurd yet oddly formal slight, one that he would never forget.

A year later, in one of those random Hollywood serendipities, Friedkin wound up at the helm of a Sonny & Cher spoof. *Good Times*, filmed in 1966 (at the height of the inexplicable Sonny & Cher craze) but released in 1967, was a rip-off of *Help!* and other Beatles romps, but without the visual pizzazz Richard Lester had brought to those productions or the surreal inspiration with which Bob Rafelson suffused *Head*, another Beatles clone featuring the synthetic Monkees.

Good Times crashed at the box office, blindsided by the emerging counterculture. By 1967, Sonny & Cher had already been rendered obsolete by the amped-up acid jams of Jefferson Airplane and Vanilla Fudge, along with the more sophisticated pop-rock sensibilities of The Beatles and the Moody Blues. As a result of this abrupt cultural shift, *Good Times* barely registered, and William Friedkin had his first Hollywood bomb.

In less than five years, Friedkin would direct four money losers in succession, casting doubt on his future in Hollywood. But with the overwhelming critical and box-office success of *The French Connection*, Friedkin now had leverage. And in Hollywood, leverage was everything. From the mailroom to the studios of WGN-TV to the offices of David Wolper in Los Angeles to a box-office smash and an armful of Academy Awards—Friedkin had raced headlong into a future that had never even been a glimmer until he was twenty-six or twenty-seven years old when Charles Foster Kane showed him the way.

"Imagine how life changes for a young filmmaker with a successful film," Friedkin wrote in his memoir. "Suddenly people you don't know invite you to dinner parties; you get scripts from every studio; executives who turned *The French Connection* down are now calling you for lunch. Or dinner. Come meet the wife. Your closest friends, agents, and business associates are overjoyed. The best tables at the best restaurants are yours for the asking. You don't travel by subway anymore, you ride in limos. Why rent an apartment or a house when you can buy or build one? It seemed to me then I was on a merry-go-round that would accelerate forever."

His drive, ambition, and combativeness, along with the wildness David Wolper succinctly described, had vaulted Friedkin to the top of a tumultuous profession. Now Friedkin was in the position to choose his next project with no strings attached. What he chose was *The Exorcist*.

CHAPTER 7

In Search of . . . Friedkin

William Peter Blatty never forgot what he had witnessed years earlier, when he sat in on that meeting between Blake Edwards and William Friedkin: professional self-immolation. In Hollywood, where dis-ingenuity and obsequiousness are mainstays, Friedkin had insisted, without concern for his bank account or his tenuous standing as a film-maker, that the *Peter Gunn* script was trash. And when Blatty entered the room, Friedkin doubled down on his attack.

"Now you must set this into context," Blatty told Nat Segaloff. "Billy had, at that time, only done one film. I'm sure that Billy will agree that it was not an auspicious beginning. This interview was extremely important. I sat back and reached for another cigarette and thought, Well, now he's going to give way and like the dream sequence when he sees how much Blake likes the dream sequence. Billy did not back off, knowing full well that he was not going to get this important job. He stuck to his guns and he didn't get the assignment. I never forgot that. That was why, when it came time to find a director for *The Exorcist*, I threatened Warner Brothers with a lawsuit because of their refusal to consider Billy."

Impressed by how Friedkin would not compromise on aesthetic principles—a rare enough stance in Hollywood in 1966 but completely unheard of from a neophyte director with a single bomb on his résumé—Blatty filed away the experience for future reference.

With *The Exorcist* greenlit and Blatty named the producer, the search was on to find a director who could wrangle the explosive material found in the novel. John Calley, head of production at Warner Bros., spearheaded the effort from the corporate end. At the same time, Blatty launched his own parallel quest for the right man to make his vision a celluloid reality.

One of the first directors Blatty approached for *The Exorcist* was Peter Bogdanovich, a hot young gun riding high on the success of *The Last Picture Show*, a multi-Oscar nominee, as well as a critical and economic triumph. Bogdanovich was in the midst of a spectacular box-office run that would eventually include *Picture Show*, *What's Up, Doc?* (which earned a stunning $66 million), and *Paper Moon*. Although Bogdanovich began his career under exploitation tycoon Roger Corman and had directed a disturbing mass shooter film called *Targets* in 1968, he was known for a light touch and an overriding interest in 1940s Hollywood studio films, especially the screwball comedies of Howard Hawks and Preston Sturges. It was perhaps this adherence to classic form that drew Blatty to Bogdanovich (and possibly their shared background in humor). In fact, Blatty inscribed a copy of his novel to Bogdanovich with a crafty bit of flattery: "If you don't make this movie," he wrote, "nobody will." Bogdanovich passed, and Blatty continued looking for a director.

As *The Exorcist* made the rounds among prospective filmmakers, the names attached to the project narrowed to a handful of Warner Bros. suggestions: Stanley Kubrick, Mike Nichols, Arthur Penn, and Mark Rydell. Nichols declined the project, believing that hinging a big-budget blockbuster on the performance of a twelve-year-old girl was a disaster in the making. Arthur Penn was teaching at Yale and was committed to the position while *The Exorcist* would be in production. Not surprisingly, Kubrick, obsessive to the core, demanded complete control of the film, including the production end, something Blatty would never surrender.

As for Rydell, he was rejected outright by Blatty, who was unimpressed by a rough cut of *The Cowboys*, starring John Wayne in his still-profitable twilight stage. By this time, Blatty was already hectoring Warner Bros. to hire Friedkin. "Again they said no," he wrote in *William Peter Blatty on The Exorcist: From Novel to Screen*, "and they asked if instead I'd be willing to consider another director whom I personally liked and who was talented and sensitive but whose work I nonetheless loathed." Blatty, who refused to name Rydell in his book (giving Rydell the bizarre pseudonym of Edmund De Vere, the 17th Earl of Oxford), felt that *The Cowboys* suffered from leaden pacing. It was a flaw Blatty could not abide. Yet Warner Bros. seemed determined to sign Rydell.

According to Peter Biskind in *Easy Riders, Raging Bulls*, John Boorman, having survived a harrowing shoot on *Deliverance*, also rejected *The Exorcist*. Boorman found the material disturbing and considered the plot sadistic. To Boorman, *The Exorcist* skirted the edge of exploitation. "I was hot," Boorman wrote about his high peak after *Deliverance*. "I had made a hit, a genuine blockbuster. The picture had not been expensive. The studio had made lots of money. I had earned myself the power to make what I wanted. Warners had bought the film rights to *The Exorcist*. [John] Calley asked me to make it. Would I read it and give him a fast answer? I found it repulsive. I told Calley it would be a film about a child being tortured. Calley said, 'You're such a snob.'" (In a strange twist, Boorman would go on to direct *Exorcist II*, one of the most vilified films of the 1970s.)

Alternative histories of *The Exorcist* are intriguing to contemplate when considering the final short list of directors. Kubrick might have taken years to finish the project (in England, no less, where the aerophobic director had moved in 1961, rarely straying from its shores). His obsessiveness often meant interminable shoots, cost overruns, and extended running times for his projects. With only two films released in the 1970s (and two in the 1980s), Kubrick seemed like anathema to the strike-while-the-iron-is-hot philosophy so popular in Hollywood.

Mike Nichols might have imbued *The Exorcist* with a fashionable pop-culture resonance—maybe a hit soundtrack song—and a more tender, less confrontational approach, one with a heavier moral than Friedkin eventually produced. After *Carnal Knowledge* (1971) opened to only fair box office, however, Nichols lost his touch, producing a series of flops over the next decade.

Penn, with his sometimes-ragged camerawork and his loose method, might have brought some black humor to *The Exorcist*, an unrelievedly grim property. But Penn had been losing his Hollywood zest for years, and his next project, *Night Moves* (1975 but filmed in 1973), would be shelved by Warner Bros. for more than a year before it was finally released to general apathy. His follow-up, *The Missouri Breaks* (1976), was an unqualified disaster when it opened, although its surreal air (along with an idiosyncratic performance by Marlon Brando) has since earned it cult status.

And there was no telling what Rydell, the least accomplished of the quartet, might have done with the material. His filmography remained largely undistinguished until 1981, when *On Golden Pond* became the second-highest-grossing film of the year (at $119 million, behind only

Raiders of the Lost Ark) and earned ten Academy Award nominations in the process. Films as varied in quality and subject matter as *The Reivers*, *Cinderella Liberty*, and *The Rose* gave no indication that Rydell could handle a prestige horror film, although like Kubrick, Penn, and Nichols, Rydell had also enjoyed a *succès de scandale* with *The Fox* (1967), featuring Anne Heywood in an extended nude sequence and a lesbian make-out session.

A frustrated Blatty finally threatened to sue Warner Bros. over the right to name Friedkin as the director. Citing the "mutual approval" clause in his contract, Blatty insisted that Warner Bros. at least consider his preferred choice instead of overriding his objections to Rydell. Obsessed with seeing his vision of God and salvation realized as faithfully as possible, Blatty had inserted a minefield of provisions into his contract that would protect him when the time came for the studio to undermine him. "I don't believe that any other novelist has been able to keep control of his screenplay," Blatty told Peter Travers and Stephanie Reiff for their book *The Story Behind The Exorcist*. "This contract gives me some important safeguards: to begin with, they have to start principal photography within two years, or all of the money and the rights reverted back to me. I had to function as producer, not only in name, but in fact. If this condition was not met, all of the money and the rights reverted back to me. If they started to film and dropped it or delayed filming for more than three months, then all of the money and rights reverted to me. You may accurately deduce that I am paranoid about studios."

Fortunately, both parties stumbled into some luck when *The French Connection* erupted on screens across America in October 1971, causing a critical and commercial sensation. Suddenly, Blatty would no longer have to scrap or sue to convince Warner Bros. that William Friedkin was what *The Exorcist* needed to succeed.

At first glance, Friedkin might not have seemed like the top candidate to direct a big-budget theological horror film. Despite the armful of Academy Awards that *The French Connection* won, it was still a relatively inexpensive *policier* with chaotic action sequences and, more important perhaps, an amoral worldview. (Ironically, when the final cut had been delivered and *The Exorcist* had become one of the most successful films of its era, Blatty would complain that Friedkin had removed the moral heart from his script.)

What Blatty wanted was the hyperrealist patina Friedkin had given *The French Connection*, a film shot completely on location, with numberless nonprofessional actors, and a versatile camera crew. While the frenetic pace of the action scenes in *The French Connection* energized the audience, Friedkin alternated them with quieter sequences—almost longueurs—depicting quotidian moments. It was this ability to work in two registers, perhaps, that drew Blatty to Friedkin.

After getting the director he wanted, Blatty surprised Friedkin one day by handing him a manilla envelope thick enough to suggest the Warren Commission Report was in it. It was a draft of the screenplay Blatty had hammered out while the novel was in production. Barely a month after *The Exorcist* had appeared in bookshops, Blatty had put the final touches on his magnum opus.

Blatty may have been pleased with himself for completing a script with such stealth and dispatch, but the response he received from Friedkin staggered him. "I think Friedkin was ill for three days after reading it," he wrote. "He just came in, said it was simply not faithful to the novel, and insisted I do a new script. He had a copy of the novel and had simply marked off the important scenes. It was so incredibly easy, yet I just did not think the novel could be translated."

In the creative battle between the word and the image, only the filmmaker regularly yields to brevity, an attribute Blatty did not possess as a novelist. Worse, perhaps, he did not possess it as a screenwriter, either. His original screenplay, more than two hundred pages of flashbacks, "superimposures," camera angles, freeze frames, stage directions, red herrings, and sermons caused Friedkin to tell him, bluntly: "Why would you do this, Bill? Your worst enemy wouldn't hand you a script like this."

Indeed, Blatty even tried dramatizing the epigraphs he had used for *The Exorcist*, including a wiretap recording of a conversation between two degenerate mobsters discussing a grisly torture session. It is a wonder he never tried filming the ISBN of the Bantam paperback. Oddly enough, he eliminated the prologue in Iraq, something he refused to do when Harper & Row had suggested it.

After rejecting the screenplay, Friedkin went home, opened a hardcover edition of *The Exorcist*, and circled scenes and dialogue from page after page, occasionally adding comments to his selections. With an eye to the screen, Friedkin jettisoned the competing subplots, minimized the murder mystery, and reduced the roles of Burke Dennings and, especially, Lt. Kinderman. Then he gave the annotated book back to Blatty for a rewrite.

Although its estimated running time would have approached four hours, the original screenplay contained didactic messaging crucial to Blatty. Later, even after the film had become a smash, Blatty resented Friedkin for cutting these homilies. "Friedkin told me that the first draft screenplay wasn't true to the novel," he told writer Mark Kermode. "But it *was*...."

Years later, they were still sparring over the final cut. In 1998, during a discussion at the Getty Museum moderated by Mark Kermode, the acerbic Friedkin responded to yet another complaint from Blatty about the mawkish ending that had been left on the cutting-room floor. 'You know, I think you're right, and I think what we should probably do is have you come on at the end of the film and say to the audience, 'Hey, this film is not a downer, folks! This is not a downer! And Karras lives on!' And the whole audience should have to be passed by you, Bill, and no one gets into the theater until you've explained the movie to them."

Blatty and Friedkin would finally revisit and compromise on *The Exorcist*, via a new version of the film that restored eleven minutes of footage left on the cutting-room floor in 1973.

CHAPTER 8

▲ ▲ ▲

The Gods of Casting

From the beginning, William Friedkin (along with publicists and the marketing team at Warner Bros.) circulated tales of supernatural forces surrounding the production of *The Exorcist*. But if unearthly powers might have affected one element of the film, it was the casting. "To this day," Friedkin said in *Leap of Faith*, a documentary on the making of *The Exorcist*, "as though there were forces beyond me, that brought things to that movie, like offerings, the whole picture was put together by the movie gods."

The four leads in *The Exorcist* were uniformly outstanding in their roles, and, except for Ellen Burstyn, none of them would ever exceed their performances for Friedkin. They seemed uniquely suited to the dark vision of *The Exorcist*.

For the role of Father Karras, Warner Bros. and Blatty targeted Marlon Brando, whose astonishing comeback in *The Godfather* after nearly a decade in the doldrums ultimately led to an Academy Award in 1972. (The mercurial Brando sent a proxy—Sacheen Littlefeather—to decline his Oscar.) According to Blatty, however, Friedkin feared being overshadowed by the now-resurgent Brando, once again considered the greatest actor of all time.

"Billy ran like the wind from star names," Blatty told writer Bob McCabe. "I proposed Marlon Brando to play Karras and Billy just hated that idea. Not because Brando wouldn't have been wonderful in the part, but because it would have been a Brando movie, and so on down the line."

And while Brando had behaved in *The Godfather*, his reputation as a loose cannon still trailed him in Hollywood, and his track record of obscure flops in the 1960s gave him the air of a box-office jinx waiting to happen. Out of all his starring vehicles since 1960—including disasters such as *The Countess from Hong Kong, Reflections in a Golden Eye*, and *Burn!*—only *Candy* could be counted as a moneymaker. Friedkin passed on Brando, who would go on to stun the country with *Last Tango in Paris*, the second-most controversial film of the early 1970s.

Another marquee name interested in the part was Jack Nicholson, who was then establishing himself as the face of New Hollywood. But Friedkin thought suspension of disbelief would be impossible with Nicholson, who, since *Easy Rider*, had become a symbol of nonconformity and skepticism. "Jack," he reportedly said, "if I saw you in a priest's collar, I would burst out laughing."

Also given a hard look was Roy Scheider, one of only a handful of top actors to eventually work with Friedkin twice. (In 1977, Scheider would headline *Sorcerer*, an extraordinary film that doubled as a financial calamity and the beginning of a career downturn for Friedkin.) Scheider had earned an Academy Award nomination as best supporting actor for his performance in *The French Connection*, and Friedkin seriously considered casting him as Karras. Among other attributes, Scheider had gravitas; the broken nose he had received as an amateur boxer in the 1940s would have justified the gym scene with Karras pounding on a heavy bag, and, finally, he would have been the only generally recognizable name on the marquee. While not an A-list actor, Scheider was on a streak that would last until the early 1980s: *The Seven-Ups, Jaws, Marathon Man*, and *All that Jazz* were a few of his standout turns in a solid decade of work. His quiet charisma, today a style as obsolete as VHS cassettes or double features, would have been a perfect fit for the downcast Karras.

This time, Blatty objected to the choice, telling Friedkin that Scheider was not sympathetic enough. Friedkin would later explain how Blatty came to that conclusion. "I was about to go with Roy," Friedkin recalled in an interview with the Directors Guild of America. "I had made *The French Connection* with him, and Bill Blatty said to me, 'I don't think he's right, I don't think Roy is—no, he's not.' It later turned out that Blatty wanted to play the part himself, because I would have cast Roy, but now again, we're going down to the wire. . . ."

Eventually, Friedkin and Blatty agreed on Stacy Keach, a newcomer with a reputation as one of the best stage actors in America. Keach, with an MFA from the Yale School of Drama, had impressed critics and filmgoers with turns in *Doc* and, especially, as the washed-up boxer Billy Tully in *Fat City*. For most of the 1970s, Keach would inspire newswire features about impending stardom—stardom that never arrived. "The trouble is that I haven't been doing enough of the so-called popular films," Keach said in 1975. "I've had myself tagged as a serious character actor because I've been involved in such plays as *King Lear*, *Hamlet*, and *Peer Gynt*."

Ultimately, Keach lost his first real opportunity to headline a popular film when fate intervened against him. William Friedkin had been haunted by a play he had seen in New York City—*That Championship Season*, written by a struggling thirty-three-year-old actor named Jason Miller, whose previous play, *Nobody Hears a Broken Drum*, came and went Off-Broadway without a sound.

Before embarking on a shaky career as a playwright, Miller had been an English teacher in Pennsylvania. As a child, he had thought about becoming a priest, and he credited his churchgoing days with inspiring his vocation. "The Latin Mass got me interested in theater," he told the Allentown, Pennsylvania, *Morning Call* in 1987. "The symbolism of the vestments and the sacraments, the high drama of the Crucifixion and the Resurrection—everything was mystical and theatrical to me. There was ceremony, judgment, forgiveness, redemption."

Miller had graduated from the Jesuit-affiliated University of Scranton and moved to New York City to pursue a precarious dream. "When I was growing up in Scranton, Pennsylvania," Miller told the *New York Times*, "New York was the capital of my imagination, the El Dorado of my mind. As soon as I was able, I started visiting whenever I could, coming with a little money and selling my blood on Delancey Street for a few dollars more, to sit and drink in the Cedar Bar, hoping that Jackson Pollock, Allan Ginsberg, or Norman Mailer would drop in."

According to a *Daily News* profile published after *That Championship Season* began buzzing in the theater world, Miller had lived a patchwork existence before achieving success. He had been a messenger, a waiter, a welfare investigator, a delivery truck driver, and had been playing dinner theater engagements in Texas. His wife had recently been handing out cigarette samples on Fifth Avenue. "I wrote several one-act plays during that run, but

I nearly gave up my acting career," Miller recalled. "I was always too short, too dark, or too Italian when they wanted an Irishman, and too Irish when they wanted an Italian. Once, I ended up as the Tin Man in *The Wizard of Oz* for six weeks, touring orphanages."

That Championship Season opened at the Estelle Newman Theater in New York City on May 2, 1972, and would eventually win a Pulitzer Prize for drama. Intrigued by Miller—and by the miasma of failure and religion pervading *That Championship Season*—Friedkin asked for a meeting. It did not go well. "It was a terrible meeting!" Friedkin told Peter Travers and Stephanie Reiff. "I was sick and had all these vitamin pills around and I think he was stoned. I looked at him and thought he was a junkie. He came, saw all the pills, and must have thought I was some kind of pill freak. We had a very tense meeting and I was not all that impressed with him."

Even after their dismal encounter, and with Keach already chosen, Friedkin could not shake Miller from his mind—that brooding, hangdog look, the quiet, almost mournful air. Then, one day, while in Los Angeles, he received an unexpected call. It was from Miller. Having finally read the novel, Miller realized just how connected he was to Father Karras. "I am that guy," he insisted to Friedkin, who instinctively offered Miller a screen test.

In the documentary *Friedkin Uncut*, Friedkin recreates the screwball dialogue he and Miller exchanged over the phone.

I said, can you catch a plane tomorrow and get out here tomorrow night?

He said, Fuck, no. He said, I don't fly. I'm not gonna get on an airplane. It'll take me a week to get out there on a train.

I said, You're really out of your fucking mind.

Still, Miller eventually showed up in Los Angeles after traveling cross-country by rail and shocked Friedkin with his audition. "I came to L.A. to do the screen test in some big old warehouse, with a papier-mâché bridge," Miller told *Cinefantastique*. "I said I didn't want to do anything from the script, I'll just improvise. So we did the scene on the bridge with Ellen [Burstyn]. Then I had to say Mass. I had every vestment for a High Mass: for the chalice they had an old grapefruit can, the Host was a Ritz cracker, and the Gospel was Blatty's book."

Despite having offered Stacy Keach the part, Miller was exactly what Friedkin had been looking for. "The camera loved his dark good looks, haunted eyes, quiet intensity, and low, compassionate voice," he wrote in his memoir. "He had a quality reminiscent of the late John Garfield."

In one of the first of many clashes he would have with the studio, Friedkin insisted on casting Miller, a Hollywood outsider known only to hard-core theatergoers in Midtown Manhattan. Although Warner Bros. balked, they eventually relented, despite reservations from nearly everyone involved. "Bill Blatty didn't want him, Burstyn didn't want him, nobody wanted him, which made me want him even more, I suppose," Friedkin told Bob McCabe. "And I got Warners to pay off Stacy Keach, which was a difficult thing to do. They had to pay him off in full."

Keach had a slightly different recollection. "I read for the part of the young priest in *The Exorcist*, performing with Ellen Burstyn and Linda Blair for writer William Peter Blatty and director William Friedkin," Keach wrote in his memoir *All in All: An Actor's Life On and Off the Stage*. "I knocked it out of the park. I just knew it. And I was right—that afternoon my agent called with the job offer . . . but she got a bit greedy, as agents are wont to do. The money was too low, she complained, so she had not agreed to the deal. She'd make a counteroffer on Monday. Over the weekend, Friedkin saw the Broadway hit *That Championship Season* and met the playwright, Jason Miller, who, Friedkin decided, had that certain something. He offered Jason the role. On Monday my agent found out she was too much, too late."

▲ ▲ ▲

According to various sources, Ali MacGraw, Jane Fonda, Anne Bancroft, Barbra Streisand, and Audrey Hepburn were all considered for the part of Chris MacNeil, the beleaguered actress whose daughter is possessed by a demon.

The multitalented Streisand, hot news since her debut in *Funny Girl* (1968), seemed an odd choice: barely thirty, she had yet to appear in a drama. As with much of what floats out of Hollywood, the famous names attached to forthcoming projects are often dangled for publicity purposes, to keep actors in the public consciousness, to pique interest in the film, or simply as a way for entertainment columnists to stay busy. Over the years, Blatty would say that he had frightened Streisand away at a party with an overzealous handshake, one of dozens of far-fetched claims he would make concerning *The Exorcist*. (This strange bit about handshakes probably was inspired by his one-time friend Shirley MacLaine, known for her firm grip.)

Hepburn, essentially semiretired, would have promised celebrity wattage; her last film, *Wait Until Dark*, released in 1967, was a surprise hit, underscoring her staying power. But she insisted that *The Exorcist* be shot in Rome, where she had relocated after a tempestuous marriage to Mel Ferrer. "No way did I want to film in Rome," Friedkin wrote, "it was impractical from every standpoint. All the other actors would have to be imported from the United States, and I didn't want a language barrier with the crew. In fact, I wanted my crew from *The French Connection*, starting with [cinematographer] Owen Roizman and [cameraman] Ricky Bravo. We asked Mrs. Hepburn to reconsider, but she declined."

As for Bancroft, she also had not appeared in a film since 1967, when she earned an Oscar nomination for playing the sultry Mrs. Robinson in *The Graduate*. Her legitimate interest in the role of Chris MacNeil was offset by the fact that she was pregnant. Warner Bros., looking to piggyback on the success of *The Exorcist* novel as soon as possible, passed on delaying the shoot for her.

For box-office purposes, Ali MacGraw might have sent *The Exorcist* into orbit—even beyond its record-breaking haul. The co-star of *Love Story*, one of the most astonishing jackpots in Hollywood history—$173.5 million against a budget of $2.2 million—MacGraw was as sought-after as any actress on the scene. And she had not yet become involved with Steve McQueen, a relationship that would keep her in the tabloids for the rest of the decade. But she was in her early thirties and, despite her performance in *Love Story*, had limited experience as an actress. With that in mind, Friedkin considered her too green for the part.

As controversial as anyone in Hollywood at the time, Fonda, whose raw, remarkable performance in *Klute* a year earlier had won her an Academy Award, likely saw Chris MacNeil as a step back. To an extent, Chris is a reactive role, and her character essentially disappears three-quarters of the way through the film, when Karras and Merrin arrive for the final confrontation with the demon. Fonda had also been attracting the kind of attention that went beyond *Variety* or *The Hollywood Reporter*. Her counterculture activism, which would culminate in the infamous "Hanoi Jane" photo in July 1972, might not have jibed with a big-budget production whose subtext, after all, was conservative. "I respect what she is doing," Friedkin said at the time, "but her strong stand on political issues would cause too great a loss in audience involvement."

Either way, Fonda was not interested. In yet another dubious anecdote, Blatty claimed that her response to playing Chris MacNeil was brutally frank: "Why would any studio want to make this capitalist rip-off bullshit?" (Fonda would later deny saying such a thing.)

That left Ellen Burstyn, a veteran television actress (she had been a regular on *The Doctors*) slowly transitioning to film in her late thirties. Alluring in *Tropic of Cancer*, haunting in *The King of Marvin Gardens*, Academy-nominated for *The Last Picture Show*, Burstyn gave Chris MacNeil individuality—something the character had lost in the translation from page to screen. In the novel, MacNeil is a more complex character, an emblem of the secular materialist whose lack of faith condemns her to accept Christ the hard way; but in the script, she becomes secondary to the possession of Regan and the climactic battle between Karras and the demon. To her credit, Burstyn fleshed out every dimension of Chris: the confident actress on set, the playful mother, the angry wife abandoned by an irresponsible husband, the shocked woman besieged by forces she cannot control or understand.

Burstyn got the role despite some corporate pushback, according to Friedkin, who, like Blatty, often seemed incapable of telling an anecdote about *The Exorcist* without including the theme of great struggles overcome by heroic feats. "The studio, by the studio I mean Ted Ashley [Chairman of Warner Bros.], was against her," Friedkin told Peter Travers and Reiff. "But he came around. There was no divine inspiration. I just think there are very few first-rate intelligent actresses around, and I was impressed with Ellen Burstyn as a person as well as an actress."

Even in 1973, when he made that comment (which sounds hopelessly sexist to modern sensibilities), Friedkin was wrong about first-rate intelligent actresses. Gena Rowlands, Julie Harris, and Joanne Woodward, among others, would all have fit the bill, but Friedkin had never been shy about his chauvinism. "I don't know too many intelligent women," he told Sally Quinn of the *Washington Post* in a 1973 feature. "In fact, I don't know any woman I'd rather talk to than a man. If I met a woman who was smarter than I was, I'd marry her or at least try to spend a lot of time with her. Of course, I don't mean to judge all women, only the ones I've had the experience of meeting. I'm really concerned about it because I happen to move in relatively sophisticated circles with women of background, experience, and education. I have never met one single woman in my life who I felt was on an intelligence or emotional level with any men I know. I have never gotten into a nitty-gritty conversation without the woman pulling out her femininity in the moment of crisis like, 'How can you talk to me like that?' or 'You never spend time with me.' The women I have met are not women whose identities are apart from men or strong enough to maintain them."

Like Shirley MacLaine (whom Blatty used as a model for Chris), Burstyn had a background in dance and a New Age outlook. Divorced, with a mentally disturbed ex-husband who stalked her, and a young son to worry about, Burstyn also reflected, to an extent, the dysfunctional family aspect of *The Exorcist*. But if there was an overriding reason why Burstyn craved the part, it was probably because of her supernatural beliefs, which went beyond her interest in Jung and Eastern religions. (Later, Burstyn would spread and solidify the nonsense of a cursed set and demonic forces surrounding the film. Her memoir, *Lessons in Becoming Myself*, is full of unexplainable incidents that took place in her life before, during, and after *The Exorcist*, making her the perfect spokesperson for the wayward occultism that has trailed the film since 1973.)

Burstyn convinced Friedkin to meet her—but away from an office or a studio set. It was as if Burstyn believed the metaphysical trappings of her house—where they eventually met—would have some sort of effect on the director. "It was a kind of hippy pad in the Hollywood Hills," Friedkin told Bob McCabe. "And she was wearing a big shift. She was very heavy-set. She was probably about fifty pounds heavier than you see in the film, and one of the first things she did was offer me some grass, which I don't smoke, have never been interested in and was sort of turned off by. But then she started to talk and tell me about her spiritual and religious beliefs. And I was very impressed with her and her knowledge of the book, and I told her at that time that these other actresses were under consideration and that the studio really wanted a star. And she said, 'Well, I believe that it's fate that I will do this part.' I said, 'Good luck to you.' And I left, never thinking that I would have to use her."

While Friedkin would offer several versions of how Burstyn wound up portraying Chris (including one where Ted Ashley laid on the floor and played an "over my dead body" routine), his comments about her weight offer a clue. "At the time she was seventy or so pounds overweight, but she was so interesting and fascinating, and she understood the part totally and knew all of the metaphysics surrounding it and everything else. But I didn't think it was going to happen. She said, 'I'm gonna lose the weight, watch and see.' So months go by, she's losing the weight, and she starts to look great."

Naturally, the most difficult part to cast was the one that drove Mike Nichols away from involvement: the role of Regan, the twelve-year-old girl who falls prey to a demon. In some ways, Nichols might have been right to beg off. The child actors who had dominated Hollywood in the past— from Shirley Temple to Judy Garland to Mickey Rooney—rarely had to manifest such psychic distress. There were exceptions, of course, such as Martin Stephens in *The Innocents* and Patty Duke in *The Miracle Worker*, but most teens and preteens dealt with everyday troubles with wide-eyed sentimentality.

For Friedkin, the right candidate to play Regan needed several qualifications, and the frustrating hunt dragged out long enough to inch him toward despair. "For four months in 1972, half a dozen casting directors around the country put hundreds of young girls, ages eleven through thirteen on videotape," he wrote in *The Friedkin Connection*. "Over a thousand girls eventually auditioned. I watched the tapes, if only for a minute or two, and personally interviewed at least fifty girls. It seemed hopeless. The question was not only whether a child could portray the character's innocence as well as her possession without self-consciousness, but how she would react to the experience itself. How would it affect her life? None of the girls I met seemed likely to overcome these obstacles."

Given Friedkin's proclivity (as well as Blatty) to embellish, it should be noted that the "one thousand girls" had, in other interviews, been pegged as five hundred, give or take a few. Still, the quandary was real. Not only did Friedkin have to cast a believable, sympathetic Regan, a girl who could withstand the darkness of the material, but he would also have to be careful about culling such an actress from the Hollywood set, where megalomaniac parents could make shooting difficult.

As preproduction advanced, casting director Nessa Hyams found herself reduced to impromptu soliciting. "We saw so many kids, I couldn't find anybody in L.A.," she told David Konow. "Billy and I used to have dinner, and he would make me get up and ask people with little girls at their table,

"Hello, you don't know me, but I'm doing a movie.' Most people would look at me like I was some horrible pervert or something!"

Finally, New York–based Juliet Taylor, who would go on to cast *Taxi Driver* and over two dozen Woody Allen films, recommended Linda Blair. From Westport, Connecticut, the vibrant Blair had starred in print ads and commercials for JCPenney, Sears, Ivory Soap, and Carefree gum. She also had walk-ons in a pair of now-obscure films, *The Way We Live Now* and *The Sporting Club*. "She was smart but not precocious. Cute but not beautiful. A normal, happy twelve-year-old girl," Friedkin recalled. "Her name was Linda Blair. Her mother was quiet, pleasant, not a stage mother. Linda was represented by an agency that suggested ten other girls to us. Not her. . . . Her main interest was training and showing horses, for which she won a lot of blue ribbons. She was a straight-A student in Westport, Connecticut. I found her adorable. Irresistible."

According to Friedkin, the auditioning process that saw Blair earn the role included frank discussions about some of the taboo aspects of the script. By gauging her reactions to such subjects as masturbation, Friedkin would determine whether Blair could handle the disturbing, demanding part.

From the beginning, the filmmakers worried about how such dark material might warp Blair, especially some of the sexually explicit taunts. "I was afraid," Blatty said during an interview with Merv Griffin. "I didn't know what traumatic effect it might have upon a child. But of course it depends upon the child. Linda is so psychologically sturdy that I think she's indestructible. She has a great deal more common sense than her elders, myself included."

Mrs. Elinor Blair had a similar outlook when asked by a reporter how she could allow her daughter, only thirteen at the time, to participate in such a bleak production. "It was just something else that had to be done," Mrs. Blair told the New York *Daily News*. "Children today are so much more knowledgeable than when we were kids. They're more sophisticated and better-adjusted. It's the parents that you have to worry about. They go to see a film and are horrified. But the children are not bothered by it as much."

Still, there was widespread concern that Linda Blair might be psychologically affected by the demanding role. To limit her exposure, the producers hired a double named Eileen Dietz to perform some of the more physical aspects of the role, including the infamous crucifix scene, and tried to shield her from the pornographic implications of her part. "She has an understanding of what this all is, but no real deep knowledge of how dirty and how vile it is supposed to be," Friedkin told Travers and Reiff. "Linda thinks that this all is a game. And I intend to keep it that way. She is capable of portraying everything with realism."

In brief scenes maximized for their telling details, Blair effectively conveyed a range of feelings and emotions leading up to her possession—she is sweet, mischievous, wholesome, forlorn, and dispirited. Finally, when the demon takes over her completely, Blair is suitably, almost flamboyantly, diabolical. Because Friedkin insisted on a relentless pace and a manageable running time, characterization throughout the film was minimal. Yet Blair managed to create a convincing, rounded personality despite a sketchy backstory. With her first appearance on-screen, Blair immediately won over the audience, earning sympathy for her future torments. Whether or not Blair deserved an Academy Award is questionable; that *The Exorcist* hinges on her exceptional performance is certain.

▲ ▲ ▲

Group Theatre veteran Lee J. Cobb topped the supporting cast. Long typecast as a heavy, Cobb plays the affable Lt. Kinderman, who investigates the death of Burke Dennings with a comic undertone reminiscent of another famous lieutenant: Columbo. Comparisons of Kinderman to Columbo (immortalized on ABC by the marvelous Peter Falk) drove Blatty haywire. With an ego as big as the budget of *The Exorcist*, Blatty would not only refute the influence of Columbo outright, but he would also lie about it. (Similarly, William Friedkin would say on a DVD commentary that "Columbo is probably ripped-off of this character," adding that Peter Falk's "characterization owes a lot to Lee J. Cobb's performance," which were two self-serving fabrications.)

"I cannot begin to convey the extent of my irritation when I read letters—and I get quite a few of them—asking if I based the character of Kinderman on Columbo," Blatty wrote. "As any plagiarist would know, the novel was written long before Columbo debuted on TV."

This is categorically false, and because Blatty was part of the industry that produced Columbo, it is likely a deliberate falsehood. In fact, Columbo had been in existence since 1960, when the Chevy Mystery Show aired an episode called "Enough Rope," starring Bert Freed as the title character.

Two years later, Columbo was recycled for a stage play starring Joseph Cotten and Thomas Mitchell. Finally, Peter Falk played the title role in a television movie that was so popular it eventually led to the creation of a regular series. That movie, *Prescription: Murder*, aired on February 20, 1968, long before Blatty created Kinderman for his novel. Within fifteen minutes of *Prescription: Murder*, Falk mentions his wife in a jokey aside, much as Kinderman would in *The Exorcist*.

What little star wattage *The Exorcist* radiated belonged to art-house favorite Max Von Sydow, the versatile Swede who had appeared in several Ingmar Bergman films and crashed the international scene in 1957 as the knight who plays chess with Death in *The Seventh Seal*. Both Friedkin and Blatty immediately targeted Von Sydow for the role of Father Merrin, the exorcist who confronts the demon with Father Karras by his side. Von Sydow had a spiritual quality that Friedkin recognized as perfect for the priest who must battle evil. "I felt the dignity he is associated with in every film he's done was important for Merrin," Friedkin told Travers and Reiff, "because the man chosen to be the exorcist is a man who has lived a pure life."

The naturalist styles of Burstyn and Cobb (both with Method backgrounds), the appealing teen mannerisms of Blair, the low-key approach of Miller, and the monolithic distinction of Von Sydow gave *The Exorcist* a decided edge over most horror films of the time. The ensemble also raised the intrinsic value of material written in questionable taste.

With the outstanding cast set, Friedkin was closer to his goal of realistically filming unbelievable events.

CHAPTER 9

This Bizarre New World: Horror Movies Before *The Exorcist*

uring its formative years, Hollywood had a few hits with spooky films, most notably those starring Lon Chaney Sr., "The Man with a Thousand Faces." (Although *The Hunchback of Notre Dame* had mass appeal, *The Phantom of the Opera* provided chills.) Not until talkies arrived, however, did horror become a stand-alone genre, like Westerns or melodramas.

In 1930, Universal Pictures, which had Chaney under contract, cast him in *Dracula*. Unable to secure the rights to the Bram Stoker novel, Universal settled instead on a 1924 stage version written by Hamilton Deane, which had caused a commotion in London. Deane, an Irish showman, anticipated, and perhaps inspired, some of the ballyhoo that would eventually surround *The Exorcist*. When *Dracula* opened in London, Deane announced that a nurse would be in attendance to help spectators overcome by fright. He also planted women in the audience, who would faint at appropriate moments, ensuring buzz about a play that made its viewers swoon.

In 1927, eccentric publisher and producer Horace Liveright brought *Dracula* to Broadway and cast Bela Lugosi as The Count. Despite the fact that Lugosi could barely speak English, *Dracula* became a success, touring the country after its engagement in New York.

When Universal released *Dracula* on February 2, 1931, it set off a creepy new trend that would last, with a brief interval, until the mid-1940s. A yeoman effort by Tod Browning—who may have lost interest in the film after Lon Chaney Sr., originally slated to play the Count, died just before shooting began—*Dracula* was an unusual curio that shocked unprepared audiences with its novelty villain, the forty-eight-year-old Bela Lugosi.

Dracula was such a smash that Universal went into overdrive looking for another nineteenth-century gothic novel to adapt. They settled on *Frankenstein*, a far more complex property than *Dracula*; nevertheless, Universal, sensing a potential bonanza, rushed into production.

With a star-making performance from Boris Karloff, an unforgettable makeup job by Jack Pierce, and a genuinely disturbing air, *Frankenstein* surpassed *Dracula* in both ticket sales and fear. Unlike *Dracula*, with a surprisingly uninspired Browning behind the camera, *Frankenstein* was stylishly filmed by James Whale, inspired by the Expressionism of Robert Wiene and F. W. Murnau. "The picture was phenomenal, smashing box-office records and igniting a storm of controversy wherever it played," wrote Michael Brunas in *Universal Horrors: The Studio's Classic Films, 1931–1946*. "Far from being regarded as the artful, literate horror classic it is now considered, *Frankenstein*, in its day, was seen as a grisly blood-soaked example of exploitative filmmaking."

After putting the ghastly and the gothic on the map with *Dracula* and *Frankenstein* in 1931, Universal Pictures ushered in a horror craze that spread across the country. Most studios jumped into the fright fad—from comedy specialists MGM to social realist stalwarts Warner Bros.—producing a wide range of chillers, including some that remain objectionable even today. Before the Hays Code arrived to sanitize Hollywood, horror films bordered the edge of polite society. Among the most disturbing of these early genre exercises were the astonishing *Freaks* (Tod Browning, 1932), pulled from theaters in record time after a public uproar; *Island of Lost Souls*, banned in Britain; *White Zombie*, an independent production that grossed $8 million dollars against a budget of roughly $65,000; the outlandish Expressionism of *The Black Cat* (Edgar G. Ulmer, 1934, and featuring one of the first Satanists on the silver screen); *Murders in the Rue Morgue*, suggesting bestiality and interspecies blood transfusions; and the outrageous *Kongo*, with enough atrocities to make the Hays Code seem reasonable.

This bizarre new world of doppelgangers, mad scientists, ghouls, hunchbacks, reprobates, mountebanks, zombies, vampires, mummies, and werewolves lasted until about 1936, when it seemed to have run its course. But in 1939, the rerelease of both *Dracula* and *Frankenstein* produced such spectacular box-office returns that studios revived the cycle. Once again, Universal led the charge, cranking out spin-offs and sequels to their classic films with the efficiency of a Ford assembly line. By the mid-1940s, Universal had so exhausted the formula that it simply switched labels: horror films became comedies, with crossover appearances featuring the comedy duo Abbott and Costello and battles royale retrospectively known as "monster rallies."

At the same time, the quiet, psychological suspense films produced by Val Lewton—*Cat People*, *I Walked with a Zombie*, and *The Leopard Man*, among others—in the early 1940s for RKO faded away. Chiaroscuro and stylized sound stages were out; high-key lighting and on-location shooting were in. Even the concept of "horror" had changed. The Eisenhower era, what poet Robert Lowell once called "The tranquilized Fifties," was soon mirrored in the films Hollywood cranked out. In the wake of mass UFO sightings and the fear of nuclear annihilation (after Russia successfully detonated an atomic bomb in 1949), Hollywood spent most of the 1950s producing sci-fi films that often doubled as Cold War parables.

Traditional horror movies essentially disappeared from neighborhood screens until imports from the United Kingdom made a bloody splash in the late 1950s. With its reboots of *Frankenstein*, *Dracula*, and *The Mummy*, Hammer Film Productions, an independent company based in London, resurrected not just the famous monsters of a previous era but the gravity implicit in the genre. Although Hammer featured an occasional gag in its films, Abbott and Costello were nowhere to be found. In addition, Hammer pushed the bounds of permissibility, drawing critical rebuke for its Eastmancolor gore and earning X certificates from the British censorship board. *The Curse of Frankenstein* and *Dracula*, both directed by Terence Fisher, had an air of maturity few American horror cheapies could match.

These period films, featuring lush set designs, voluptuous women in low-cut dresses, graphic makeup, and far better actors than could be found pantomiming in *Creature with the Atom Brain* or *War of the Colossal Beast*, took both sides of the Atlantic by storm. And no sooner did Hammer begin raking in the money than the expected cloning began. Surprisingly, the conveyor belt did not materialize in a major studio but from a production house notorious for its cheesy output aimed almost exclusively at the exploding teen market. In the late 1950s, American International Pictures (AIP) released such low-budget offerings as *Drag Strip Girl*, *I Was a Teenage Werewolf, Hot Rod Gang, Daddy-O, Diary of a High School Bride, Invasion of the Saucer Men,* and *Reform School Girl.*

In 1959, B-movie maven Roger Corman convinced the déclassé AIP to pry open the studio coffers for a series of Gothic films loosely based on the tales of Edgar Allan Poe. To ensure name recognition, AIP made Vincent Price the centerpiece of most of these adaptations. After years as a bit player in Hollywood, Price finally made it to headline status in 1953 with *The House of Wax*, a 3-D novelty film directed by Andre de Toth (who, ironically, was blind in one eye). But it took a few more years before Price became synonymous with horror films. *The Fly*, released in 1958, was another surprise hit, and Price rarely appeared in mainstream dramas again. In 1959, his filmography was decidedly grim: *House on Haunted Hill, Return of the Fly, The Tingler,* and *The Bat* (which was more of a mystery thriller).

Two of these productions—*House on Haunted Hill* and *The Tingler*—were directed by William Castle, a veteran huckster specializing in gimmick horror films targeting high school seniors. Castle, the man behind such marketing ploys as handing out life insurance policies to ticket buyers who might "die of fright" and zip-lining glow-in-the-dark skeletons above a giggling audience, typified the schlocky nature of the genre at the time.

Corman and AIP consciously tried to change that, with solid box-office success if mixed aesthetic results. From 1960 through 1964, Corman directed eight Gothic melodramas with Poe as their cornerstone. (*The Haunted Palace*, released in 1963, used H. P. Lovecraft as its source, but exploitation specialists thought nothing of false advertising.) With better production values than the average drive-in film and a recognizable star headlining, the Poe cycle was unusual in its dedication to quality. Shot in wide-screen, using scripts by Richard Matheson, Charles Beaumont, and Robert Towne, and with the same philosophy as Hammer regarding buxom starlets (even casting Hammer mainstays such as Hazel Court, who starred in three AIP Poe films), this series stood out in the early 1960s, when *Psycho* had made everyone scramble over the mass-killer-with-a-Freudian-complex genre. "What I was trying to do was bring back the concept of the gothic horror film, which was not original to me, obviously," Corman told *Film Comment* in 2016. "But that type of film had fallen out of favor, so for a young audience it was a new type of film, and I felt that would appeal to them. And always with Vincent [Price] playing the lead, it would be a young man and a young girl playing the second leads, so we did have the name and the stature of Vincent, but we would have a young leading man and leading lady in their twenties to appeal to a teenage audience."

Unfortunately, the American dollar did not stretch as far as the British pound. Nor did AIP have its own sprawling studio (as Hammer did) or, given their location in Southern California, ready access to a Gothic mansion. In fact, for *The Pit and the Pendulum,* AIP rented their castle piecemeal from various production companies and assembled it, like an oversized Lego kit, on a soundstage. But sets were the least of the problems Corman faced. Wooden acting (aside from Price, who had his own limitations), wayward accents, erratic soundtracks, stock footage, florid dialogue, and an overabundance of fake cobwebs gave the cycle a campiness AIP may not have intended. Corman, however, seemed to sense how the overripe material edged burlesque. As the series went on, he seemed unable to maintain the gloomy tone and began injecting the films with farcical elements, possibly in hopes of attracting the wandering attention of the teen audience now flocking to beach-party films starring Sandra Dee, Annette Funicello, and Frankie Avalon. Both *Tales of Terror* (an anthology) and *The Raven* were spoofs, with the sad-eyed Peter Lorre humorously ad-libbing throughout.

Corman (as well as other cut-rate producers) also began casting geriatric stars of the 1930s and 1940s, men with some connection to the early horror canon—Boris Karloff, Lorre, Lon Chaney Jr., Basil Rathbone, and Ray Milland—primarily for comic effect. To an extent, these veterans of the Golden Age had been resurrected by television, which began airing the horror classics in the 1950s, giving Hollywood its first taste of ancillary revenue. The drawback was that producers with even smaller budgets than AIP began hiring these senescent ex-stars for progressively worse fare. To their credit, Karloff, Lorre, and others, for the most part, avoided the true bottom feeders, such as the duo of Herschell Gordon Lewis and David Friedman, whose atrocious *Blood Feast* (1963) established the gory splatter movie, or various fly-by-night hucksters who produced such classics as *Hand of Death*, *The Leech Woman*, *Hillbillies in a Haunted House*, *Night of Bloody Horror*, and *The Incredibly Strange Creatures Who Stopped Living and Became Mixed-Up Zombies*, among dozens of other similar exploitation titles.

These amateur auteurs, whose sole aim was to earn bookings at drive-ins and a handful of grindhouses, could barely use a light meter or understand focus, but they nevertheless dominated the disreputable genre at its lowest levels. Occasionally, singular films were produced under similar circumstances—crude, inconsistent, with spotty acting and editing, but effective nonetheless, such as *Night Tide* and *Carnival of Souls*. But most serious horror films in the early-to-mid-1960s were imported: *The Innocents*, *The Haunting*, *Burn, Witch, Burn!*, and the occasional Hammer release.

Other than Corman, the exception to this rule was Alfred Hitchcock, whose horror and gothic bona fides had been established with *The Lodger* (1929), *Rebecca* (1940), and *Shadow of a Doubt* (1943), and who had gone over the top with *Psycho*, certainly the most influential horror film in history.

Produced on a micro-budget and released in June 1960, *Psycho* terrified audiences with its tawdriness, its sympathetic killer, its nightmare score (courtesy of Bernard Herrmann), its unrelieved tension, its twist ending, and its shocking shower scene, which resulted in the death of the headline star only forty minutes into the film.

Paramount, which had Hitchcock under contract, had no interest in backing such a risky and risqué project—it negotiated an unusual financial deal with the director and limited itself to distribution. Most of the financing came from Hitchcock himself, through his television production company, Shamley. The result was a financial windfall no filmmaker had ever seen before. With a 60-40 split on profits, Hitchcock made millions of dollars on *Psycho* at a time when the cost of the average movie ticket was roughly seventy cents.

Anticipating *The Exorcist* by more than a decade, *Psycho* also caused an uproar in and out of theaters. Reports of faintings and freak-outs at screenings became common, and the lines of hopeful ticket buyers stretched for blocks. Also like *The Exorcist*, critical response to *Psycho* ranged from outrage to bewilderment to acclaim.

Mixed reviews from *Time*, *Esquire*, the *New York Times*, and the *Boston Globe* contrasted with raves from *Variety*, the New York *Daily News*, and *Newsweek*. The *Chicago Tribune* seemed to sum up the consensus of *Psycho*: "Despite the second-half rally, the film is not the best of Hitchcock because of its uneven quality taken as a whole."

Although William Friedkin never stopped resenting Hitchcock for the necktie affair in 1965, he never hid his admiration for the erstwhile "Master of Suspense." In a 2003 interview with the American Film Institute, Friedkin clarified his debt to Hitchcock: "He's the greatest, I mean look, nobody better in filmmaking. That's it. Stops and starts right there, basically. He encompasses all the vocabulary." Indeed, Friedkin patterned the slow build of *The Exorcist* after the suspenseful but relatively sedate first half of *Psycho*. And Friedkin likely considered what Hitchcock once said about *Psycho* deliberately evoking an emotional response from the viewer: "That's the whole device. After all, the showing of a violent murder at the beginning was intended purely to instill into the minds of the audience a certain degree of what is to come."

But the two films diverge widely on aesthetic intent. Where *The Exorcist* is a fairly predictable and mechanical exercise, *Psycho* subverts audience expectations at every opportunity—even before principal photography began. By casting teen idol Anthony Perkins as a cross-dressing serial killer, Hitchcock sadistically dashed the illusions of countless high school girls. In addition, Janet Leigh, at the time a gossip column mainstay because of her marriage to universal heartthrob Tony Curtis, lost the star treatment when she was slaughtered in a motel shower less than halfway through the film.

Although *Psycho* was stylish, superbly acted (except for the inert John Gavin, whom Hitchcock nicknamed "the Stiff"), and lively, it spawned most of its imitations from a cesspool of drive-in schlockmeisters (surprisingly, Hammer produced some watchable knockoffs across the Atlantic). That meant that the American horror scene remained undistinguished and largely dedicated to cheap thrills for teens between sessions of heavy petting.

Until Roman Polanski made his American debut.

▲ ▲ ▲

In 1967, two years after making international headlines with *Repulsion*, a tour de force of psychological terror, Roman Polanski arrived in Los Angeles to helm *Rosemary's Baby*, one of the landmarks of horror cinema.

Looking to revive the fortunes of a struggling Paramount, new VP of production Robert Evans, still in his thirties, saw *Rosemary* as the kind of cultural hot property that would transcend the entertainment pages of daily newspapers and give the studio a new, edgy identity. To ensure that *Rosemary* would rise above the usual genre hokum, he ousted William Castle as director and insisted on replacing him with Polanski, a European art-house stalwart. As producer and owner of the film rights to the novel, Castle, a twenty-year veteran of B quickies, had grandly envisioned himself escaping the carnivalesque world of gimmicks (*Emergo, Percepto*) and teen screamers (*House on Haunted Hill, The Tingler, 13 Ghosts*) and vaulting into respectability behind the camera on *Rosemary*.

In the 1960s, Castle, alongside Roger Corman, had been the leading purveyor of horror films in America that were, by varying degrees, a cut above typical drive-in fare. Despite the low-rent nature of most of his output, Castle had a fair eye for setups and a knack for casting. In the 1940s, Castle directed a pair of solid films noir, *When Strangers Marry* and *Undertow*, but a head-to-head comparison with Corman, however, would leave Castle as a perennial runner-up. His unique brand of schlock and hoopla served him well but rarely captured the adult demographic. Castle also had unfulfilled artistic ambitions. "I've just paid $150,000 for something fantastic," he announced in early 1967. "I bought Ira Levin's book, *Rosemary's Baby*, which I predict will be a bestseller. I plan to film it as a sophisticated thriller—exciting, different. It's going to take me completely out of what I've been doing."

Evans and Paramount CEO Charles Bluhdorn had other ideas, however, and they did not include handing over the adaptation of a best-selling hardback to a man who, in 1964, had Joan Crawford swinging an ax in the ludicrous Grande Dame Guignol *Strait-Jacket*.

An urban gothic with an unnerving current of black humor running through it, *Rosemary's Baby* is a superbly mounted film whose multilayered meanings and sly ironies reward repeat viewings. Essentially the first Hollywood horror film executed as an A-list project since the Universal era, *Rosemary's Baby* outstripped all other genre exercises in production values, theme, acting, and style; from that point of view, *Rosemary's Baby* is as close to a watershed film the genre has ever produced after its initial development in the 1930s.

Among the first wave of New Hollywood films, *Rosemary's Baby* prefigured the controversy the nascent movement would generate in coming years. Its taboo subject matter (persecuted woman gives birth to a demon baby) would have been scotched just a few years earlier by the Production Code. Brief nudity, a supernatural rape scene, and a downbeat ending also might have disturbed the moral sensibilities of entertainment puritans. As it is, *Rosemary's Baby* earned a "Condemned" designation from the Catholic

League and was banned outright in a few theaters when it opened in June 1968.

Its lurid plot, breezily unraveled by Ira Levin in the novel, becomes, among other things, a meditation on paranoia. Here, on the well-heeled Upper West Side of New York City, Satanism is embodied by Roman and Minnie Castevet, an eccentric elderly couple who, along with other members of a local coven, plot to use Rosemary Woodhouse (played by Mia Farrow) as a surrogate for Lucifer. Her husband, played by John Cassavetes, joins the coven in exchange for success as an actor, a bargain-basement Faustian pact meant to mock the cheapjack values of the striving American. *Rosemary's Baby* is gaslighting with a sinister twist—one that Roman Polanski made clear in subsequent interviews and writings: "For credibility's sake, I decided that there would have to be a loophole—the possibility that Rosemary's supernatural experiences were figments of her imagination."

With the Summer of Love rapidly degenerating into the chaos and disorder of 1968, *Rosemary's Baby* seemed almost attuned to the pessimistic times. It was a gold mine, paving the way for future horror films with more serious intentions, if not themes.

Not only is *Rosemary's Baby* a pivotal film for the development of the horror genre, but it is the key influence on *The Exorcist*, both the novel and the film. Indeed, the ambiguity Polanski aimed for in *Rosemary's Baby* inspired Friedkin to add a few enigmatic scenes to *The Exorcist*. William Peter Blatty, who viewed himself as some sort of apostle, was incapable of obliquity; he was mostly interested in sermonizing. With Friedkin as a go-between, *The Exorcist* lost most of its religious pamphleteering in the cutting room. The result was what Friedkin had intended—an escapist film whose commercial possibilities superseded moralizing. "I'm not making a commercial for the Catholic Church," he told Blatty.

In the future, Friedkin would make dubious claims about the ambiguity of *The Exorcist*, but his debt to *Rosemary's Baby* was nonetheless unmistakable.

PART II

CONJURING TERROR: FILMING *THE EXORCIST*

CHAPTER **10**
▲ ▲ ▲

Roll Camera, Roll Sound, Rolling

With a budget of just under $5 million and an optimistic shooting schedule of eighty-five days, *The Exorcist* began principal photography on Monday, August 14, 1972, in New York City.

The first scene of what would often seem like an ill-starred production occurred at Goldwater Memorial Hospital on Welfare Island (now Roosevelt Island) in the East River. Here Karras visits his mother (played by Vasiliki Maliaros) in what resembles a psychiatric ward. To reach his mother, Karras, with a visible look of distaste, must circumnavigate a crowd of mentally ill patients. As a metaphor for his faltering faith, Karras has his Roman collar stripped away by one of the inmates.

William Friedkin once claimed that the shuffling figures in robes and gowns in that scene were real patients, but eccentric character actor Joe Spinell offered up an even stranger version of the on-screen talent. "Billy Friedkin, who I did extra work for in *The French Connection*, hired me on *The Exorcist* as like the second assistant director," Spinell told *Psychotronic Video* magazine. "I used to go and cast all these crazy people out of the nuthouses here (New York City). They had me do this because I would go places other people wouldn't go."

Among the other sequences completed in New York were: the dormitory scenes between Karras and Father Dwyer (Fordham University, The Bronx), the boxing gym scene where Karras whales on a heavy bag (Elmhurst, Queens), and the scene where Karras visits his mother in her squalid neighborhood (West 48th Street). The chilling subway scene, where Karras is revulsed by a beggar (and which reveals the depths of his distress), takes place at the 34th Street Penn Station stop.

What marks most of these locations—beyond how vivid they are as real spaces—is a sense of desolation. In pre-gentrification New York City, still a few years away from being declared a national Sodom, the seedy, shabby, and sickly atmosphere corresponds to what Karras feels emotionally: despair.

▲ ▲ ▲

Meanwhile, at the Ceco Studio, on West 54th Street, a large crew set about round-the-clock construction of the main set: a detailed replica of the Georgetown house described in the novel. Almost immediately, *The Exorcist* was delayed when Friedkin dismissed his set designer, John Robert Lloyd after Lloyd had already completed the interiors. Friedkin was not only unhappy with the technical limitations of the set, but he was particularly incensed by the proposed color scheme. "Shortly after the interior of the 'MacNeil House' started construction, what I saw shocked me," he wrote. "There were curved archways, not common in a colonial interior; the ceilings were too low to allow overhead lighting; the rooms are too small to allow for depth or complex staging; and worse, there were paint samples on the walls: pink and chartreuse!"

Although Lloyd had collaborated with Friedkin on *The Night They Raided Minsky's* and *The Boys in the Band,* his work on *The Exorcist* bordered on incompetence. When asked by Burstyn what was wrong with the set, Friedkin replied, "Among other things, the goddamn walls are too short! If I shot up from a low camera angle, I'd be shooting off the set."

Friedkin subsequently hired Bill Malley, an inexperienced designer with only a few television credits. The whole structure—which was partially a trick set built to accommodate the practical effects that would dominate the second half of the film—was disassembled, redesigned, and rebuilt, costing the studio tens of thousands of dollars, and delaying the interior shoot from August 14 to September 25.

This early setback was a sign of things to come for *The Exorcist,* which suffered unexpected delays from illness, technical malfunctions, and the trial-and-error process of achieving innovative special effects.

▲ ▲ ▲

In late October, production moved to Georgetown, where the events of the story take place. Taking advantage of the appropriate weather, Georgetown gives *The Exorcist* a suitable autumnal feel, the windswept leaves hinting at the turmoil to come. An upper-crust neighborhood, Georgetown as a setting also reflects how secular pursuits—wealth and materialism—cannot insulate Chris MacNeil from the dark forces that assault Regan. "It is amazing how Blatty set this particular story in a given place which does exist," Friedkin told Travers and Rieff. "He caught the life and feelings of that place which certainly influence all the characters in the story. The places were all there and quite accessible. Georgetown has never appeared in a feature film, but it has marvelous qualities for this type of film."

With its cobblestone streets, its Colonial- and Federal-style architecture, and its Jesuit trappings, Georgetown is more than just a picturesque milieu. As the first Roman Catholic University in America, founded in 1789 by Bishop John Carroll and the Jesuit Society, Georgetown University functions as a symbolic battleground: the demon has infiltrated not just a particular family or a particular house but a religious stronghold, so to speak, magnifying the stakes at hand.

All the horrors of *The Exorcist* took place in a stately Federal-style revival house, built in 1950 and located on 3600 Prospect Street, in Georgetown, scouted by William Peter Blatty and David Salven before filming began.

While 3600 Prospect Street seemed like the perfect location, Friedkin could not convince its owner, a seventy-three-year-old socialite named Florence S. Mahoney, to fling its doors open for Hollywood. "When I first went to see her, she was very sweet, but she wanted no part of this movie," Friedkin wrote in the *Los Angeles Times*. "We couldn't pay her enough money. She'd never heard of *The Exorcist*, and she turned me down."

It took the intervention of Jack Valenti, president of the Motion Picture Association of America, for Mahoney to agree. As a lobbyist and supporter of various health causes (her unstinting advocacy was largely responsible for expanding the National Institutes of Health), Mahoney had links to the DC power structure, including Valenti, who had once been Special Advisor to President Lyndon B. Johnson.

Since the early 1950s, Mahoney had been using her Georgetown home as a high-society salon, inviting scientists and politicians to dinner parties for far-ranging conversations. At the time the production showed up, Mahoney was receiving Democratic presidential nominee George McGovern between events. "Mahoney knew nothing about movies," Friedkin recalled. "She didn't see movies. She hated the idea of a film crew in her house while she was hosting [George] McGovern there during the [1972 presidential] campaign." Even after assenting to Valenti, Mahoney would only allow Friedkin to shoot exteriors, forcing him to reconstruct the interiors in a New York City studio and compromise his obsession with realism.

Bill Malley was tasked with recreating the look of the Mahoney lifestyle. "Together with the set decorator, Jerry Wunderlich, he made the house interior look as good as the original," Friedkin wrote. "Wunderlich was able to rent master paintings, fine rugs, and period furniture."

Another problem, one that Friedkin could solve without help, was the geography of the house in relation to the stairs. "When I got there, I realized that . . . the flight of stairs was about twenty yards away from the side of the house where the bedroom window was, where the priest jumps out at the end and is supposed to come out the window and land right on the stairs . . . ," Friedkin said in an interview with the Directors Guild of America. "We're filming outside, but we had to build an extension, a false extension from her house to the stairs, which contained the girl's bedroom, which was nothing more than a platform that was later interiored on a set in New York, but I had to bring the house closer to the stairs and use a long lens to show, like, Lee J. Cobb going up the stairs, and then you'd see the window very close to where he's standing. But that's a long lens that's bringing the window closer to his body. He was maybe still fifteen yards away from that window."

Those steps, where Father Karras plummets to his death (and where Burke Dennings had suffered the same fate, off-screen), serve as a grim iconographic reminder, or totem, to horror fans worldwide. Given the droll name "The Hitchcock Steps" during production, we first see them in a fuzzy wide shot that fails to suggest their role in the film, a rare case of Friedkin not overworking the foreshadowing element so prevalent in *The Exorcist*. "We shot it early in the morning, so the steps are very hard to see," Friedkin told WTOP in 2015. "It's not until later in the film that I feature them, but at that point, if you know where the steps are and you look for them, you can probably pick them out. It's about ten minutes in."

Establishing the steps as a motif was difficult in that early shot because of technical limitations. "It was the best zoom Panavision made at the time, but it was obviously underexposed, done at a time of very low light levels. It had about a 20:1 zoom ratio," Friedkin continued. "If I was doing it today, I'd use a drone! There's a lot of very effective shots, very stabilized as well, from drones now. Tiny, little handheld drones that contain these GoPro cameras, and that's what I would have done today."

Although not nearly as famous as the *Psycho* House (as the Universal Studio Tours bills the Bates Residence), 3600 Prospect Avenue still draws visitors and has become a common selfie background. In 2015, Friedkin and Blatty attended a ceremony to unveil a commemorative plaque. A few years later, the steps became an official historic landmark in Washington, DC.

▲ ▲ ▲

On a February Sunday morning, before sunrise, a disaster occurred that would hit *The Exorcist* trifecta: delaying production, increasing the budget, and, finally, boosting the "curse" narrative. That was when a fire broke out at Ceco Studios, leveling the set. After associate producer David Salven awoke him in the dead of night with a phone call, Friedkin rushed to the set. "By the time I arrived, the stage was filled with smoke," Friedkin recalled. "Firemen everywhere. The set was in ruins, along with all the expensive artwork, furniture, and rugs. The question of how the fire started was never adequately explained. There was a lengthy investigation by the insurance company, which paid off on the theory that because the stage was old and there were pigeons flying around in the rafters, a pigeon may have flown into a light box, causing a short circuit. I was frightened and confused, for the first time since we started production."

Like so many of the unexpected happenings that took place during filming, the studio fire made its way into the twisted publicity campaign, more unprincipled grist for the supernatural mill. The practical result of the fire at Ceco was another delay in filming; the MacNeil residence would have to be reconstructed, marking the third time that the costly set, filled with antiques, original paintings, and upper-crust furniture, was built.

CHAPTER 11

A Very Intense Set

Reckless and boorish on the set of *The French Connection*, Friedkin surpassed himself for bad manners while filming *The Exorcist*. After *The French Connection* dominated the Academy Awards, Friedkin, now the reigning Best Director in America, began believing that he was beyond such trivial concerns as budgets, schedules, producers, safety protocols, feelings. This megalomania would eventually culminate in the catastrophic production of *Sorcerer* in 1977, a boondoggle from which Friedkin would never recover. (As far as New Hollywood pandemonium is concerned, only *Apocalypse Now* outstrips *Sorcerer*.)

While the shooting schedule for *The Exorcist* was initially set for eighty-five days, chaos and delays would cause the film to drag on for nearly a year. Along the way, Friedkin fired several key collaborators, injured two of his stars, alienated crew members, taunted the studio, slapped an actor, and ordered William Peter Blatty barred from postproduction. Even for the New Hollywood era, when loose cannons such as Bob Rafelson and Dennis Hopper left behind a legacy of chaos, Friedkin stood out for his antics.

"He screamed and yelled at people, he was the worst," Jim Nelson, a sound mixer, told Peter Biskind. "I went from a seven-year contract as his associate producer to the guy he hated most in the world—in two minutes. He made [Bob] Rafelson look like Donna Reed. Bob wanted his own way, but he wasn't vicious. Billy was vicious."

Another crew member, who wanted to maintain anonymity, also gave Biskind dirt on the erratic Friedkin. "He is the only guy I ever saw shake hands with someone with gusto and a smile, and then turn as he was exiting past that person, and say, 'Get this guy outta here.'"

The heat in Iraq, the cold during the exorcism scenes, the time-consuming makeup applications, the delays that more than tripled the originally scheduled eighty-five days, the erratic behavior of a director whose fuse was so short you needed tweezers to handle it—*The Exorcist* was an uncomfortable experience for most involved.

"It was a very intense set," Linda Blair recalled. "There was very little laughter."

Shooting *The Exorcist* was not only intense; it was dangerous. In an era when Burt Reynolds, to his everlasting regret, legitimately went over a waterfall while canoeing in *Deliverance*, Friedkin pushed his cast to the limit in assorted callous ways.

When cynically promoting *The Exorcist* as a cursed film, Friedkin often mentioned the accidents that had befallen the cast and crew during filming. He would say, more than once, that Ellen Burstyn had wrenched her back and had been sidelined for two weeks. But this was nothing more than a way to play up the supernatural marketing aspect while minimizing his role in what happened to Burstyn. It was Friedkin, in his zeal for authenticity, who had injured Burstyn, a woman who had been nominated for an Academy Award just a year earlier. "He likes to manipulate actors, he likes tricks," Ellen Burstyn said about the methods Friedkin employed. "But he was always great with me, except when he permanently injured my spine."

As an exclamation point to the infamous crucifix scene, Burstyn takes a superhuman blow from Regan that sends her crashing to the floor. Fit with a harness controlled by a stunt coordinator, Burstyn was at the mercy of her director for that sequence. After an initial take, Burstyn remonstrated with Friedkin about the risk of injury. In her memoir *Becoming Myself*, she described how Friedkin ignored her appeals.

Billy called, "Cut. We go again."
  I asked why.
  "Because your scarf covered your face when you landed."
  I felt scared. I didn't want to do another take. But I was a girl who couldn't say no. Not to a director and certainly not to Billy, the King.

I said, "He's pulling me too hard. Could he not pull me so hard?"

"Well, it's got to look real," Billy replied rather forcefully.

"I know it has to look real, but I'm telling you he's pulling me too hard. I could get hurt."

The stuntman stood on my left slightly behind me, listening and waiting for instructions. Billy was on my right. There was a pause. Then Billy looked to the stuntman and said, "All right, don't pull her so hard." Then he moved away and behind me so he and the stuntman were face to face. I couldn't see them. But I felt them. I felt an exchange between them behind my back. I saw only the blinding light in my eyes and the surrounding blackness.

On the second take, Burstyn went airborne. "I got yanked to the wooden floor hard. Much harder than the first time. I didn't land on my buttocks this time, but on my sacrum. It smashed into the hard wooden floor and I screamed in pain, louder than I've ever screamed in my life. It was the worst pain I've ever felt. I looked to Billy to yell 'Cut.' He did not. I saw his hand touch the camera-man's elbow. I saw the lens move closer. Billy wanted to use this real pain. I felt fury rise through my whole being and although I couldn't stop screaming, I managed to choke out the words, 'Turn the fucking camera off.'"

Marcel Vercoutere, the special-effects man who had rigged the stunt, explained that Friedkin often wanted to go beyond the miming of emotions. "Ellen Burstyn smacked the wall, landed on her hiney, and didn't care for it at all," he told writer Thomas D. Clagett. "And the look on her face was to kill. Acting there had ceased."

That a world-class actress who had trained with Lee Strasberg and would win an Oscar in her next starring role would need to cease acting seems counterintuitive, but Friedkin, who has publicly denigrated actors as a class (a shortcoming he had in common with Hitchcock), thought nothing of maiming one of his top cast members.

"After *The Exorcist* finished filming, I began seeing an orthopedist for my back," Burstyn wrote. "This was the beginning of a lifelong line of doctors and practitioners who would treat my back and the arthritis that developed in the scar tissue."

What makes this incident even more troubling is that the scene is not essential to the overall film. It is not a plot twist, it is not a reveal, it is not a set piece. Physical requirements for disaster sequences, Western brawls, foot chases, sports movies, and other kinetic scenes meant to be showstoppers involve a certain amount of risk when doubles are not involved. But a backhanded blow, albeit one from a possessed teen, hardly merits hazardous treatment of an actress.

Ninety percent of the shots in *The Exorcism* are not "real," yet, somehow, Friedkin was looking for realism in a spot that caps the already shocking and gruesome crucifix scene, which culminates with Regan twisting her head around. Of course, Regan knocking her mother for a loop emphasizes just how malevolent she has become under possession. Her first violent outbursts in the film are directed exclusively at doctors and psychiatrists; abusing her mother signals the final stage of her transformation from a conduit of evil to the evil itself. But that point had just been established with Regan mutilating herself with the crucifix and grabbing her mother by the head and shoving her face into her bloody crotch. A dangerous stunt is overkill, and a dangerous stunt deliberately manipulated by a filmmaker who did not respect boundaries is something else altogether. "It was way beyond what anyone needs to do to make a movie," Burstyn said.

In the subsequent clash of reality that is a characteristic of Hollywood citizens, Friedkin denied that Burstyn was ever injured, although she had been, indeed, taken from the set via ambulance, eventually returning on crutches. Burstyn also detailed her lifelong back troubles in several interviews and appearances, as well as in her memoir. None of that seemed to dissuade Friedkin from trivializing her distress. "That's bullshit!" Friedkin growled to *The Independent* in 2003. "She's on stage right now, doing a one-woman show. Burstyn never missed one day's work as a result of that shot in *The Exorcist*. She is a drama queen and journalists play this up. You guys love this stuff. . . . She'll say to me jokingly, 'You know, I really hurt my back.' I hurt my back getting out of bed!"

Next on the casualty list was Linda Blair, the thirteen-year-old girl Friedkin claimed to have protected from the opening shot. A particularly vigorous bed-thrashing sequence left Blair, like Ellen Burstyn, with permanent back troubles. As with Burstyn in her tumbling scene, Blair was strapped into a harness (made possible by metal body molding) controlled out of sight by Marcel Vercoutere. "Everything was hooked up inside the bed itself," he told *Fangoria*. "I'd just lace her into it. She had no control of herself, whatsoever. If I wanted her to lay down, she'd lay down. She had no control of herself. I was the devil!"

This low-tech system did not consider how much the violent thrashing would affect the apparatus. "My back was damaged during *The Exorcist*," Blair told Mark Kermode in 1989. "Filming some of the bed-bouncing scenes, some of the metal equipment came loose and damaged my back. They sent me various doctors and masseuses, and anyway, a child's body will heal, and I was very strong. But it was tough work."

Repeated takes slowly began to unravel the harness lacing, eventually producing serious pain and leaving Blair crying after the ordeal was finally over. Video footage of the incident shows Burstyn rushing to the bed to comfort Blair. Vercoutere once again gleefully describes the result of his brutish methods and reiterates his bizarre notions regarding acting. "By that time, she had had enough, and she wants out, and she says so, 'Make it stop! He's trying to kill me!' It's in the movie. That's when the acting ceases and realism starts," he told Thomas D. Clagett.

Worse than the cavalier attitude Vercoutere had about abusing actors was the fact that Friedkin might have encouraged it. "When she started screaming 'Let me out,' Billy said 'Go.' And that's what worked. She was saying 'Let me out'—she really wanted out. She was getting thrashed, you know. But that's what looked good on film. It worked for that."

One of the strangest rumors from the production was that Linda Blair had suffered a nervous breakdown during filming. Given the nonsense *The Exorcist* crew openly spewed to the press (as well as behind the scenes, no doubt), it would not be surprising if someone involved with the film had leaked such a story for publicity. Friedkin had already set a standard of cheap ballyhoo with his suggestion, repeated to anyone within earshot, that the production was cursed. He also insisted on having priests bless the sets (this from a man who had been bar mitzvahed, no less). Then there was the balderdash about "inexplicable" phenomena. "There are strange images and visions that showed up on film that were never planned. There are double exposures in the little girl's face at the end of one reel that are unbelievable," he told *Castle of Frankenstein* magazine, proving that no outlet was too small for his unique brand of hooey.

When Janet Maslin of the *Boston Phoenix* asked Friedkin outright: Was Linda Blair under psychiatric care during production? His response was enigmatic. "Of course not," he said. "I don't believe in psychiatry, in the terms in which you've mentioned it. If you're under psychiatric care you're there to get help for an illness, but it ain't going make you go out and act in a movie like *The Exorcist*."

A major selling point for *The Exorcist*, and something Friedkin harped on almost as much as he harped on supernatural forces infiltrating the set, was the groundbreaking special effects. But neither of the effects that hurt Burstyn and Blair was particularly innovative; both involved ropes or harnesses and a puppet master off-screen. Yet both effects seemed poorly designed for the participants. "That was a bad experience," Burstyn told *The Guardian*. "I don't feel that I was complicit in it because I told [Friedkin] not to do it. When I think about it now, why weren't there pads on the floor, why weren't there pads on my back?"

Injuring not one, but two, eventual Academy Award nominees from his own film, both of them female, puts Friedkin somewhere on the lamentable roster of brutish and abusive directors, along with, among others, Carl T. Dreyer, Fritz Lang, Henry Hathaway, Otto Preminger, John Ford, Alfred Hitchcock, Henri-Georges Clouzot, Stanley Kubrick, Bernardo Bertolucci, David O. Russell, Lars Von Trier, and even Vincent Minelli, whose whirligig torture of Lana Turner in *The Bad and the Beautiful* produced a stunning scene at a serious psychological cost.

▲ ▲ ▲

Although William Friedkin was one of the young guns threatening to overthrow the studio system completely, he was fond of an Old Hollywood prank: He liked to shoot guns on the set, inspired by George Stevens, who startled his cast on *The Diary of Anne Frank* by firing blanks from the rafters of the soundstage. As with Stevens, who earned an Academy Award nomination for *Diary*, Friedkin was looking to spark unease and surprise on the set. "I shot blanks on the set a few times just to get the actors in a mood where they were all keyed up," Friedkin told Bob McCabe. "And it works. It works every time you do that. They were cap pistols and it was a technique that was not invented by me. I read that George Stevens did that when he filmed *The Diary of Anne Frank* to make the actors who were portraying the Frank family terrified on-screen when they were supposed to be listening to the sirens of the German police cars. And, of course, when you're filming an actor's reaction to something when they're supposed to be terrified—say it's a police car—you don't often play the sound on the stage. They have to act it; they've got to fake it. One of the toughest things to fake is genuine fear. A lot of actors don't understand that. A lot of actors will say I don't need all those devices, I'm an actor, I can act it. And in every single case, I always let the actor do it first without any supplemental device: 'Okay, you're supposed to be afraid, you're seeing God knows what, a demon appear in a room or whatever, go ahead—Action!' And it's generally shit or unbelievable or over the top because what directing is, for the most part, is providing an atmosphere in which this stuff can unfold. Sometimes it's an atmosphere of great tranquility, other times it's chaos. If what you're trying to portray on the screen is chaos, as a director you generally have to create a chaotic environment to get the ultimate reaction to something like that."

Jason Miller found the tactic insulting. He nearly whiplashed in a scene where a ringing telephone startled him. What Miller is reacting to in the film is a gunshot from the trigger-happy Friedkin. According to Miller, Friedkin used a shotgun. "That really pissed me off," Miller recalled to McCabe. "I told him, I said, 'Never do that again. I'm an actor. I don't need these artificial stimulants.' I was in that room all alone, and my son was in the hospital, and I was a little jumpy then. [Friedkin] had me sitting there and he had this absolute silence in the room and I'm listening to the tape and trying to decipher it when the phone rings. He wanted my reaction to the phone to create some kind of tension in the scene. So he and I did it a couple of times and on the third or fourth take the phone rings. I pick it up and ahhhh! This shotgun goes off, this close to my head. I said, 'You son of a bitch. How dare you do that? What if you went a little too far to the right?' And Friedkin said, 'It's all right, we've got Jack Nicholson in the wings.' I had to laugh. It was a good line."

▲ ▲ ▲

Like his New Hollywood peers, Friedkin was not interested in casting stars and preferred specific looks or auras. Jason Miller had never appeared on-screen before, and Linda Blair had a pair of walk-on roles in minor productions. As Francis Ford Coppola did in *The Godfather* and Steven Spielberg would do in *Jaws*, Friedkin would often cast amateurs as well. There are many amateurs in *The French Connection* and probably more in *The Exorcist*, mostly among the priests who appear in the film, although nonactors also play the derelict in the train station and Mrs. Karras. Amateurs have their drawbacks, of course, especially those with more than just bit parts. Father William O'Malley, at the time a teacher at McQuaid Jesuit High School in Rochester, New York, played Father Dyer, who appears in several extended sequences as a central character: drinking with a dejected Father Karras at Georgetown, playing piano at the party, and, in a scene that required far more than O'Malley could give, performing the last rites over a mortally wounded Karras at the foot of the Hitchcock steps.

It was well after midnight when the scene began shooting. More than a dozen takes later, Friedkin approached O'Malley for a brief conversation, in which he asked O'Malley if he trusted him. O'Malley said yes. "He had never been an actor," Friedkin told Stephen Galloway of *The Hollywood Reporter*. "It was his first and only film. He might have done some plays in school. He had to break down and cry at three or four o'clock in the morning on a freezing cold night when the crew had worked for sixteen hours that day and he had to give the last rites and, according to the script, burst into tears. He couldn't do it. He couldn't get there. There was nothing I could say to him that would get him there. He had no technique. So I resorted to something that I had read that many directors have done before me over the years."

Howard Newman described what followed in his book *The Exorcist: The Strange Story Behind the Film*: "Friedkin then nodded to the sound-man, who yelled, 'Speed,' just as the cameraman boomed, 'Rolling.' With that Friedkin hauled off and belted O'Malley right across the face. Stunned, the priest turned around and went through the scene a final time. With a trembling voice O'Malley absolved Karras for the last time, his hands shaking and tears welling up in his eyes. As Karras died, O'Malley threw himself down on the bloody corpse sobbing uncontrollably. 'Cut!' yelled the delighted Friedkin, who ran over to the shaken priest, grabbing him up in his arms and planting a big kiss right where he had struck him."

While slapping an amateur may seem extreme (even in the 1970s), Friedkin was obsessively driven to produce results that would stand out on the screen. Despite the superb final take, the crew was shocked at what Friedkin had done—after all, O'Malley was a priest—but the actor himself claimed to be appreciative. "He belted me to get my adrenaline going, and I'm eternally grateful to him," O'Malley told David Konow. "He made all the difference in the world. It's awfully difficult to spill your guts with all those people standing around smoking at 2:00 in the morning, looking at their watches, hoping they'll get to bed. You give your best friend the last rites fifteen times in a row, you're just doing it by the numbers, and all of a sudden he rocked me to my heels, got out of the way, and I knew instinctively what I was supposed to do."

CHAPTER 12

▲ ▲ ▲

Held Hostage in Iraq

He may have had to recreate the MacNeil house in a studio, but William Friedkin was determined to film the prologue in Iraq, thousands of miles away, to achieve the verisimilitude he felt was key to the film.

Already alarmed at the delays and cost overruns accrued over more than two hundred days of shooting, Warner Bros. beseeched Friedkin to set up in the Mojave Desert and not endanger the crew in an unstable country. Of course, Friedkin insisted on making the studio—and everyone else involved—sweat.

As is customary for Blatty and Friedkin, both men claimed to have been responsible for making *The Exorcist* the first Hollywood film ever shot in Iraq. For his part, Blatty gave an account that focused on his personal magnetism. "I was the one who arranged to get them into Northern Iraq because I spoke Arabic," Blatty told Bob McCabe. "I went to the Iraqi embassy day after day romancing someone in the consulate's office and showing him how I, an American, spoke Arabic." This highly unlikely scenario is typical Blatty— once again, he has come to the (fantasy) rescue. If not for the fact that Iraq broke diplomatic relations with the United States in 1967 (in protest of the United States supporting Israel during the Six-Day War), this tale would have been one of the more dashing Blatty would spin in a lifetime of spinning tales.

Characteristically, Friedkin offered a version that foregrounded his resourcefulness and ingenuity. In his memoir, Friedkin said he once again called upon the well-connected Jack Valenti to pull political strings on behalf of the production and set up a meeting with a United Nations representative from Iraq. Like Blatty, but with much more pizzazz, Friedkin loved even embellishing something that may have been true. After agreeing to hire and train Iraqis in exchange for the right to film in Mosul and Hatra, Friedkin described a few more colorful requests from the UN representative: "We want your makeup person to teach Iraqis how to manufacture movie blood," and "We want you to donate a print of your film *The French Connection* to the Iraqi government."

Along with a small crew (assistant director Terrence Donnelly, Max Von Sydow, Dick Smith and his assistant, Rick Baker, and a few others), Friedkin likely arrived in Baghdad in late June or early July of 1973. In Northern Iraq, where filming would take place, Friedkin met with Yazidis, whose beliefs he promptly mischaracterized as soon as he found a reporter willing to listen. Further adventures, or misadventures, delayed production again, nearly a year after the first interruptions began in New York City.

Thanks to the unforgiving summer heat, which can reach 120 degrees in Northern Iraq, the crew was limited to filming in the early mornings and late evenings, when the blistering sun was weakest. Under these broiling conditions, Max Von Sydow, with a layer of makeup that caulked his pores, suffered the most. "Von Sydow would go into the makeup tent at 3 o'clock each morning, and Dick Smith and Rick Baker would work on him until it was time to start filming," Friedkin recalled. "He would keep the makeup on during our daily hiatus of about seven hours; then Baker and Smith would freshen him up for the evening shoot. At the end of the day, they would peel the makeup off, and torrents of sweat would pour from his face. This took an hour, so he would get three hours sleep each night, and then nap during the afternoon."

Eventually, Von Sydow gave the notoriously meticulous Friedkin a simple mandate: the director would have only four more days to work with him. After that, Von Sydow would pack his bags and leave.

But the most harrowing delay occurred when a failed coup threw the entire country into turmoil. On the day *The Exorcist* team arrived in Hatra, Iraqi handlers visited Friedkin and informed him that shooting was postponed until further notice and that the crew members were confined to their hotel. "The crew became frightened and concerned. We were being held hostage," Friedkin wrote. "This went on for four days, with assurances from the Baathists that it had nothing to do with us and would soon be remedied. Our nervousness turned to panic when, on the fifth day of what was essentially a friendly captivity, we were told what happened."

What happened was the kind of international intrigue that might have sprung from a Graham Greene novel. A pair of high-profile kidnappings engineered by Colonel Nazem Kazar, director of the national security department, served as a preamble to overthrowing President Ahmed Hassan al-Bakr. At the time, al-Bakr was en route to Iraq from Poland, but a flight delay kept him from an assassination attempt. When Kazar failed to get his accomplices to act in time, he fled with his hostages. Captured before he could reach the Iranian border, Kazar and his co-conspirators were executed en masse a few days later.

A more humorous setback transpired when a giant Pazuzu statue, designed by Bill Malley and shipped from the States, never arrived. Eventually, a production member tracked it to Hong Kong. Of course, Friedkin took the opportunity for some more supernatural spin, telling Travers and Reiff: "It was packed in a 10-foot-high crate. How do you lose something like that? How does it get to Hong Kong instead of Iraq?"

Another mystery about the Iraq shoot concerns just how long Friedkin and company remained there. Even time spans were subject to the tricky Friedkin touch; his repeated claims to have been in Iraq for three months are dubious. (Dick Smith, in an interview with *Fangoria*, contradicted Friedkin bluntly: "We were supposed to shoot over there four days, and we wound up being there four weeks." Bob McCabe estimated the crew was in Iraq just short of six weeks.)

According to the timeline he set out in *The Friedkin Connection*, six weeks after arriving in Iraq (four weeks of prep work and two weeks of shooting), the production shut down for a few days due to the botched coup. That coup took place on July 1, 1973, and the first wave of mass executions of the participants occurred on July 7, putting Friedkin, by his estimate, in Iraq as early as the third week of May—before he received permission to shoot there. (To muddle the logistics even further, Friedkin testified at the Senate Subcommittee hearings on June 21, 1973, speaking on behalf of the Directors Guild of America concerning anti-obscenity laws.)

If Friedkin did, indeed, spend three months in Iraq, then he would have returned to the United States sometime in the middle of September, which would not only have made postproduction for a complicated film scheduled for release at the end of December impossible, but it would have nullified the obligation to shoot during the hottest months of the year.

The difficult conditions, combined with the political turbulence of a country constantly in crisis, left Friedkin somewhat remorseful for his decision to shoot on location. "I went to Iraq because I thought it would be wonderful for the movie," he told David Konow. "But I endangered people's lives. I was a schmuck. Today I would shoot the opening in the Mojave Desert with a lot of guys in bedsheets."

At the time, perhaps, Friedkin might have thought the hardships were worth it.

CHAPTER 13

The Transformations of Dick Smith

F ew other specialized artisans in film have had the impact on their fields that Dick Smith had on special-effects makeup. "Fifty years ago, when I decided to become a makeup artist, it was an entirely different world," he recalled for *Filmmakers Newsletter*. "For a Yale graduate like myself to choose this career was absolutely unheard of. I mean, no one even knew there were such things as makeup artists in those days. I only found out when I picked up a book on makeup and thought, 'This would be neat.' But it seemed crazy to me to make this decision because I had no obvious artistic skills and, on top of that, I didn't really believe that I had the talent to become a makeup artist. A while later I did become a successful TV makeup artist—but there was a little voice inside of me that said, 'You know, you were just there at the right time, in the right place,' that sort of thing. It took me years, years to become a good makeup artist and to get to the point where I accepted that I was a top makeup artist."

Not only was Smith a top makeup artist, but he also revolutionized the industry, developing new techniques such as applying prosthetic applications in sections, allowing for more range of motion than a mask would. While working on *The Godfather*, Smith also invented the makeup effect, a combination of traditional prosthetic work and mechanical, or practical, effects. When Sterling Hayden takes two bullets to the head (and one to the throat) in *The Godfather*, gunshot wounds in Hollywood were changed forever, or at least until the end of the New Hollywood era, when studios began depicting violence with a cartoonishness in line with video games and the general infantilizing of the film industry.

Along with John Chambers, Smith was the bridge between the old guard of Lon Chaney Sr., Jack Pierce (whose *Frankenstein* and *Mummy* creations remain indelible), John Fulton, and George Bau and the technologically advanced pyrotechnics of 1980s FX masters Rick Baker, Rob Bottin, Craig Reardon, Stan Winston, and Chris Walas. Most of the latter, of course, were proteges of Smith at one time or another.

For *The Exorcist*, Smith excelled at both makeup and, with help from Marcel Vercoutere, showstopping effects that have remained in the collective consciousness of filmgoers for half a century.

When Smith first met Linda Blair, he was displeased: she was simply too appealing. "Now as you know," he said, "Linda Blair has this cute, apple-cheeked face with a little butterball nose—healthy, healthy, healthy! I would have loved to make her look gaunt, ghoulish, and wasted, but there was just no way. One cardinal principle in makeup is that you can add to a face, but you cannot subtract."

After a seemingly endless round of making life casts of Blair, Smith began working on a look that would transform her from a bubbly All-American teenage girl into a fearsome demonic presence. Smith finished his work, which he considered suitably disturbing, and Friedkin rejected it. "The only problem with Billy was the fact that he had no sense of diplomacy, no tact," Smith told author Pascal Pinteau, "if he did not like something, he would just say so bluntly!"

Once the production got underway, Smith would return to the drawing board, so to speak, over and over. He worked long hours, with a single assistant (a young Rick Baker, who would become a makeup-effects superstar in the 1980s), seven days a week, until a blowup with Friedkin drove him to quit on the set. The pace and the demands Friedkin made had left Smith, like so many other crew members, exhausted. But Smith returned the next day to settle matters with Friedkin and to negotiate the occasional day off.

Ultimately, the makeup became another major stalling point for the production, when Smith had to scrap the prosthetics he had spent months designing. "All that work went down the drain," Smith told Bob McCabe. "Billy had to change his shooting schedule since we couldn't go on with these until I made the changes. It was several weeks before we were able to go further with it."

Eventually, Friedkin and Smith settled on a strategy for Blair, one rooted in a gradually disintegrating appearance that, in keeping with the overall philosophy of realism, could retain a certain plausibility despite its supernatural origin. "For the more advanced stages of possession, we worked from the fact that in the masturbation scene," Smith told *Cinefantastique*, "the possessed child has mutilated herself extensively. Billy was kind of cute; you never actually see that she has cut her face, but there's blood all over the place and she certainly could have. So in the later stages of possession, her makeup played on the fact that her face had been cut up, with festering, pus-filled wounds and so forth."

Indicative of the meticulous attention to detail required for the job, Smith spent hours each day applying makeup to Blair, who sat in a chair as patient as any thirteen-year-old girl had a right to be. "She was remarkable throughout the whole thing," Smith said to McCabe. "Linda was quite an adult young lady. . . . She was really very very patient. Of course it was boring for her to sit for two hours in the morning while this stuff was put on. So she asked if she could have a television set. So what we did was put a small set on a shelf on the wall behind her, so she could look in the makeup mirror and see the set."

According to Smith, Blair was fond of *The Flying Nun* and often moved her head if he blocked her view while applying makeup. "God bless Dick Smith," Blair told McCabe. "Nothing could have prepared anybody for what that experience was going to be. Maybe an adult might have taken better to it. I was always very good about it. Billy's decision was he didn't want it to look like I was wearing a mask, so Dick Smith would continue to chip away at the pieces and there were several different pieces on my face."

Even in the 1970s, when Smith was at his peak, the job of a makeup-effects artist was often trial and error, requiring an offbeat inventiveness, a restless pragmatism, and a solitary DIY process that occasionally led to surprise breakthroughs.

From the relatively primitive Golden Age materials and ingredients, such as spirit gum, greasepaint, cotton, putty, and adhesive tape, Smith experimented with seemingly arcane substances such as toupee glue, gypsum, Liquitex, and acrylic. One scene in *The Exorcist* pushed Smith to his ingenious limits. When the script called for the words "Help me" to materialize spontaneously on Linda Blair's stomach (an instance of "dermal branding," inspired by the marks that supposedly afflicted Ronald Hunkeler), Smith began brainstorming.

After designing a torso appliance for Blair, Smith had to figure out how to make the letters appear. He settled on spraying carbon trichloroethylene on the torso because it made foam expand on contact. "I made some tests on various foam rubbers, and I noticed that in some cases, when the foam dried, the expansion would disappear without leaving a trace," he told Pascal Pinteau.

By using a heat gun to accelerate drying, Smith could carve the words into the foam and then erase them quickly. "I got the idea to film the whole thing in reverse. During the shooting, we first starched her clothes so that they would not move when the heat gun above her would blow hot air on the appliance. I would trace the letters with a brush on the appliance to make the foam expand, we would then roll the camera while the heat gun was on letters which disappear within a minute. When the film was run backward, the effect was great. But Billy thought it ran too long and inserted a cutaway, and I thought it sort of made it look like it was fake."

In the famous scene where Karras is splattered with green bile, a tube rigged to shoot a mixture of pea soup and oatmeal was aimed too high. As a result of a slight miscalculation (or, possibly, a Friedkin scheme), Jason Miller was hit right in the face with this grotesque homemade substance that was also kept warm on the set to maintain its consistency. The reaction Miller gives—shock and disgust—is not acting but a natural response that Friedkin elected to use in the final cut.

To achieve this spewing effect, Smith heat-formed sheets of plexiglass into thin tubes that also doubled as retractors that held the mouth open at the edges. "The retracting part connected with the device that went into her mouth that held the nozzle," Smith explained to *Cinefantastique*. "Now all of this had to be made as thin as possible because over it I had to apply a very thin foam latex mask which included the lower lip, and mouth corners to cover this thing where it went into her mouth. The final effect then, with the makeup and all, and a wig on top to cover the harness that held it all on, was a very good duplication of the demon makeup with the mouth open. She couldn't close her mouth at all. This wasn't exactly comfortable to wear, of course."

There remains some question about this entire sequence and how it was achieved. Although Friedkin repeatedly boasted that all effects were live-action, without any opticals, Smith claimed that his contraption was replaced by artificial means. "Later on, I found out that Billy changed his mind and matted in straight jets of vomit over my carefully planned effects!" (Another oddity is the fact that it is clearly Eileen Dietz in one frame of the sequence.)

The most shocking scene of all—when Regan MacNeil, now fully under the power of the demon, twists her head around for the first time—was achieved by a primitive form of animatronics: a full-size mannequin with a small electronic system placed in its skull and governed by a remote control. It took six weeks for Smith and Rick Baker to fabricate the mannequin.

Dick Smith described the process to *Cinefantastique*. "I molded Linda's body in sections and made a dummy which was basically latex filled with polyurethane foam, a soft foam," he said. "I did try to have the joints at the arms and legs bendable so that we could alter the position somewhat. The head and shoulders were made out of a polyester resin because they had to be rigid enough to install the mechanism to make the head pivot smoothly."

Beneath the bed a pole ran through the dummy allowing it to rotate the head, which was detachable. To give the dummy a more lifelike appearance, its eyes were mechanical and were activated off-screen via remote control by Marcel Vercoutere.

Today, this effect seems rudimentary, especially considering the sophisticated animatronics developed in its wake (not to mention the subsequent arrival of CGI), but at the time, it was breathtaking. First, its occurrence was unexpected, given what had preceded it. In that sequence, which began with everyday objects flying around the room in a supernatural tempest, Regan had already masturbated with the crucifix, forced her mother down onto her bloody crotch, punched her across the room, and tried to crush her with a chest of drawers. A final outrage seemed unlikely, but Friedkin, as was his custom, went full throttle.

The second time Regan rotates her head, however, with Father Merrin reading from the Roman Ritual, it not only reeks of overkill but is less realistic as well. During the crucifix scene, the entire mannequin is revealed, giving it an illusion of human solidity. But in the exorcism scene, a blanket partly conceals the mannequin. Consequently, it resembles a bust instead of a body, canceling out the life-casting realism of the crucifix scene.

There is also the gratuitous nature of the 360-degree redux: once is a shock, twice is a lark. William Peter Blatty had always disagreed with the second head-spinning scene. "When I pointed out to Billy Friedkin that in such an eventuality, the head would likely fall off and that 'supernatural' was not synonymous with 'impossible,' the head turn was modified in the editing room. I still believed it to be excessive and unreal, but audiences loved it, proving me an idiot once again." (The modification Blatty referred to was a cutaway from Regan—and her mutinous head—to a shot of a stunned Father Karras watching at the foot of the bed.)

Although Smith worked hard to get the perfect look for Linda Blair, his real challenge was transforming Max Von Sydow, the handsome forty-four-year-old Swede, into an old man on the verge of death. Because Friedkin intended to shoot close-ups of Von Sydow without the use of filters, Smith would have to work overtime on developing a naturalistic appearance that could withstand the scrutiny of the camera.

In a career that would eventually span over fifty years, Smith aged stars as varied and luminous as Laurence Olivier, Marlon Brando, Walter Matthau, David Bowie, and F. Murray Abraham. His tour de force, however, remains the transformation of Dustin Hoffman (then thirty-two) into a 121-year-old Jack Crabb in *Little Big Man* (1970).

To age Von Sydow by thirty years, Smith used every trick he had learned over the decades. He added freckles, liver spots, wrinkles, creases, puffiness, and even a wattle. "Max had a more elaborate makeup, more time consuming, and in some ways more tricky," Smith told Travers and Reiff. "His makeup took three hours every day. In fact, it was more difficult for me to age Max Von Sydow in *The Exorcist* than it was to age Marlon Brando in *The Godfather*. . . . Max and Marlon are about the same age: in their forties. But the technique I used on Marlon did not work for Max—he has a different kind of skin. He had to be older than Brando, too. I used appliance makeup on Max. The makeup is put on in sections called 'appliances.' I don't use masks. There can be as many as a dozen sections applied to a face. The sections overlap, and that way I get the best possible fit and the greatest flexibility. The secret of really good character makeup is that the appliances be flexible and thin enough to allow the actor's expressions to come through."

Once again, Smith struggled with the erratic Friedkin, whose desires and instructions were often contradictory from one day to the next. (That would be proven in postproduction when Friedkin dismissed Lalo Schifrin.) At one point, Friedkin demanded that Von Sydow get a haircut, which Smith protested because a shorter style would expose some makeup. After the haircut, Friedkin complained that the makeup was visible, precipitating an argument that sent Smith packing for the umpteenth time. "There were a couple of times where the conditions were such that I wanted to quit and did virtually tender my resignation," he told Pascal Pinteau.

In no time, he had returned to the set, patched things up with Friedkin, and produced a remarkable metamorphosis of Von Sydow. "Although tight close-ups were used without diffusion, most people did not realize Max was heavily made up," Smith proudly told writer Anthony Timpone for his book *Men, Makeup, and Monsters*.

When Friedkin decamped to Iraq with a small team, Smith went along as an essential crew member: he had to keep Von Sydow from melting in the desert heat.

CHAPTER 14

Cold Rooms and Levitations: Special Effects in *The Exorcist*

Once the production returned to New York from Georgetown to shoot the crucial exorcism scenes, the setbacks multiplied, and the budget further spiraled out of control. At the time, Friedkin explained that the delays were unavoidable because of the cutting-edge special effects planned for the spectacular climax. "We are attempting to do, on camera, what has never been done before," he told Travers and Reiff. "We're not using opticals or any traditional way of doing things. The objects we've devised will move in ways that have never been tried before. It costs a lot of money and requires a lot of experimentation. We've had a lot of failures so far."

The special-effects team, led by Marcel Vercoutere, had been given a head start on the production, in hopes of perfecting the difficult challenges presented by a script that called for, among other things, cracking walls, projectile vomit, head-turnings, a rocking bed, and levitation.

Today nearly every effect seen in *The Exorcist* would be CGI, from the most complex—the levitation—to the seemingly innocuous—visible condensation. And while some feats created in 1973 now seem hokey (the head-turning, for example), digital technology cannot easily replicate the verisimilitude of tangible objects and occurrences. Nobody, including Vercoutere, knew if the effects would work on camera, a distinction that overrides the physical success of a stunt. For *The Exorcist*, the effects had to translate realistically on the screen, something that CGI repeatedly fails to accomplish.

To achieve the visible condensation of the actors, Vercoutere turned one of the bedroom sets into a giant refrigerator, using fiberglass insulation and powerful air-conditioning units. "I brought in two 15-ton compressors and put them up on the stage roof," he told *Fangoria*. "And I made a cocoon that fit around her bedroom. That was 40-feet square and 20-feet high. Then we refrigerated it. In the morning we would go in there to shoot it; it would be about 10 degrees below zero. We shot at zero."

During the Golden Age of Hollywood, the studios, just as they owned back lots and had entire carpentry staffs on the payroll, kept a location specifically for Arctic conditions. "From the 1930s through the 1960s, large bricks of ice were manufactured in the Glendale icehouse, in which scenes requiring cold air, snow, and visible breath were photographed," Friedkin wrote. "*Lost Horizon, The Magnificent Ambersons*, and many other films were shot there, but it had long since been closed."

When filming began in the "cold room," a difficult shoot became much more arduous for the cast and crew. Linda Blair described her miserable experience to Mark Kermode. "There were these huge meat-packing-plant cooling fans. And they kept them on all night long and so in the morning it'd be below zero, then they would light the set and it would come up to zero, and then when it would reach something like 17 degrees above, they'd have to turn the fans back on. . . . Everyone else got to wear snowsuits; I had a nightgown on. There were times I could wear long underwear, there were times I could not. There were times the blankets were on me, many times they were not. Was it cold? Yes. Did I like it? Not much. That's probably why I hate cold so much nowadays."

The artificial atmosphere made it harder to shoot extensively (Friedkin complained that after averaging twenty to thirty setups a day on *The French Connection*, he was down to three or four on *The Exorcist*), which also created a fitful pace. "By the time the movie lights are on [for] an hour and a half, the temperature would climb up to above 32 degrees, and we would have to stop everything and start up the air-conditioning units again," Friedkin told Travers and Reiff. "We had to shut them off during shooting because they made too much noise. Even after we shut them off, it took fifteen minutes for the sound to settle down so we could record again. We'd come down to the set in the morning, and if the units weren't working properly, we were stuck!"

Friedkin lost another day of shooting after he reviewed the first rushes of the cold room scenes and saw that the condensation did not appear on camera. "When we screened the first dailies from the cold room," he wrote, "no breath was visible! Like rain, we learned, breath doesn't photograph unless it's backlit or side-lit. We had to redo the entire day, with Owen [Roizman] setting small lights on the floor around the room, focused on the actors' breath."

Owen Roizman, the ace cinematographer on the film, found these sequences problematic to stage. "The most difficult part of the effects was the breath," he told Dennis Schaefer for the book *Masters of Light: Conversations with Contemporary Cinematographers*. "Showing the frost on the breath was the most difficult thing. And that's because we decided not to work with backlight. The reason for that was because we were always looking up so many times. We didn't want to get too involved and have to constantly change lights. So, what we had to do was have an electrician control a light, which was hidden behind an actor most of the time, and project it to catch his breath as it came out of his mouth but without hitting the actor's face."

The eerie plumes of visible condensation became another layer of surface realism that added to the total effect of *The Exorcist*. These details, worked over by Friedkin almost obsessively, are often ignored or seemingly misunderstood by critics, who believe they come at the expense of logic and characterization. And while Friedkin has been reliably deficient in those areas ever since *The French Connection*, one of his primary interests as a filmmaker is the graphic evocation of a specific milieu—the grimy Manhattan and Brooklyn streets in the 1970s, the godforsaken jungles of South America (with the Dominican Republic and Mexico as stand-ins), the Boston underworld of the '40s and '50s, the shocking S&M leather scene in New York City, the gritty outer limits of Los Angeles, even the shady subculture of college basketball. "What I try to do before each film is immerse myself totally in many peripheral or tangential phases of the subject before I make it, so I'm literally swimming in it before I expose a frame of film," Friedkin told writer Eric Sherman. His dreamworld vision of *The Exorcist*, rooted in realistic details that accrue over two hours and leave the viewer subconsciously engrossed, is a by-product of this fanatical immersion.

Other drawbacks from the refrigeration included some that were both surprising and time-consuming. "Billy would get the damn thing down to zero Fahrenheit," Dick Smith told Bob McCabe. "It was so cold that one morning we came in and there must have been excess humidity in the air because there was a layer of snow over the whole set."

While most of the crew wore nylon ski jackets, Jason Miller and Max Von Sydow wore only long underwear beneath their vestments. Their faces and hands were exposed to subfreezing temperatures. Both men made dashes to a heated room off-set to thaw out, causing further delays. For her part, Blair would lie in bed with an electric blanket underneath her.

As clumsy as Marcel Vercoutere was with humans, he was a whiz with inanimate objects. His live-action practical effects combined engineering, illusion, physics, and carpentry to produce what had only been suggested in the past or, worse, cartoonishly rendered by the still-primitive art of optical effects. Except for two or three scenes, stop-motion, dissolves, superimpositions, double exposures, rear projection, matte compositions, and shaking cameras were prohibited from *The Exorcist.*

While the bedroom was designed to be "wild" (with removable walls) it was also designed to tilt, slant, and roll. Although rumors of the set being balanced on a bowling ball circulated for years (mostly by Howard Newman in his hyperbolic book *The Exorcist: The Strange Story Behind the Film*), Vercoutere revealed the mechanics behind the sliding room in a 1983 interview with *Fangoria.* According to Vercoutere, the bowling-ball idea had been floated as a possibility. "That was the original concept," he said. "But I didn't like that because we just got a rocking motion, like you were on a ship. And being from California, I know what an earthquake feels like. So we put the entire thing on pneumatic wheels. We could put the whole crew, camera dollies, and everything on there and the room wouldn't move. If you put it on the bowling ball and shock-loaded the corners, you would have a weight problem. And we switched to pneumatic wheels. It went sideways, like an earthquake. I could start slowly, or knock everybody down. Just with a violent pull."

During the exorcism scene, the calamitous moments when the MacNeil house quakes, cracks, and seems on the verge of collapse are astonishingly effective, giving the viewer an almost immersive sense of impending catastrophe. The spider-webbing cracks that appear spontaneously on the ceiling and doors were an added detail that both surprise and convince the viewer of just how hellish things are in the bedroom.

"I used regular plaster and laid it out in wire mesh," Vercoutere said about this effect. "Then I went to the top of the ceiling with a rounded level bar, then, when I pushed down on it, the wire mesh would just stretch. Then the plaster would all crack. We had full control over when we wanted it to crack or how much."

Vercoutere rigged the doors using the same basic principle, although they were made of balsa wood, with rubber sheets installed to prolong the stretching effect until breaking point.

The trick beds Vercoutere designed for the majority of the torments Regan underwent were obviously not Simmons models. And where most thirteen-year-olds would probably sleep in a twin or a full, Vercoutere designed what looks like a queen-size to accommodate the extensive rigging. Even that was not enough for Vercoutere. "Well, I had three beds," he said. "There were so many things involved with the bed, that I couldn't involve all the gags and gimmicks in just one bed."

Vercoutere explained how he achieved some of the rollicking effects in the bedroom to *Fangoria*. "Oh, the floating bed? That was done by weights and a beam that went from the back of a headboard, through the wall. It was all counterweights on the other side. And of course the bed was reinforced. Then we had a piece of wallpaper that covered up the crack in the wall, like a roll-up shade."

Of all the practical effects in the film, perhaps none is as convincing or mesmerizing as the levitation scene, which amazed an audience in 1973 and 1974, when such a thing had never been seen on the silver screen before.

Taking his cue from P. T. Barnum and William Castle, who both perfected the art of bunkum as publicity in their respective fields, Friedkin insisted that the levitation scene in *The Exorcist*—a remarkable visual effect made all the more so for its novelty—was achieved through the use of what he called "magnetic fields."

In fact, this scene, designed by Marcel Vercoutere, was executed by a simple mechanical system involving piano wire. "I think it was number 8 piano wire," Vercoutere told Bob McCabe. "Three threads. Then I rigged the bed so that when she came down into it, the bed recessed, so it looked like all of her weight was coming down into it. I could take her up and pull her around. It was done with counterweights; I had her same weight off-stage so I could work it with one hand. The object was to do it as smoothly as possible."

An Unholy Racket: Sound Design

I n 1953, when William Friedkin graduated from Senn High School—he did not drop out or, conversely, graduate at sixteen after skipping two grades, as he alternately claimed—his yearbook photo notes that he was a member of the Psychology Club. In his post-auteur career, which followed the failure of *The Boys in the Band*, Friedkin advocated populist entertainment based on economic returns. "I have no image of myself as an artist," he said. "I'm making commercial films, I'm making a product designed to have people buy it." For Friedkin, part of that process meant the psychological manipulation of the audience.

To that end, Friedkin made sound design a core element of *The Exorcist* and deliberately crafted it to be as nerve-racking as possible. While *The Exorcist* has some innovative audio effects, its primary attribute is volume: Friedkin meant to bludgeon the audience with a pounding, shrieking, alienating soundtrack that would raise its collective blood pressure. This strategy is based purely on a reflex physiological reaction and has almost nothing to do with plot, acting, script, or even directing.

Cacophony is the key to the opening scenes. In the Iraq prologue, there are multilayered sounds of pickaxes, sledgehammers, wheelbarrows, and shovels, creating a dissonance that peaks with the clanging of a forge as three blacksmiths work over a piece of iron. (Although the actual excavation is absurd. Even in the 1970s, no archeologist would oversee such frenetic and potentially destructive activity at a historical site. The dig is another example of Friedkin exaggerating claims of authenticity. In his DVD commentary for *The Exorcist*, Friedkin claims that the excavation was "real.") Other disturbing sonic effects in the prologue include the thunderous roar of a dro-shky that almost flattens Merrin, the snarling dogs, the magnified sounds of bees (recorded by Jack Nitzsche) emerging when Merrin examines the Pazuzu sculpture, the percussion and singing at the bazaar, the haunting, howling wind that dissolves into Georgetown.

A perfect example of this deliberately manipulated noise is the hospital scene, where Regan endures an arteriography that sounds like a 747 taking off. In the novel, Regan underwent a brain scan, but to Friedkin, such a process was humdrum. "Brain scan is computer," he told Travers and Reiff, "and a computer is not cinematically exciting." Instead, Friedkin overdubbed a hellish racket during the procedure that became the first torture sequence Regan would undergo. "As she cringes with pain," Colin L. Westerbeck Jr. wrote in *Commonweal*, "enormous machines lurch and clank with a mechanical vengeance more horrific than anything unseen spirits have done to her so far."

(According to some reports, it was this agonizing scene that disturbed contemporary audiences the most, precipitating legitimate faintings and walkouts. Which is fitting, considering that the sequence—with its excruciating noise, its suffering teen protagonist, and its unexpected squirt of blood—was specifically designed to generate a visceral response. If Friedkin bordered on schlock throughout *The Exorcist*, he crossed the line into exploitation with the arteriogram [not morally, but aesthetically] by graphically emphasizing a nonessential scene, one that lasts nearly three minutes, strictly for its yuck factor. His defense of the arteriogram has always been the same: the film had to show how far medical science would go before its methods could be ruled out in favor of God.)

Contemporary reviews often noted how loud *The Exorcist* was in theaters and what an excruciating physical experience it was to watch and hear the nonstop shock sequences of its last half hour.

When asked by the American Film Institute about the excessive volume of the film, Friedkin affirmed that it was by design. "Yes, that's how I want the sound, very loud," he said. "I figured it took me three months to get the soundtrack. It might as well be loud. As a matter of fact, I have set the sound level in each of the theaters where the picture is playing, in the twenty-four opening engagements."

Insisting on setting the sound level at twelve, however, brought some objections. "The manager of the National told me that he had gotten some complaints, that it was a little too loud, could we set it at eleven?" Friedkin told the American Film Institute.

Just as Friedkin used "subliminal cuts" (borrowed from sources as diverse as Alain Resnais, Sidney Lumet, Hitchcock, Kubrick, Donald Cammell, and Nicolas Roeg) to unsettle viewers, he also used chaotic sonic devices to torturous psychological effect.

In distorting sound throughout the film, Friedkin ensured that *The Exorcist* had both a conscious and subconscious effect on its audience. The unceasing din caused anxiety at the surface level and, at the same time, created a sense of dread that seemed to grow intrinsically.

Alfred Hitchcock used non-diegetic sound to disturbing effect in *The Birds*, but Friedkin likely modeled his sonic techniques on *The Haunting*, directed by Robert Wise and released in 1963. One of only a handful of genuinely creepy horror films released in the early 1960s, *The Haunting* used imaginative sound effects to suggest paranormal activity as well as the tortured state of mind of the protagonist. Wise incorporated a broad arrangement of synthetic noises as expressionistic devices to establish a mood of terror and would follow it with a diminuendo. Friedkin followed a similar approach with *The Exorcist*.

By alternating between quiet lulls and unexpected roars, Friedkin assured himself of an audience perpetually on edge, anxiously awaiting the next shock. "Very often in the film I use absolute dead silence," Friedkin told *Film Score Monthly*. "No sound at all. The entire concept, visually as well as in terms of sound, is made up of contrasts—light and dark, warm and cold, quiet and noisy. And usually in direct contradiction."

Judging by the widespread terror *The Exorcist* caused, Friedkin had made a shrewd choice. Still, in conceiving a soundscape that relied on mechanical prompts, Friedkin left himself open to charges of sensationalism. And this criticism came not just from the exalted pages of *The New Yorker* or *Cineaste* but, incredibly, even from William Peter Blatty. His overall assessment of the film, driven by bitterness over the final cut that Friedkin had delivered, seemed both harsh and ungrateful. "On the other hand," he told Douglas E. Winter after a withering rundown of the film, "one can't argue with success. The film of *The Exorcist* will always remain a phenomenon, but it will never be a classic. It's just a roller-coaster ride—as elegant a roller-coaster as you can find, but that's all it is." Keep in mind that Friedkin had made Blatty tens of millions of dollars, enough to keep him comfortable for the rest of his life, especially when the ancillary age arrived—network broadcasts, cable repeats, Laserdisc, VHS, DVD, and Blu-Ray sales (as well as rentals), rereleases, and sequels. In fact, Blatty had made so much money that he produced little that was not connected to *The Exorcist* in the last forty years of his life.

▲ ▲ ▲

One of the key sonic elements in the film is the voice of the demon, embodied, most of the time, by Mercedes McCambridge. But Friedkin had to tinker long and hard before he finally settled on her as the solution. To create the demon's voice, Friedkin initially turned to an old crony from his WGN days in Chicago, Ken Nordine, beatnik, spoken word artist, and voice-over wizard. Over the years, Nordine had released several *Word Jazz* albums and had collaborated with artists as diverse as the Fred Katz Group, Billy Vaughn, Fred Astaire, H. P. Lovecraft, and Laurie Anderson. "A lot of what I know about sound came from listening to Ken," Friedkin told Nat Segaloff. "So he was the first one I reached out for, and we paid Ken a lot of money to go out and experiment. He was going to go out and use computers to mix the voice with animal sounds and come up with that distortion. At a certain point Ken played some tapes for me . . . and it basically sounded like Ken Nordine doing a demon voice. It was wrong. But what it told me—while I'm listening to this voice that is trying to sound demonic, which basically sounds comic—is that I had to go for a kind of unnatural sound, neither male nor female. Otherworldly. But what is otherworldly?"

CHAPTER 16

Demon Speak: "I pulled a scarf around my neck . . . and almost strangled."

issatisfied with what Ken Nordine had produced, Friedkin began brainstorming. It turned out that Mercedes McCambridge fit the "otherworldly" role to twisted perfection. "I had no idea if she was still alive," Friedkin told Bob McCabe, "but I remembered her from dramatic radio, which used to be a staple of American life. Radio drama was a very important part of American cultural life when I grew up. I was very influenced by radio drama, and one of the great voices on radio was Mercedes McCambridge. Terrific actress, great voice. I asked my production manager to find out where the hell she was and if she was still alive."

At fifty-seven, McCambridge was not only still alive, but she remained as intense as ever, and she took Method acting to an extreme in what amounted to an off-screen role for *The Exorcist*. "She worked for, maybe, three weeks doing the demon voice. She was chain-smoking, swallowing raw eggs, getting me to tie her to a chair—all these painful things just to produce the sound of that demon in torment," Friedkin told *The Guardian*. "And as she did it, the most curious things would happen in her throat. Double and triple sounds would emerge at once, wheezing sounds, very much akin to what you can imagine a person inhabited by various demons would sound like. It was pure inspiration."

The woman who seemed to burn through the screen in *Johnny Guitar* (and who also violently upstaged the Golden Age headliner, Joan Crawford, in every scene) was not about to start sleepwalking now—being lashed to studio furniture notwithstanding. Recalling some of what she had learned from Stanislavski, McCambridge exploited her chronic bronchitis, found motivation in her Catholic background, and drew on physical actions to enhance her performance.

Then she went even further. "For the groaning sounds," she told the *New York Times*, "I pulled a scarf around my neck, tight, and almost strangled." When Regan projectile vomits on Father Karras, McCambridge unsuccessfully generated sounds until, finally, after a certain amount of trial and error, she settled on the ghastly solution: spewing forth a vile concoction whose ingredients included overripe apples and raw eggs. "On the soundtrack you can hear the bumps that the apples and yolk make!" she recalled in her memoir. "I had to do it many times before it was absolutely right. It made me so dizzy and weak that I would have to lie down for an hour between throw-ups, and then I'd go back and have another go at it."

The horrific voice she produced (with some help from a mixing board), with its diabolical phrasing, was the stuff of nightmares for those who heard it in the theater and an exhausting ordeal for the actress who generated it. "Except for playing *Who's Afraid of Virginia Woolf* on Broadway, I think *The Exorcist* stint was the hardest work I've ever done," McCambridge said. "I mean real physical work! There were nights when, after recording all day, I was afraid to drive over the pass from the Valley to my home in Westwood. I was so wiped out I couldn't be sure of handling the car. So I would sleep in a motel near the studio."

That impassioned effort, which bordered on lunacy, was one reason why McCambridge came to despise Friedkin when he denied her a credit on the film.

Later, Friedkin would say that McCambridge, a recovering alcoholic, also drank whiskey to coarsen her voice. While this is a possibility, it seems far-fetched. McCambridge had not been your run-of-the-mill Sunset Boulevard lush: she had years of hospitalizations behind her, blackouts, and suicide attempts. On the eve of her forty-seventh birthday, "fresh out of lifeness," and rarely anything but drunk, McCambridge swallowed every pill she could find in her medicine cabinet and was dejected when she woke up in a Santa Monica hospital.

She testified at a 1969 Senate subcommittee hearing on alcoholism, and in 1971 she served as the first honorary chairman of the National Council on Alcoholism. In the mid-1970s, she redoubled her efforts as a spokesperson, attending seminars, participating in telethons, even hosting "An Evening with Mercedes McCambridge," where she spoke about her ordeals. In her fanciful 1981 memoir, *The Quality of Mercy*, McCambridge does not mention deliberately diving off the wagon—all in the name of art. In the end, the story of McCambridge drinking whiskey is probably more mythmaking by Friedkin, who spent nearly fifty years telling improbable tales about *The Exorcist*.

▲ ▲ ▲

Other elements Friedkin added to the audio included the sounds of squealing pigs, the amplified buzzing of bees, voices played backward, and the clang and hum of general industrial operations. His real secret weapon, however, may have been Mexican Foley artist Gonzalo Gavira, who had impressed Friedkin with his work on a pair of Alejandro Jodorowsky films, *El Topo* and *The Holy Mountain*. It is Gavira who sells the showstopper: Regan twisting her head around, to the astonishment of the audience. To mimic the sounds of bones cracking while Regan turns and turns, Gavira held an old, cracking leather wallet filled with credit cards up to a microphone and began to manipulate it in sync with a film of the action rolling on a screen in the recording studio.

Until just a few days before opening, Friedkin fiddled with the mix, putting the finishing touches on an audio onslaught that left audiences reeling. For their efforts alongside Friedkin, Robert "Buzz" Knudson and Christopher Newman won an Academy Award for Best Sound.

CHAPTER 17
▲ ▲ ▲

Sticking Pins in a Bill Friedkin Doll

Having overthrown Paul Monash to earn sole credit as producer (in order to protect his vision of *The Exorcist*), William Peter Blatty saw his role shrink into a ceremonial title almost immediately.

After denying Ellen Burstyn the use of a limo when she had arrived at an airport, Blatty squared off with an annoyed Friedkin, who felt that penny-pinching the actors was detrimental to the shoot. "I didn't know what a producer was supposed to do," Blatty told Peter Biskind, "but I knew one thing, I was supposed to watch the budget." At the end of the confrontation, Friedkin, in his best New Hollywood manner, dared Blatty to fire him. Blatty obliged, on a street corner in Manhattan, no less. "My intention was very simple," Blatty told Biskind. "I was stupidly trying to do what I assumed a producer should do. I thought, Monday morning, Billy and I will patch it up and we won't have any more of these ambiguities about who's running what. But Monday morning, the studio sent in a team of seven attorneys for Billy, plus his agent, to hold his hand and assure him I had no legal right to fire him. I was defeated. I went to The Sherry-Netherland where Billy was staying. If Billy didn't want to cope, suddenly his throat was too sore and inflamed. He got psychosomatically ill, couldn't talk. We patched it up, interspersed with spritzes of medicine from his spray bottle. I told Warners, 'From this point on I am not responsible.' And of course from that point on the budget went from four million two to twelve million something."

Cost overruns soon became headline material for *The Exorcist*. To the critics of that era, spending obscene amounts of money on a film bordered on immoral, especially in light of the current state of the national economy (i.e., stagflation), a point of view as outmoded now as phrenology or the Hollow Earth Theory.

An easy way to agitate the combative Friedkin was to question him about the ever-expanding price tag of a film that had operated as a closed set for months. "There is a guy working for one of those papers who'd like to win the Pulitzer Prize for writing the real story of *The Exorcist*," William Friedkin told Peter Travers and Stephanie Reiff. "Obviously, *The Exorcist* is one of the most talked about and anticipated films ever made. It went way over budget and nobody denies that. The woods are filled with guys who would like to take that and twist it down people's throats just to ruin the film business."

While there had been blockbuster productions in the recent past, such as road-show spectaculars *Ben-Hur* and *The Ten Commandments*, these films had epic ambitions and an acknowledged scale. *The Exorcist* was a horror movie—not a genre in which studios gambled—and one plagued by delays and unforeseen expenses. "I'm sure they were sticking pins in a Bill Friedkin doll," Friedkin told Peter Biskind. "But I made as though I was working on the Sistine Chapel, and they never really bothered me."

With the memory of overpriced bombs such as *Mutiny on the Bounty* and *Cleopatra* still relatively fresh, critics eyed *The Exorcist* with a combination of disbelief and malice. Sabotaged by Marlon Brando, *Mutiny* went millions over budget, in the process supplying never-ending material for columnists. Of course, hardly anything in the studio era compared to the nightmare production of *Cleopatra*, whose budget surpassed $30 million in the early 1960s, more than a quarter billion dollars when adjusted for inflation.

Even after the success of *Rosemary's Baby*, there were few mainstream Hollywood horror movies produced, and those also piggybacked on best-selling properties: *The Mephisto Waltz*, *The Possession of Joel Delaney*, and *The Other* all sold well as hardcover and paperback novels. Minimizing risk by adapting proven sources reflected how pragmatic studios could be, but this strategy never went over the top in horror until *The Exorcist* began shooting. None of those three horror films had budgets approaching what Warner Bros. spent on *The Exorcist*. Indeed, *The Exorcist* cost more than 1970s all-star disaster-fests such as *Airport*, *The*

Poseidon Adventure, and *Earthquake*. *The Towering Inferno*, co-headlined by Steve McQueen and Paul Newman (two of the biggest stars of their day) and featuring explosions, fires, and the relentless destruction of sets, cost only $3 million dollars more than *The Exorcist*. As hard as it is to believe today, given how much of it was filmed in a studio with an inexpensive cast, *The Exorcist* cost more than *The Godfather*, *Jaws*, and *Star Wars*. As the first blockbuster Hollywood horror film, *The Exorcist* was something new, and, as such, it was also something completely unexpected.

Although Warner Bros. had several positives about *The Exorcist* to consider—it was based on a blue-chip property, it was helmed by the reigning Academy Award winner for Best Director, the dailies were impressive—they were leery nonetheless and stepped in, occasionally but ineffectually. "The movie was running way over," said Warners executive Dick Lederer. "He was driving them crazy, because he was absolutely intent on getting it exactly the way he wanted, and there were terrible technical problems, to freeze the set so that icicles would form, until he got it he wouldn't quit. The cost was going up and up. It was scary."

Associate producer David Salven described one such instance to author Thomas D. Clagett: "I remember one time when a couple of Warner Brothers executives said we're over schedule and over budget. It was around $4 million dollars to start and came in at about $11 million dollars, but the difference is that everything that went into the picture is up on the screen. Anyway, the studio guys asked Billy, 'What do you think we should do?' His answer was, 'I would suggest you fire me.' Now how do you answer that? He was being Billy Friedkin. It's his plus side. He could say fire a grip or get rid of a truck or we won't eat lunch tomorrow. Instead, it's 'Fuck it. We're doing everything to the best of our knowledge and capability. Otherwise fire me.' That stops the meeting. It's either you're fired or how do you like the food in New York?"

Without a functioning producer on set, Friedkin had carte blanche on a multimillion-dollar enterprise. Only during the height of the New Hollywood era was this possible. In the late 1960s and early 1970s, filmmakers—even some rebellious ones—received producer credits, but few ran roughshod over studio reps. Those freewheeling days, as Friedkin would eventually experience firsthand, would soon come to an end.

CHAPTER 18

Diabolus in Musica

With the December 26 release date closing in, Friedkin was under pressure from every aspect of the production. One of his key worries was the soundtrack, which had to complement, somehow, the sonic terror he was developing on the mixing boards.

Initially, Friedkin had pursued Bernard Herrmann to score the film. The curmudgeonly Herrmann, widely considered the best film composer in history, was sixty-two years old and, after decades of conflict with the industry, now worked primarily out of London. In 1941, Herrmann had been part of the most brazen debut in the history of Hollywood when he arranged the soundtrack for *Citizen Kane*, the masterpiece that had originally inspired Friedkin to become a director. Herrmann had already worked with Orson Welles in the Mercury Theater, and just as Welles had revolutionized film in America, Herrmann had changed music as well. Having won an Oscar in 1942 for *The Devil and Daniel Webster* (when he was just thirty-one years old), Herrmann spent the next three decades being comically overlooked by the Academy, with *The Man Who Knew Too Much*, *Vertigo*, *North by Northwest*, *Psycho* (believe it or not), and *Fahrenheit 451* apparently unworthy even of a nomination. To his credit, Friedkin recognized the towering achievements of Herrmann even if the erratic voting committees did not.

In another standard Hollywood truth-or-fiction moment, the meeting between Friedkin and Herrmann has produced multiple versions, but there is only one version advanced by Friedkin that marginally exaggerates his own standing. "I showed him a rough cut and he loved the picture, and he wanted to do it, except he would not work in California," Friedkin told Elmer Bernstein in an interview for the American Film Institute. "He didn't like California's musicians. He didn't want to work in Hollywood. He had been through all that and to hell with it." This story ends with Friedkin declining to work with Herrmann based on time and distance.

Every other retelling by Friedkin of this meeting raises his status in the story, which means, axiomatically, that a negative anecdote is closer to reality. According to Nat Segaloff, Herrmann traveled to Los Angeles to screen *The Exorcist*, where the following scene ensued:

"I want you to write me a better score than the one you wrote for *Citizen Kane*," Friedkin said, according to one story.

"Then you should have made a better movie than *Citizen Kane*," Herrmann replied, and returned to London.

Whatever happened between Friedkin and Herrmann left *The Exorcist* without a composer.

Enter Lalo Schifrin, who executive producer Noel Marshall had recommended. It turned out that Friedkin had known Schifrin for years. Before moving to Los Angeles, Friedkin had befriended Schifrin in Chicago, where the composer made tour stops as the musical director and pianist for Dizzy Gillespie. "And I admired both his playing and his compositions . . . his work as a jazz artist," Friedkin told *Film Score Monthly*. "And then he came out to Hollywood and established himself as one of the best composers out here."

A supremely gifted pianist, Schifrin would write and appear on several Verve releases, including *Gillespiana*, a full arrangement infused with Latin and African touches, as well as *Carnegie Hall Concert*, featuring a thunderous version of "A Night in Tunisia." He had already earned accolades in Hollywood for his work on *Cool Hand Luke*, *Bullitt*, *Dirty Harry*, and *THX 1138*. The accolades would stop, at least momentarily, with William Friedkin.

A 1999 *Film Score Monthly* article by George Park revisited the fallout between Friedkin and Schifrin, highlighting a communication breakdown that eventually led to the rupture of a long-standing friendship.

At first, Schifrin thought that Friedkin was happy with his direction after Warner Bros. had produced a trailer accompanied by a passage that Schifrin had composed. Everyone involved, including Friedkin, loved the music. But the trailer was so disturbing—visually and sonically—that the studio decided to spare the public from seeing it. A two-minute nightmare, the trailer, already on the edge of nerve-racking, was made unbearable by the music—dark, intense, pulsing.

But Friedkin, whose communication style often veered between terse and cryptic, despised what Schifrin subsequently produced. "I felt that *The Exorcist* score should be atonal and minimalist, like a cold hand on the back of your neck," he wrote in his memoir. "I wanted abstract chamber music because I felt a big orchestra would overwhelm the film's intimacy."

Instead, Schifrin gathered an ensemble for a recording session in late October that delivered "wall-to-wall noise." Whatever Friedkin thought he might get out of Schifrin, he was unprepared for what he heard on the stage that day. "I was in shock and appalled because it was the precise opposite of all that I had told him I felt that the film needed," Friedkin told *Film Score Monthly*. "It was percussive, loud, bombastic. It was hocking away with a huge orchestra."

Friedkin and Schifrin discussed the score, first dispassionately, then heatedly. After calling Warner Bros. exec John Calley to mediate, Schifrin was fired—less than two months before the release date.

"This case was a mutual understanding, that we didn't understand each other," Schifrin told George Park, "and I left very resentful because nobody warned me that I had to be a little bit more subtle. They raved about the music I did for the trailer, so I went in the same direction. So when the director himself told me, 'This doesn't work,' I got mad. And he got mad. And we ended in a terrible way."

Even the sidelined Blatty erupted at what Friedkin did to Schifrin, and he added it to his running tally of grievances. "Unfortunately, I was not there. I was barred from that," Blatty told *The Hollywood Reporter*. "But in view of the fact that the music had been approved the week before by the director, and since the session was all paid for, it would seem of necessity, in my opinion, to be another reckless action. Only 20 percent of the session had been completed."

It was one thing for Friedkin to dump Schifrin based on incompatible visions, but the director also smeared Schifrin by repeatedly linking his score to demeaning terms such as "marimba music" and "samba." Schifrin, from Buenos Aires, found himself typecast despite producing work without a hint of South American influence. As churlish as Friedkin was by nature, his gratuitous insults of a world-class musician are more problematic than most dustups because they are based apparently on falsehoods. There seemed to be an illogicality to some of his reactions. When David Salven and Bud Smith tried to convince Friedkin to let Schifrin complete the score for future use by the studio (the musicians and recording time were already paid for), Friedkin erupted: "Fuck the money, fuck the music, fuck everything!"

Years later, Schifrin would hint at a deep-rooted personal grudge that had driven Friedkin to sabotage his work. "The trailer was terrific, but the mix of those frightening scenes and my music, which was also a very difficult and heavy score, scared the audiences away," he told *Score Magazine* in 2016. "So, the Warner Brothers executives sent Friedkin to tell me that I must write a less dramatic and softer score. I could easily and perfectly do what they wanted because it was way too simple in relevance to what I have previously written, but Friedkin didn't tell me what they said. I'm sure he did it deliberately. In the past we had an incident, caused by other reasons, and I think he wanted vengeance. This is my theory."

Indeed, Friedkin was not content to fire Schifrin; he would boast about it. "Lalo Schifrin could denounce me every day on the front page of the *New York Times*," he seethed to Janet Maslin of the *Boston Phoenix*. "I would rather see that in bold headlines two inches thick every day for the rest of my life than have one note of his miserable soundtrack in my picture! I would rather be sued in court by him, I would rather have him put out a contract for me than have one note of the music he wrote for *The Exorcist* in the film. And it is not in the film because it was terrible, it's that simple."

In 1998, a twenty-fifth anniversary "Special Edition Deluxe Set" VHS and DVD release of *The Exorcist* included among its bonus materials a CD featuring the soundtrack of the film—including a suite recorded by Schifrin. For the first time, the public could hear the original, discarded soundtrack, the "Mexican mariachi" score, as Friedkin had put it in *Easy Riders, Raging Bulls*.

The eleven-minute track featured on the CD begins with a haunting Tantum ergo Sacramentum sung by what sounds like an adolescent girl before segueing into an eerie passage with abstract tones. A dramatic string orchestra, reminiscent of certain elements Bernard Herrmann used in *Psycho*, follows, jarring and dissonant, occasionally using *col legno battuto* for emphasis.

Frenzied, foreboding, and feverish, *Suite from the Unused Score to The Exorcist* (as it is now known) is unlike any other music produced for a horror film. This was before the elaborate soundtracks for horror movies had become standard (think of the bare-bones score of *Psycho*, with only strings, or the simple lullaby motif that runs throughout *Rosemary's Baby*, along with its creepy chants). Only Hammer, with their heavy, Romantic arrangements, consistently tried adding ornate music to horror films. Even so, Friedkin correctly recognized the mismatch between the film and the score. Schifrin had created a powerful soundscape that threatened to over-whelm not only the film but also the carefully crafted audio manipulations and effects so important to Friedkin. Pairing the score with the film—which are both assaultive pieces at their cores—would have been overkill.

"A ten-year friendship was over," Friedkin wrote about Schifrin in 2013. "Whenever our paths cross, we avert our eyes. We haven't spoken to each other for forty years."

(A similar fate afflicted the relationship between Ken Nordine and Friedkin, whose friendship stretched back to the 1950s. Nordine, whose voice for the demon had been nixed by Friedkin, was forced to sue Warner Bros. for payment. In 1979, he finally settled out of court for an undisclosed amount. His relationship with Friedkin did not survive their luckless collaboration.)

Now short a composer and the time to find a replacement, Friedkin scrambled to create a patchwork soundtrack. He hired Jack Nitzsche—once the right-hand man of Phil Spector and a former member of Crazy Horse and the Rolling Stones—for sound texture and a few atonal pieces. Then Friedkin invited David Borden, a minimalist composer, to contribute a few cues. Only snippets of what Nitzsche and Borden produced appear in the final cut of *The Exorcist*, however; at some point, Friedkin had decided to assemble what he would call a "music score by Tower Records."

Friedkin rounded out the rest of the film with the same classical compos-ers he had recommended to Schifrin as inspiration: Krzysztof Penderecki, Hans Werner Henze, George Crumb, and Anton Webern. (In retrospect, Penderecki is a sly addition when one considers that his opera, *The Devils of Loudon*, about possessions and exorcisms, debuted in 1969.)

But Friedkin was still searching for a lullaby piece for the film, a haunting melody, preferably something with keyboards. A stack of records provided by Warner Bros. (which received albums from all over the world from labels looking for exposure) gave Friedkin his next rendezvous with Kismet. He began searching for his elusive lullaby randomly. "Auditioning music this way is called 'needle dropping.' I began to play through the stacks, listening for no more than several seconds before changing discs. I did this several hours a day, and on the fourth day I was ready to give up. Wearily, I selected a disc called *Tubular Bells*, written and performed by Mike Oldfield."

A rock prodigy, Oldfield first recorded when he was fifteen years old. Not long after his debut, Oldfield joined ex–Soft Machine frontman Kevin Ayers, playing bass and guitar on a few of his early solo releases. At eighteen, Oldfield began working on his magnum opus, an album titled *Tubular Bells*. It took Oldfield more than nine months to record, under stressful circumstances for the teenager, who was heavily using drugs. Oldfield also played numerous instruments himself, including glockenspiel, Farfisa organ, guitar, piano, bass, timpani, flageolet, and the title instrument, working feverishly to multitrack all the disparate sounds.

Released on May 25, 1973, *Tubular Bells* was a groundbreaking album: a forty-nine-minute instrumental (split into parts on each side of the vinyl disc) that established its own genre: New Age. Celebrated in England for its unique fusion of progressive rock and classical music, *Tubular Bells* became an oddball smash in the United States when a fragment of it appeared in *The Exorcist*. Virgin pressed a single of "Tubular Bells" in 1974, which sold by the tens of thousands. At a time when the Billboard charts were far more adventurous than they are today, "Tubular Bells" peaked at number seven.

"Why did my music become associated with what was probably the scariest movie ever about the supernatural?" Oldfield wrote in his autobiography *Changeling*. "It's just one of those synchronicity things, I think. There are musicians that make music purely for entertainment, be it rock music or ballads. I can, and sometimes do, make that kind of music, but when I feel I have really fulfilled my purpose of being a musician, my music doesn't turn out like that at all. In my mind, for music to really work it's got to be something completely different; it's got to have something like a spiritual connection. Obviously, that piece of music from *Tubular Bells* must have had that dimension, otherwise the director, William Friedkin, wouldn't have seized on it."

Tubular Bells was the first album released on the newly launched Virgin Records label and would eventually sell more than sixteen million copies worldwide. Only twenty years old when *The Exorcist* made him rich, Oldfield was too depressed and anxious to enjoy the fame that usually accompanied such a windfall. Richard Branson, head of Virgin, tried unsuccessfully to get Oldfield to tour or at least grant interviews to music journalists. "But all I was interested in was flying my model aeroplane . . . and covering the telephone with a pillow," Oldfield wrote. "It was all I was capable of at the time; if I could have fast-forwarded my personality by ten years, I probably would have been overjoyed to do what they wanted. After some time, several months or a year, they gave up and the phone stopped ringing."

In stitching together an ad hoc soundtrack, Friedkin had provided another pop touchstone for *The Exorcist*. "Tubular Bells," with its eerie melody and its curious 15/8 time signature, is instantly recognizable as the "theme" of *The Exorcist* and has become musical shorthand for the sinister and haunting.

CHAPTER 19

Merciless: In the Cutting Room

After shooting was complete, William Friedkin geared up for the most excruciating—and exhilarating—aspect of postproduction: editing. With hours of footage from Iraq alone, Friedkin would have to shape hundreds of setups into a coherent narrative. It was a process he relished. "Editing is the most exciting part of filmmaking for me," he told the American Film Institute. "I would be an editor full-time if I can make as much money at it, if I can live the same lifestyle, as I do by directing."

To deliver a cut in the limited time remaining before the opening date of December 26, Friedkin created an assembly-line team that worked punishing hours. In his memoir, Friedkin recalled the frenzied process. "I hired four editors—Jordan Leondopoulos, Evan Lottman, Norman Gay, and my old pal from Wolper, Bud Smith, to whom I assigned the Iraq sequence—plus two assistants for each, and rooms side by side," he wrote. "Each editor was given different scenes, and I would go from room to room making changes for at least twelve hours a day, six days a week. Once an editor finished one scene, he'd take on another. This was an unprecedented, potentially chaotic way to edit a film."

This breakneck pace arose because Friedkin insisted on asserting his dominance over a shoot without a producer. In *Easy Riders, Raging Bulls*, Peter Biskind described how editing *The Exorcist* became a race against the clock. "With most films, the editor is at work assembling a rough cut while the director is still shooting. But Friedkin was so determined to control every aspect of the production that he hired an editor with no feature experience and refused to cut film for the entire eight- or nine-month production."

Still, this seemingly haphazard approach underscored how Friedkin thrived on pressure and how he viewed filmmaking as a strenuous adventure, pushing the limits of what was possible. With all its delays and injuries, *The Exorcist* was much more arduous than *The French Connection*, and in a few years, *Sorcerer* would top them both. Even with time and circumstances conspiring against him, however, Friedkin never lost sight of his visual principles. "To me, editing is more exciting, more interesting, more discovery prone, more important than any other facet of filmmaking. You can, literally, blow a good film in the cutting room, or make a film better than it is, or ruin stuff that was well shot to begin with—you can just ruin it. I find that the attitude in the cutting room that works best for me is to be merciless. I've reached the point now where I don't have to psych myself to do it; I just view the stuff as total shit; I divorce myself from the guy who directed it. I become another person, in effect. You literally have to split yourself in two at that point. And you have to forget about all of the troubles that you had getting that shot, all the difficulties you had and achieving that performance on take twenty-eight, or whatever it was, and say, 'This doesn't work. This doesn't make it!'"

In the cutting room, Friedkin had a distinct vision, inspired not only by his admiration for Alfred Hitchcock and Michelangelo Antonioni but also by his documentary background and, most important, perhaps, his understanding of what contemporary moviegoers wanted to see. "I like quickness on the screen," Friedkin told Travers and Reiff. "I like things to happen fast. It is my feeling that the audience is two steps ahead of most filmmakers. So what I try to do is play a little game with that intelligent audience I have in my head. I look at the film and see, as usual, that we're going along A-B-C-D. But the audience, given A, is already at D. So I say, let's go straight to D. If we're wrong, at least we won't be boring anybody."

With his ruthless editing style, Friedkin ultimately sacrificed a few plot points along the way, including some that were sacred to William Peter Blatty. He used the same methodology for *The French Connection*, cutting several scenes that might have given more depth to Popeye Doyle. An overriding interest in speed and pace meant jettisoning character development, a trademark Friedkin rarely abandoned, and one whose apotheosis is apparent in his superficial action film *The Hunted* (2003).

For *The Exorcist*, there was another, more practical reason to hack away at scenes, and it had nothing to do with aesthetic considerations or running time. As Friedkin put it to Mark Kermode: "One of the things I was conscious of doing while editing *The Exorcist* was to keep it moving and not stop in one place anywhere, where the audience could say, 'Oh, wait a minute, fella....'"

The Exorcist is full of undeveloped subplots or scenes that lead nowhere. This is especially true concerning the murder of Burke Dennings, which takes place off-screen in the hopes of building mystery around it. By then, however, the audience is already conscious that Regan is possessed by an evil force that will likely explode at any moment.

The party scene early in the film is responsible for the biggest lapse in narrative logic found in *The Exorcist*. After Regan urinates in front of the guests, she is next seen being comforted by her mother, who tells her, "It's just like the doctor said, it's nerves. And that's all. OK? You just take your pills and you'll be fine, really. OK?"

William Peter Blatty, still in his monetization phase, had not yet bared his fangs about the damage Friedkin did to his sacred vision when he wrote about this scene in his 1974 book *William Peter Blatty on The Exorcist: From Novel to Film*: "Audiences are jarred when Chris refers out of nowhere to Regan taking pills 'just like the doctor said' at a point in the film where they have yet to see Regan being examined by a doctor, are in the dark about why she might have gone if in fact she did, and have no idea what kind of pills she might be taking."

According to Blatty, the first cut that Friedkin delivered in late September was roughly two hours and twenty minutes long. It was that version, the one with theological explanations and an upbeat ending, that William Peter Blatty saw and approved. But when Warner Bros. advised Friedkin to trim the running time and to drop the anticlimactic finale, he agreed. Without input from Blatty, who had been, after all, barred from the editing room, Friedkin went to work with his typical merciless exactitude. Out went more than a reel of footage, including material Blatty considered sacred.

These cuts, without his approval, left Blatty convinced that *The Exorcist* had been irreparably marred. "The film today is considered a classic," he told Bob McCabe sometime during the late 1990s. "The film I saw at 666 Fifth Avenue was a masterpiece. That's the difference."

CHAPTER 20

▲ ▲ ▲

The Mysterious R

By the late 1960s, the collapse of the studio system (and with it, the Production Code, which had regulated morality in Hollywood since 1934) had allowed auteurs and schlockmeisters alike to push the boundaries of what was permissible. Grindhouse films, Russ Meyer sexploitation romps, brutal imports such as *Witchfinder General*, the occasional independent horror film (including *Night of the Living Dead*), and "hicksploitation" fare for the Southern market played with little oversight from the MPAA or even local municipalities in the Bible Belt.

In November 1968, the Motion Picture Association of America adopted a voluntary ratings system, hoping to quell the controversies surrounding lightning-rod films such as *Who's Afraid of Virginia Woolf*, *Blow-Up*, and *Bonnie and Clyde*. To MPAA president Jack Valenti, the steady move to adult content was not only inevitable but commercially desirable for Hollywood. Nudity, graphic violence, and raunchy language were the only things television could not offer an increasingly housebound audience. Since "the idiot box" first began diverting eyeballs from the silver screen, Hollywood had tried numerous strategies to retain viewers, including novelties such as stereoscopic (3D) thrillers, and technological innovations such as CinemaScope. Sex and violence was the latest strategy.

When Michelangelo Antonioni refused to eliminate nudity from *Blow-Up*, MGM released the film without MPAA approval through a subsidiary, Premier Productions. *Blow-Up* became an art-house hit in 1967, and the MPAA became increasingly peripheral.

As if in response to *Blow-Up*, Senator Margaret Chase wrote a feature in *Reader's Digest* calling for a Senate Committee to determine a ratings classification system that would protect the public from indelicate films. "In fairness to the MPAA," she wrote, "I must say that most of our movies— including a good number unfit for children—are not made by members of that organization, nor are they submitted for a code seal of approval. Thus, the door to degeneracy and sadism is still wide open."

Even President Lyndon B. Johnson weighed in, signing a bill to establish the Commission on Obscenity and Pornography in October 1967. Aimed mostly at smutty paperbacks and raunchy magazines, the Commission hinted at targeting other mediums. As journalist Ted Lewis put it in the New York *Daily News*, "In addition, [the bill] constitutes a warning to the motion picture industry about off-color productions."

With the battle over free expression and censorship blazing, and the fear of legislative control over filmmaking, Valenti made his move. Where television had to abide by FCC regulations, Hollywood had only its own self-regulatory apparatus—the Production Code—to worry about. There was nothing television could do about government oversight, but Hollywood had only its toothless house censors to manage. Because the studio system had already collapsed, opening the market to independents and freelancers, Hollywood could no longer control distribution and, similarly, the MPAA found itself bypassed more often. The Production Code was scrapped altogether, replaced by a classification system based on age guidelines and designated by letters: G, M (for "mature audiences"), R, and X. An R meant no one under sixteen would be admitted without a guardian, and the X meant no one under sixteen would be admitted at all, eliminating a significant percentage of paying moviegoers. (The ages for R and X films would be raised more than once in subsequent years.) On November 1, 1968, the new ratings system went into effect, allowing both permissive subjective matter and stricter self-regulation. Major studios would voluntarily submit their films to the MPAA for ratings approval.

In keeping with the accelerating times, and to attract the new class of suburbanites dotting America, Hollywood shifted to previously unthinkable themes and images. In 1969, *Midnight Cowboy* became the first—and only—X-rated film to win an Academy Award for Best Picture, and a few years later, *Last Tango in Paris* raised the bar for risky and risqué cinema, causing its own share of walkouts and nausea despite Oscar nominations for Marlon Brando and director Bernardo Bertolucci.

The first films stamped with the pristine X were imports: *The Girl on a Motorcycle* (1968, United Kingdom), featuring an international cast of Alain Delon and Marianne Faithfull; and *Birds of Peru* (1968, France), with the tragic duo of Jean Seberg and Romain Gary on board.

Then came *Midnight Cowboy*, whose X did not prevent it from winning Academy Awards for Best Picture, Best Director, and Best Adapted Screenplay. The stunning success of *Midnight Cowboy* flipped everything on its head: how could cinematic art without explicit sex or violence be unsuitable?

A handful of years into its existence, the MPAA system remained embattled, with *Midnight Cowboy*, *Tropic of Cancer*, *Carnal Knowledge*, *The Last House on the Left*, and *Last Tango in Paris* creating a stir due to disagreements over their ratings classifications. The producers of *Tropic of Cancer* went so far as to sue the MPAA over the X rating it received.

Despite all the commotion surrounding the ratings controversies of the late 1960s and early 1970s, no one was prepared for *The Exorcist*, not only because it had graphic special effects never attempted in film but because it had also completely avoided interference from the MPAA. Somehow, *The Exorcist* sidestepped an X rating, reportedly because its clear-cut religious theme of good overcoming evil appealed to Aaron Stern, chairman of the MPAA ratings board. According to William Friedkin, *The Exorcist* received no pushback from the MPAA, a shocking outcome, given its vulgarity and bloody crucifix masturbation. In his memoir, Friedkin reported what Aaron Stern told him after Stern viewed a rough cut of *The Exorcist*: "Listen, I've just seen *The Exorcist*. It's a great film. We're going to give it an R, and I'm sure we'll catch heat for that, and so will you, but this is a movie that should be seen as you made it, so we're not asking for any cuts."

That R rating guaranteed that the first wave of moviegoers had no idea what was in store for them when they sat down with popcorn sacks that would soon double as emesis bags. Not only would an X rating have limited the number of teenagers who saw the film, but it would also have served as a warning to general audiences. After all, that ominous "X" would have separated *The Exorcist* from *My Fair Lady* and *The Sound of Music*, yes, and at the same time, made it clear that even freethinking viewers of difficult adult fare such as *Five Easy Pieces* and *The Panic in Needle Park* should also take heed.

In the 1970s, R-rated films were far more permissive than today, and the MPAA regularly faced criticism for its inconsistency from both filmgoers and filmmakers. When *The Last House on the Left*, the risible debut of Wes Craven, opened with an R rating in 1972, it shocked citizens everywhere it played. A crude exploitation film meant for the bottom of double-bills on the drive-in circuit, *The Last House on the Left* spurred outrage and even the occasional protest from concerned citizens. Indignation in Wethersfield, Connecticut, for example, forced one movie theater to make its own edits to the film, overseen and approved by a Chief Circuit Court Prosecutor and a police officer. (There were also stories about projectionists so appalled at what they were exhibiting that they made impromptu cuts to the reels in the booth.)

But *The Last House on the Left* was cobbled together by a team of amateurs and a fly-by-night distributor. Its makers, Craven and producer Sean S. Cunningham (who had previously worked on a porn film and a subgenre known as a "white coater"), viewed *The Last House on the Left* as hackwork that would pay a few bills for them and disappear from circulation within a week or two. *The Exorcist*, by contrast, was a hyped $11–$12 million extravaganza produced by one of the largest studios in the world and directed by a man whose last outing had won five Academy Awards. It was a prestige film about an outré subject previously relegated to low-budget productions in the United Kingdom. Only Roman Polanski had been able to make world-class cinema out of the inherently pulpy materials of a satanic plotline.

Most critics and reviewers agreed that *The Exorcist* did not deserve its R rating, believing its crucifix scene was more than enough to earn it an X. "The film contains brutal shocks, almost indescribable obscenities. That it received an R rating and not the X is stupefying," wrote Roger Ebert.

More cynical observers found the situation dubious. Vincent Canby of the *New York Times* and John Simon of *Esquire* led the charge, noting that the scale of the production, and the major studio backing it, Warner Bros., were the likeliest reasons *The Exorcist* had eluded cuts. "William Peter Blatty, who produced the film and adapted his best-selling novel for the screen, has succeeded in leaving out very few of the ridiculous details that, I suspect, would have earned a less expensive, more skeptical film an X rating instead of the R rating that mysteriously has been achieved," Canby wrote.

Naturally, John Simon was the most ruthless in highlighting the transactional nature of the ratings system and the productions it oversaw. "Disturbing, too, is the . . . R rating for a film that would have surely been X-rated had it not cost a major Hollywood studio a fortune," he wrote. "Valenti, Stern, and Co. have a way of becoming most accommodating when survival of the industry whose hirelings they are is at stake."

In her *New Yorker* condemnation, Pauline Kael also made the connection between the soft rating and the budget: "If *The Exorcist* had cost under a million, or had been made abroad, it would almost certainly be an X film, but when a movie is as expensive as this one, the MPAA rating board doesn't dare to give it an X."

Responding to a letter written to the *New York Times* by Washington-based journalist Roy Meacham, who warned about the traumatic effect *The Exorcist* might have on children because of its R rating, Jack Valenti defended the MPAA. "*The Exorcist* is essentially a horror film," he wrote. "Much of what might concern some people is not on the screen: it is in the mind and imagination of the viewer. A film cannot be punished for what people think because all people do not think alike. What might repel and frighten some people might not do the same to others."

The visceral, even delirious, response from audiences to what they saw on the silver screen confirmed what parents, film critics, and moralists believed: the MPAA had seriously blundered with its delicate treatment of *The Exorcist*.

▲ ▲ ▲

The Exorcist was not the first release to cause a furor. *The Birth of a Nation*, the innovative 1915 D. W. Griffith epic that doubled as a KKK recruitment ad, set off riots when it was released and was banned in several states.

In the 1920s, professional bluenoses objected to Hollywood—and films, in principle—seeing amorality and corruption in every flickering microsecond of celluloid. Eventually, grievances and threats led to the adoption of the Hays Code, which policed films with a heavy hand from script to rough cut.

It was, appropriately enough, horror films that caused some of the first mass controversies in Hollywood. *Frankenstein*, the second of the mighty

Universal Pictures monster cycle, appalled the first audiences to see it, and its disturbing murder scene (when the playful monster tosses a little girl into a lake, thinking she will float like flower petals) was excised from some prints immediately. Kansas and Massachusetts censored the film, and the occasional patron fled the theater after seeing it. *The Hollywood Reporter* assessed *Frankenstein* as follows: "Universal has either the greatest shocker of all time—or a dud." It took only a few days for the first phrase to prove accurate.

A year later, *Freaks*, directed by Tod Browning, who began the horror boom in 1931 with *Dracula*, was so revolting to viewers that MGM yanked it from several theaters across the country amid complaints. If Browning thought that portraying a sideshow troupe in mostly everyday situations (at least until the unsettling last reel) would elicit sympathy from the public, he was badly, humiliatingly mistaken. America was not ready for a revenge film whose stars included The Armless Wonder, The Human Skeleton, Pinhead, and The Boy with Half a Torso.

Aside from *Scarlet Street* (1945) and Italian neorealism films, there were minor uproars involving *The Outlaw* (1943, Jane Russell offensively— depending on your point of view—spilling out over her top) and *The Moon Is Blue* (1953, speaking hitherto verboten words such as "virgin" and "pregnant"). Films featuring Sidney Poitier were also deemed unwholesome in the South.

As the McCarthy era progressed, puritanical objections became more popular. In the 1950s, the moral panic over juvenile delinquency culminated in Senate Subcommittee hearings targeting horror comic books in the first of a slew of panics that would eventually include rock 'n' roll, Dungeons and Dragons, video games, heavy metal, VHS tapes, and 976 phone numbers. The film industry also suffered from collective hysteria: the fear of juvenile delinquency sparked backlash against *The Wild One* (1953), banned in Memphis and Calgary, Alberta, Canada. That led to greater opprobrium for *Rebel Without a Cause* (1955), with its alienated teens and fatal "Chickie Run."

In June 1960, *Psycho* changed everything with its elaborate twin murder sequences: the astonishing shower scene, which time has diminished but was almost unbearable in the days when simply flushing a toilet was prohibited, and the tour de force slashing, on a staircase, no less, of Martin Balsam. Audiences shrieked, hyperventilated, and, in some cases, fled the theater.

When the roiling late Sixties rolled around, with the studio system in ruins and permissiveness in the arts peaking, Hollywood could barely go a month without some moral controversy. The outcry that greeted *Psycho* upon its release in 1960 was nothing compared to what would happen just a few years later. *Lolita*, *The Pawnbroker*, and *Blow-Up* prefigured the creative explosions soon to come. The eruptions began in 1967 and would not cease for years: the agonizing, slow-motion bullet-ballet finale of *Bonnie and Clyde*, the triumph of Satan in *Rosemary's Baby* (with its nightmare rape scene), the endless blood-squib explosions of *The Wild Bunch*, the sexual taboos of *Midnight Cowboy*.

The Exorcist opened during a short span of releases—from 1971 to 1975—when several topflight directors found themselves causing enough controversy to force some municipalities to react based on obscenity laws that allowed them to apply community standards to films. (For example, in the future, *The Exorcist* would be rated X in the District of Columbia and Boston, two cities that overrode the official R rating.) *Carnal Knowledge* (Mike Nichols, 1971); *Straw Dogs* (Sam Peckinpah, 1971); *A Clockwork Orange* (Stanley Kubrick, 1971,); *The Devils* (Ken Russell, 1971); and *Last Tango in Paris* (Bernardo Bertolucci, 1972) all triggered backlash of varying intensity. And these were just the respectable productions. Disreputable low-budget quickies such as *The Last House on the Left*, *Three on a Meathook*, and *Texas Chainsaw Massacre*, combined with the rise of porno chic, kicked off by *Deep Throat* (1972), also contributed to an atmosphere of permanent affront.

Still, at the major studio level, nothing could compare to *The Exorcist* for mass hysteria, and no one, it seemed, was prepared for what would follow.

CHAPTER 21

▲ ▲ ▲

"*Exorcist* Literally Makes Filmgoers Sick"

On December 26, 1973, *The Exorcist* opened in twenty-four theaters dotted across the United States (compare that to the 4,802 screens that *The Lion King* reboot graced in 2019) and immediately struck a dark national chord.

Within days of *The Exorcist* opening, stories began to emerge of audience reactions that had not been seen in more than a decade, ever since *Psycho*, with its infamous shower scene, had left filmgoers shrieking in their seats. But *The Exorcist* went far beyond what even the menacing combination of Alfred Hitchcock and Norman Bates could produce. No one had ever seen such a response to a film before. Between rowdy overflow crowds, protests from parents and religious groups, and hundreds of spectators carried out from theaters in various stages of hyperventilation or insensibility, *The Exorcist* provoked startling reactions that, in some ways, resembled collective hysteria.

Local newscasts across the country dispatched reporters and camera crews to theaters, where they invariably encountered overwrought spectators who had abandoned *The Exorcist* within minutes of the houselights dimming. Some newsreels included raw footage of women collapsing, unconscious, in the lobby; others featured interviews with dazed, often distraught, theatergoers blubbering about the terrifying ordeal they had just suffered.

On January 2, 1974, the *Boston Globe* ran a headline that summed up the alarming trend: "Exorcist Literally Makes Filmgoers Sick—Especially the Fainthearted." Richard Tritter, a spectator interviewed by the *Globe*, described a night at the theater like no other. "During the movie four people vomited, including one policeman," he said. "This movie goes beyond anything that has ever been done before."

Wherever *The Exorcist* played, these disturbing reports followed, along with unusual circumstances rarely associated with moviegoing. Indeed, for a few months in 1974, *The Exorcist* reinvented the entire experience of moviegoing, a process that had been virtually static for more than half a century, since the first film palaces began opening in the 1910s. Now ushers added smelling salts to their flashlights and blazers. Security guards with bullhorns herded shivering crowds into orderly lines behind velvet ropes. Ambulances reportedly sped away from several theaters, carrying distressed spectators who had suffered heart attacks. In New York City, a mini-riot erupted outside of Cinema I when an anxious crowd, waiting for hours in frigid temperatures, realized that tickets might sell out yet again. At the Brentwood Theater in St. Louis, police arrived to quell disorder on the streets, where Officer John Donelli encountered "Mass chaos at the entrance door, which was a definite public safety hazard."

Two weeks into this collective delirium, the Associated Press offered a reason for some of the pandemonium unfolding during screenings of *The Exorcist*: "An immediate problem is that the film received an R rating from the MPAA when it should have been rated X, according to many theater managers."

It is also worth noting that some of these incidents were probably staged. Because *The Exorcist* had a limited opening (only twenty-four total theaters, mostly in urban centers), there was a small pool of theater managers who could be talked into cooperating with publicity reps. In the 1970s, when there were no pre-order apps, assigned seats, or internet sites for publicity, grassroots marketing was a major part of PR strategy.

Dramatic audience reactions had been faked before, most notably on behalf of the original *Dracula*, a risky film gambit that drove Universal executives into planting stories about faintings in the press. To further lure the morbid, Universal even parked ambulances outside of certain theaters.

The incidents surrounding *The Exorcist* were certainly, to an extent, exaggerated, as publicist Joe Hyams admitted to Bob McCabe: "Did I play it up? Sure, I played it up in the sense that people wanted to know how many people got sick last night. I would inflate the figures. That was my job. There was nothing I could do to kill that picture, so I'd lie a little."

The buildup by the filmmakers themselves—in addition to the expected hype of a studio—was both unusual and cynical. Alfred Hitchcock, of course, promoted his share of silly campaigns, but the methods Friedkin used were closer to the zany stunts of William Castle and the splatter impresario Herschell Gordon Lewis.

While William Peter Blatty made the rounds solemnly warning about the palpable threat of Satan (sounding like fellow crackpots and hucksters Hal Lindsey and Mike Warnke) and misleading the public about the Hunkeler case, Friedkin was far more outlandish in pursuit of cynical ballyhoo. Friedkin may have been a member of the New Hollywood, but his Barnumesque methods stretched back to the days of the first studio heads, men like Marcus Loew (born 1870), Adolph Zukor (born 1873) and Carl Laemmle (born in 1867). He borrowed the "top-secret" film-set schtick from Hitchcock, oversold the cursed production angle, made the special effects sound as if mystical forces were involved in creating them (during a lecture in Georgia, Friedkin told the audience that "magnetic fields" produced the levitation scene), and invariably reminded anyone with a pad and pen or a tape recorder that the set had been blessed by Catholic priests several times.

Even to the readers of *Castle of Frankenstein* (presumably a vested audience), Friedkin sliced the occult baloney extra thick. "We were plagued by strange and sinister things from the beginning," he announced. (Compare *The Exorcist* crew to Martin Sheen, who starred in a Santeria flick in 1989, *The Believers*, and said this during a publicity tour: "Such nonsense. I have no interest at all in the occult, in tribal hocus-pocus. I took this movie for one reason only—because John Schlesinger is a master filmmaker.")

If there were staged faintings written up by credulous or dubious reporters, however, professionals with reputations to protect vouched for plenty of confirmed events. Among them were doctors, psychiatrists, and priests, all of whom confirmed disturbing trends and events in the aftermath of *The Exorcist*.

According to some of these observers, fainting, vomiting, and even heart attacks were some of the milder side effects of viewing *The Exorcist*. A Chicago psychiatrist named Dr. Louis S. Schlan, medical director of River

Edge Hospital, reported that two of his patients had been in restraints for over a week after seeing *The Exorcist*. Four more of his patients, all women, reported being in the grip of Satan. Dr. Schlan, who described these women as suffering from "demonopathic hysteria," offered an informal second-hand assessment on a befuddling late twentieth-century phenomenon: fear of being possessed. "My professional colleagues who have seen the film agree that there is no way you can sit through it without receiving some lasting negative or disturbing effects," he said.

To an extent, Dr. Schlan was correct. As *Exorcist*-mania swept across America, a corresponding rise in claims of possession accompanied it. Requests for exorcisms flooded Catholic dioceses and parishes; phone calls seeking help overwhelmed priests. "Just look at the mass hysteria that occurs in the theaters, with people getting sick," The Most Reverend John Ward Bishop of the Los Angeles Diocese told UPI less than a month after *The Exorcist* opened. "The devil is the in thing today. Some people are starting to believe they have been possessed by the devil simply from reading the book and seeing the film. We're getting more calls than ever before, from people who think they have been possessed."

Even the cast suffered from this new craze. "After the film opened," Friedkin told David Konow, "Jason [Miller] and I were living in New York and we'd be walking down the street and people would come up and grab him by the arms, 'Father, it's my son, you have to help me.' He would have to tear himself away. 'I'm not a priest, I'm an actor.' He went into seclusion for a while. He couldn't walk the streets."

Lost souls also harried some of the priests who played small roles in the film. In his 2001 book *American Exorcism*, which documents the beginnings of the exorcism rage in the early 1970s (when William Peter Blatty published *The Exorcist* and kicked off the dark trend) to its millennial development, Michael Cuneo spoke to both Father Thomas Bermingham and Father William O'Malley about their troubles after playing bit parts in the film.

"Making the movie was strange enough, but the aftermath was completely bizarre," recalled Bermingham. "I knew very little about exorcism and demonic possession prior to helping Blatty do research for his book and working on the movie, but when the movie came out, I found myself on the hot seat. People saw my face and my name on the screen, and they assumed that I was the answer to their problems. For quite a while dozens of people were trying to contact me every week. And they weren't all Catholics. Some were Jewish, some Protestant, some agnostic, and they all believed that they themselves or someone close to them might be demonically possessed. These were truly desperate people, and I did my best to meet with as many of them as possible and discuss their problems. Of course, I approached these discussions with a great deal of skepticism. . . . Simply because someone tells you they're possessed doesn't mean they are; almost always, in fact, this is an indication that they're not. Of all the people who came to me, not one struck me as being genuinely possessed. I arranged psychological counseling for some people, but this was sometimes a big disappointment for them. They assumed, because of my association with the movie, that I'd be able to resolve their various difficulties with an exorcism. The funny thing is, I wouldn't have been able to do this even if they were possessed. I've never even participated in a genuine exorcism, and I certainly don't regard myself as qualified to perform one."

Like Father Bermingham, Father O'Malley was also credited as a technical advisor on the film, but he had a much larger on-screen role and was, thus, far more recognizable to the possession-hungry masses. "I was teaching at a Jesuit High School in Rochester at the time, and for a while the phone wouldn't stop ringing," he told Cuneo. "In the movie I played Father Bill Dyer, Damien Karras's cutesy and solicitous Jesuit friend, and many people seem to assume from this that I must be some kind of world-class expert on exorcism. They called looking for an instant fix—pleading with me to expel their own demons, their kids' demons, even their cats' demons. It's not that I rule out the possibility of demonic possession. As the saying goes, 'There are more things in heaven and earth, Horatio, than can be dreamed of in your philosophy.' But this movie seems to have set off some really strange vibrations."

If the public confusing actors with their roles seemed bizarre, it might have been superseded by countless bewildered persons gathering at the locations of *The Exorcist*. Not exactly a tourist mecca, Georgetown University, where several scenes from *The Exorcist* were shot, saw a sudden influx of visitors curious not only about the campus and its Jesuit tradition but also about the possibilities of salvation from demonic forces.

One of the strangest responses to *The Exorcist*, however, came from the Zodiac Killer, who had terrorized the Bay Area for years by committing a slew of murders and then mailing ciphers and deranged yet oddly poetic screeds to local newspapers. He had laid low for at least three years before returning to the public eye; it was a viewing of *The Exorcist* that lured him back into the spotlight.

On January 24, 1974, the Zodiac Killer sent a note to the *San Francisco Chronicle* that read, in part, "I saw + think '*The Exorcist*' was the best saterical (sic) comidy (sic) that I have ever seen." This letter, considered an authentic communication from the most infamous unidentified serial killer in American history, seemed to mock the widespread fear *The Exorcist* had produced. Real evil, he seemed to be saying, is secular, like the atrocities he had carried out in Benicia, Vallejo, and San Francisco in the late 1960s. Hollywood hair-raisers such as *The Exorcist* were cartoonish by comparison. As if to demonstrate his point, The Zodiac Killer also added a nightmarish postscript: "If I do not see this note in your paper, I will do something nasty, which you know I'm capable of doing."

Real-world terrors—reflected in urban decay, several high-profile assassinations, fallout from race riots of the late '60s, the shootings at Kent State, the atrocities of My Lai, and rising crime rates—were, indeed, both distressing and proliferating. Still, years of everyday horrors had failed to dull the overwhelming cinematic effect of *The Exorcist*. As Stephen King put it in his study of horror and culture, *Danse Macabre*: "The country, in fact, went on a two-month possession jag."

▲ ▲ ▲

What *The Exorcist* sparked went far beyond the arts sections of daily newspapers. "Devils Seize Public Fancy," announced the *Los Angeles Times*. The *Minneapolis Star* ran a three-part series on exorcisms in Minnesota, and the New York *Daily News* gave the history of demonic possession a multipage spread in a Sunday edition. For its February 11 issue, *Newsweek* devoted a cover story to "The Exorcism Frenzy." *Time, Texas Monthly, New Scientist, Christianity Today*, and *People* all weighed in on the disturbing trends that *The Exorcist* had initiated. Editorials from Lowell, Massachusetts, to Sacramento, California, alternated between bemoaning Hollywood excesses and praising *The Exorcist* for returning faith to the national forefront via a nauseating drama.

For the evangelical set, there was nothing metaphorical about *The Exorcist*; it was not a parable or even an edgy attempt at entertainment.

No, *The Exorcist* held a tangible and sinister power. At first, Billy Graham, king of the revivals, called *The Exorcist* "spiritual pornography" and cautioned that the film reflected a growing collective malaise in America. "The enthusiasm at the box office for *The Exorcist*," he said, "is symptomatic of a jaded society, reaching further for sensory thrills." Then Graham reevaluated *The Exorcist* and its effects, hinting that the film itself radiated devilry. "I would warn everyone to stay away from *The Exorcist*," Graham wrote in a syndicated guest column. "Man is not ready to deal with the evil forces it delivers."

While Graham and others decried *The Exorcist* as literal devilry (presaging the backward-masking trend of the 1980s, when evangelicals claimed that Led Zeppelin, Ozzy Osbourne, Judas Priest, and other rock bands hid demonic messages in their songs), more-rational observers worried about the effect such a grim fad would have on vulnerable psyches. "I've received dozens of calls from people who are horribly frightened or so confused that they have begun to lose their grip on reality," said Reverend Richard Woods, a Dominican priest at Loyola University. "I know of two kids who came out of the movie thinking that they were possessed."

In Denver, a deranged man fled a theater showing of *The Exorcist* and staggered to the Cathedral of the Immaculate Conception, in disarray. "He was half-naked—with bare feet and no shirt—and clearly distraught," Reverend James W. Rasby told the *New York Times*. "We called an ambulance, but he was so upset that it took the police, the attendants, and two priests to get him into it."

Eventually, in 1975, *The Exorcist* would even appear in the *Journal of Nervous and Mental Disease*, in an article titled "Cinematic neurosis following *The Exorcist*: Report of four cases." By then, it was clear that the number of cases that qualified as "cinematic neurosis" would escalate into the hundreds.

"People are coming from all over to see the chapel to hear mass, to discuss exorcism," said Reverend Edmund G. Ryan, SJ "I've even been asked whether the Jesuits produced the movie as publicity, and I answer with a resounding 'NO.' We've received numerous calls wondering about a cousin, sister, or other relative, whether they might be possessed."

Reverend Woods, who also wrote a book called *The Occult Revolution* (1971), which traced the growing belief in the supernatural, sounded overly optimistic about the wave of exorcism demands. "These requests for exorcists generally come from people who are to some degree emotionally disturbed," he told the *Chicago Tribune*. "The age of psychology long ago replaced the age of demons."

What followed in the wake of *The Exorcist* refuted modern religious viewpoints (such as those of Reverend Woods) and exposed the suggestibility of millions of Americans.

Even Father John Nicola, who acted as an advisor on *The Exorcist* and believed in demonic possession, worried about the vulnerability of the gullible. "I am afraid that such a phenomenon as mass hysteria could result, that teenage girls could identify with Linda Blair, the girl who is possessed in the movie," he said. "Indeed, psychiatrist friends tell me they have already had some cases because of the movie."

▲ ▲ ▲

From the viewpoint of the filmmakers, of course, the most important metric was box-office receipts. *The Exorcist* was not just a hit; it was a phenomenon, with crowd control an essential part of the filmgoing experience. During its initial run, *The Exorcist* would gross $66 million domestically and an additional $46 million internationally, making it at the time the most profitable film in Warner Bros. history. For nearly twenty years, *The Exorcist* held the top spot as the highest-grossing R-rated film in history until *Pretty Woman*, a slick romantic comedy starring Julia Roberts as a hooker with the cliché-stamped heart of gold, became a surprise sensation for Walt Disney Studios (!) in 1990.

As incredible as it sounds, however, Warner Bros. left millions of dollars on the table with its handling of *The Exorcist*, having underestimated the power of the source material (the best-selling book by William Peter Blatty, which, by 1974, had sold more than six million copies) and the Academy Award track record of the New Hollywood prodigy William Friedkin. The limited release was a startling and costly miscalculation that Warner Bros. regretted less than a few days after the film opened. Although films often opened exclusively in large markets first and then trickled out across the country (depending on reviews and early returns), mainstream genre films could count on wide releases. A year after *The Exorcist* began terrifying audiences, *Jaws* opened in 450 theaters. Unsure of what they had in *The Exorcist*, the studio hedged its bets, hoping that steady returns would allow the film to recoup its oversized budget over time. To make matters worse, Warner Bros. booked *The Exorcist* in those scant twenty-four theaters as exclusive six-month engagements.

In the early 1970s, before cable television and the home-video market added ancillary income that Hollywood wanted to exploit as soon as possible, films remained in circulation as long as local theaters reported continued interest. (*The French Connection*, for example, played in theaters for well over two years.) Today, with streaming, films are often pulled from theaters within weeks. To the disgust of Friedkin, Warner Bros. had chosen a safety-first strategy that backfired spectacularly when demand far outstripped supply. "They didn't see this thing coming," Friedkin told Peter Biskind, scoffing at Warner Bros. and short-sighted studios in general. "They didn't see *Star Wars* coming. [*Star Wars* also saw its potential underestimated by executives: it opened in fewer than forty theaters in 1977.] These were things that happened to them. They didn't make them happen. Imagine what *The Exorcist* would have done had it opened like *The Godfather* or *Jaws* a couple of years later."

Warner Bros. may have committed another gaffe when it skipped the traditional audience preview, which recorded feedback from select viewers in certain markets. Bypassing these test screenings favored the new maverick directors, who despised subsequent studio suggestions (or outright meddling) based on the answers to questionnaires handed out to random moviegoers. Naturally, as one of the top rebels in Hollywood, Friedkin was against audience previews—especially for *The Exorcist*. "If *The Exorcist* had previewed, it would never have come out," he told Biskind. "Because people would have written on cards, this is terrible, you have a little girl masturbating with the crucifix, you dirty bastard. The kind of note we got anyway, afterward. But if we'd gotten them before, it would have died."

In retrospect, Friedkin was likely mistaken. If Warner Bros. had stuck with the custom, they would have seen preview audiences gasp, scream, weep, faint, vomit, and flee—all sure indicators of, if not a box-office hit, then of a film that would generate enough free publicity just from the test screenings to justify a wider release.

CHAPTER 22

▲ ▲ ▲

The Critics, in Conflict

ecause of its limited opening (which coincided with the holidays), *The Exorcist* received fewer regional reviews than the typical Hollywood noisemaker. And because soon the talk would not be about the film itself but its effect on the public, critical response was quickly rendered inconsequential.

Early notices from newspapers in major cities were mostly positive, with the standout exception being the *Washington Post*, where Gary Arnold went nuclear. "Appallingly effective on the surface," he wrote, "*The Exorcist* is appallingly worthless beneath the surface."

There were other dissenters in the popular media. Vincent Canby at the *New York Times* seemed bewildered by the whole affair: "The care that Mr. Friedkin and Mr. Blatty have taken with the physical production, and with the rhythm of the narrative, which achieves a certain momentum through a lot of fancy, splintery crosscutting, is obviously intended to persuade us to suspend belief. But to what end? To marvel at the extent to which audiences will go to escape boredom by shock and insult."

A few weeks later, Canby would solidify his confusion by writing another piece with the headline: "Why the Devil Do They Dig '*The Exorcist*'?" The mystery of how such "claptrap" could win over audiences eluded Canby.

After some musings about the vacuous peripheral characters, the lack of narrative development, and a digression about self-reflexivity in cinema, Andrew Sarris of the *Village Voice* concluded his critique philosophically: "*The Exorcist* succeeds on one level as an effectively excruciating entertainment, but on another, deeper level it is a thoroughly evil film."

Unlike Sarris and Canby, other daily reviewers were less interested in cinematic nuances and more attuned to the film's emotional impact. "*The Exorcist* is, I think, the most blatant shocker ever produced," wrote Kevin Kelly of the *Boston Globe*, "a horror story about demonic possession so artfully made that it succeeds in rattling mind, body, and spirit long before its hoarse, black litany is exhausted."

Not yet the most famous film critic in America, Roger Ebert seemed ambivalent about the enthusiasm surrounding *The Exorcist*, but his four-star review in the *Chicago Sun-Times* recognized its cathartic force. "If movies are, among other things, opportunities for escapism, then *The Exorcist* is one of the most powerful ever made," he wrote. "Our objections, our questions, occur in an intellectual context after the movie has ended. During the movie there are no reservations, but only experiences. We feel shock, horror, nausea, fear, and some small measure of dogged hope."

Besides James Agee (dead for nearly twenty years), the only critic Friedkin publicly lauded during the aftermath of *The Exorcist* was Charles Champlin. Whether coincidental or not, Champlin wrote an extended hurrah for *The Exorcist*. "The movie plays, spectacularly, as a jolting drama which can be enjoyed (in the most flexible sense of the word) as an adult suspense shocker with overtones," he wrote in the *Los Angeles Times*.

Surprisingly, the normally prudish Gene Siskel, who would condemn countless films based on violence, gave *The Exorcist* what the industry calls a "rave." "Through technical virtuosity at every level . . . *The Exorcist* becomes more than a shocking movie: a film with a strong, positive force. I loved it."

Roger Grooms of the *Cincinnati Enquirer* was stunned by *The Exorcist* as a horror film. "I must tell you that I believe few confrontations in the history of cinema can equal the final twenty minutes of *The Exorcist* . . . ," he wrote. "As a devotee of the cinematic macabre, I believe those final moments will rank with anything even attempted in the genre."

In the *San Francisco Examiner*, Stanley Eichelbaum first noted (with the gullibility that would steadily increase over the next decades) the absurd "curse" before favorably comparing *The Exorcist* to the film that had influenced Blatty and Friedkin more than any other: "Their two-year effort (hexed by a strange chain of circumstances that kept delaying the production) has resulted in a brilliantly realized film, more riveting and convincingly horrible than anything that's been done in the genre. The effect is devastating, it makes *Rosemary's Baby* seem like *Mary Poppins*."

If the daily reviews were mixed but skewed positive, the highbrow film journals were uniformly dismissive. Because of printing schedules, these journals had more time to ruminate over *The Exorcist* than the newspapers did, and they used this delay to sharpen their knives. On nearly every possible gauge—religious, political, Marxist, sociological, feminist, and aesthetic—the scholarly voices rose, en masse, to excoriate *The Exorcist*.

In *Film Quarterly*, critic Michael Dempsey lambasted both the film and its supporters. "*The Exorcist* is the trash bombshell of 1973, the aesthetic equivalent of being run over by a truck," he wrote. "Evidently a lot of people think that great art is supposed to be like this; if it shocks them it must be brilliant."

Dempsey also shrewdly noted how *The Exorcist* had its roots in the horror genre as it existed throughout most of the 1960s and early 1970s. "Despite their pontificating about Greek tragedy, the mystery of faith, and Good vs. Evil, director William Friedkin and writer-producer William Peter Blatty have actually made a gloating, ugly exploitation picture, a costlier cousin of those ghoulish cheapies released to drive-ins and fleapits almost weekly in major American cities."

To Ruth McCormick of *Cineaste*, the film was only part of an overall objectionable package; she also cited the open arrogance and sanctimony of the filmmakers: "Writer-producer William Peter Blatty and director William Friedkin, at first surprised by the widespread popularity of their work, soon became convinced that they were great popular artists, comparing themselves to the likes of Shakespeare and Aeschylus."

Another swing of the critical hatchet came from Stephen Farber of *Film Comment*, who summed up his general viewpoint succinctly: "*The Exorcist* is not the first bad movie to be a hit, but it is a new kind of blockbuster; it represents a new extreme in the cinema of cruelty."

The weeklies and glossy magazines such as *New York*, *Time*, *Rolling Stone*, and *Newsweek* were also divided, but two of the most visible reviews savaged Friedkin and Blatty.

Writing in *The New Yorker*, Pauline Kael, the most famous film critic in America at the time, assailed *The Exorcist* and even ridiculed Blatty for his personal engagement with the occult. "Shallowness that asks to be taken seriously—shallowness like William Peter Blatty's—is an embarrassment," she wrote in her lede. "When you hear him on TV talking about communicating with his dead mother, your heart doesn't bleed for him, your stomach turns for him."

Like some of the quarterlies, Kael believed that *The Exorcist* was an exploitation film camouflaged in piety. Her take on the novel informs her reading of the film: "Like the pulp authors who provide flip-page sex, he provided flip-page torture, infanticide, cannibalism, sexual hysteria, werewolves. The book is a manual of lurid crimes, written in an easy-to-read tough-guy style yet with a grating heightening word here and there, supposedly to tone it up." To Kael, the blunt religious messaging meant to separate *The Exorcist* from run-of-the-mill fright films is superficial.

Even more ruthless than Kael (if far more erudite) was the infamous John Simon, a writer so bloodthirsty that three hundred of his peers and victims once signed an ad in *Variety* charging him with a slew of critical improprieties. Simon had long been the most acerbic critic in America (in his collection *Reverse Angle: A Decade of American Films*, Simon approved only 15 of the 245 films he reviewed), and *The Exorcist* never stood a chance when he assessed it for *Esquire*.

Just as Kael had, Simon first ripped Blatty (whom he repeatedly referred to as a hack) for his insistence that he had been communicating with his dead mother for years. Then he turned his venom to the film, targeting Friedkin for his meticulousness during shooting. "Such perfectionism at the service of trash takes on a lurid, almost indecent character. Still, Friedkin has a crass expertise with which he can keep the average moviegoer from laughing at the absurd goings-on, and he certainly gets great performances, not from his actors—who (except for Jason Miller and Lee J. Cobb) are defeated by the material—but from his special-effects and makeup men, who carry the film."

Neither Blatty nor Friedkin reacted well to negative reviews. Throughout the making of the film, throughout its publicity, throughout its theater run, throughout its afterlife, Blatty and Friedkin behaved with a pomposity, crassness, and self-importance rare even in Hollywood (at least publicly). Whether against the Academy, a few crew members, Warner Bros., or even each other, Friedkin and Blatty were always ready to ridicule. And the critics became loud targets for them.

"I have a theory of criticism: if a film is liked by the critics and the audience, it's probably a great film," Friedkin told Travers and Reiff. "If a film is liked by the audience, but not by the critics, it's still probably a great film. If a film is liked only by the critics, it is a piece of shit film!"

Of course, in a few years, Friedkin would direct a slew of films that fit none of those categories.

Critical assessments about *The Exorcist* that fell short of reverence annoyed Friedkin, but they were a sign of sub-humanity to the megalomaniac Blatty. Especially if they were written by eggheads concentrated on the East Coast. It was not enough for Blatty to say that he had no respect for critics or for him to respond to their points; that would have been insufficient for his imperial outlook. "There is a very small, elite group among the New York critics who neither sow, nor reap, nor perform any socially useful purpose," Blatty said in the kind of purple prose that saturates his novel. "They are malignant lilies of the field."

No matter how split the critics were, the public was united in its grim fascination with this turbulent film about a demon possessing a twelve-year-old girl in Washington, DC. In fact, they were more than fascinated. They were, in some cases, driven to hysteria.

PART III

"WHAT AN EXCELLENT DAY FOR AN EXORCISM"

CHAPTER 23

Evil Against Evil: Reading the Film

From the opening scene of the sun darkening on the horizon in Iraq, *The Exorcist* builds a sense of palpable dread, reinforced by repeated motifs and an eerie atmosphere accentuated by imaginative montage and a nightmare soundtrack.

In the novel, the Iraq prologue gives the narrative a powerful, nearly cosmic jump start. Here, Father Lancaster Merrin unearths an amulet of the demon Pazuzu at an archeological dig and recognizes it as an omen of tribulation. (Decades earlier, Merrin had successfully exorcized Pazuzu in Africa.) Although characteristically weakened by overwriting and inapt metaphors, the Iraq section shows Blatty at his most effective. Both portentous and atmospheric, Blatty sets the stage that foreshadows the horrors to come while evoking the primordial nature of the eternal struggle between the forces of dark and light.

Similarly, the film establishes not just its ominous atmosphere, but it also introduces its supernatural underpinnings. During a busy archeological dig, Father Merrin discovers a Saint Joseph medal buried in the earth; a few moments later, he finds a small amulet of Pazuzu, "King of the wind demons." These objects signal the uncanny events about to unfold a world away in Washington, DC. An ancient evil, emphasized by the archaeological dig and by the location—Iraq, informally known as the cradle of civilization—has materialized before Father Merrin.

To Merrin, the discoveries at the excavation site trigger uneasy feelings and incidents: the Saint Joseph medal is a baffling metachronism, the sights and sounds of the dusty streets take on a sinister cast, evoking what Baudelaire might have called a forest of symbols, a droshky nearly kills him, and the clock stops when he returns to his office.

Father Merrin is not only depicted as a man destined to square off with his archenemy—Pazuzu—but as a man whose mortality is at hand. He says goodbye to his colleague with an air of finality, takes his nitroglycerin tablets, with trembling hands, and, later, he nearly gets trampled by the droshky. The future is both grim and limited for Merrin.

"The Iraq scene introduces to you what kind of man Father Merrin is," Friedkin told *Cinefantastique*. "The man who is called in as an exorcist. It establishes, in a kind of abstract fashion, that Merrin gets a premonition that he is going to have to perform an exorcism."

Friedkin also used the prologue to establish a series of motifs. "It's not apparent why you're seeing it, but later when you think about it, it all becomes clear," he said. "So I used it to foreshadow things visually. That sequence foreshadows things that occur later. For example, in my mind, the picks that you see being pushed into the ground foreshadow the crucifix being driven into the girl's vagina. The dirt oozing out in several shots foreshadows the vomiting. And I clearly shot every sound and sequence to foreshadow something that you see and hear later. Another example of this is the blacksmith sequence. The anvil sound is in the exorcism and the blacksmith who only has one eye, his eye resembles the little girl's eyes when they go up into their sockets."

Shot by Billy Williams (Owen Roizman had been diagnosed as diabetic and remained in New York), the Iraq sequence is notable for its exquisite pictorial beauty. "Once you see the footage you'll know it's staggering," Friedkin told Travers and Reiff before the film was released. "The look of the locations is extremely exotic, for there are no motorcars to ruin the effect. For the most part, we were in Nineveh, Hatra, and Mosul. There's a fragment of a bathhouse that has been excavated belonging to the Assyrian king Sennacherib. The site is just magnificent in its appointments and in the ingenuity of the design. We use the actual stone carving, fragments of heads, and statuary in the film. It just would have been impossible to recreate the look of Iraq."

Indeed, the scenes in Mosul, Hatra, and Nineveh are spectacular. The prologue also reflects just how skilled Friedkin was at montage and how he consciously applied what he had learned from Antonioni throughout

The Exorcist. In an interview with the American Film Institute, an effusive Friedkin outlined the lessons Antonioni taught him. "Jesus Christ, I mean, like *L'Avventura, La Notte,* and *L'Eclisse,* these movies, they moved. *Blow-Up* is great. They moved differently; they move, like, laterally. One reason they move laterally is because Antonioni almost never repeats a shot. And that's what I learned from Antonioni: Don't ever repeat a setup. Most films are shot, you know, over here, boom, over there, boom, over here, boom, and they gotta keep repeating those three setups. That's why you know what's going to happen."

Not everyone understood the meaning of this exotic preamble, however. In fact, some of the top film critics were unable to connect the Iraq sequence to the rest of the narrative; it was as if Andrew Sarris was unfamiliar with the concept of a prologue altogether. If Friedkin had often been knee-jerk about critics, he was sometimes justified in his antipathy for them.

"The prologue shows that there is nothing more terrifying than evil when it is unavoidable," Blatty told Bob McCabe. Later, in his book, Blatty would mock Harper & Row for asking him to cut the prologue from the novel. Of course, Blatty had cut the sequence himself from his original 226-page script (which is equal to roughly four hours of screen time) and only reinstated it when Friedkin reproached him.

▲ ▲ ▲

Although Friedkin had eliminated most of the extraneous subplots from the novel and the original screenplay, he made one personal addition: the Saint Joseph medal that strangely materializes at the Mosul dig and reappears, inexplicably, throughout the film.

William Peter Blatty was mystified by this historical incongruity and made his bewilderment known at length over the years. "I didn't go to Iraq for the filming of those opening scenes," Blatty told William Baer for the book *Classic American Films: Conversations with the Screenwriters,* "and when I saw the rushes for the first time, I said to Billy, 'What's that Saint Joseph's medal doing in that four-thousand-year-old archeological site?' And he just looked at me and said, 'Resonance.' Then he turned around and walked away. So that's all I can tell you about it. Maybe it's best left at 'resonance.'"

Friedkin gave a more complicated, if unpersuasive, explanation about the Saint Joseph medal to McCabe. "I was looking for something akin to the obelisk in *2001*," he said. "Something from another time and place that keeps appearing in different guises. That's not from the novel. Something that would transcend time and space and place and was a kind of talisman that gave unity across many continents and across many different periods of time because I felt this work could be looked at as a kind of prophecy with a timeless quality. A quality of not only the mystery of faith, but the mystery of fate. How fate unites people from disparate worlds, brings them together over a highly charged dramatic event that ultimately affects all of their lives, even though they're brought together from various persuasions, various countries, various points of view, whatever."

While Friedkin struggled to clarify the meaning of his inspiration, its link to *2001* is clear. Kubrick was one of the few contemporary directors Friedkin openly admired, and he would specify *2001* as a film he found particularly influential. But Friedkin overstates his case. The Saint Joseph medal does not have the relevance to *The Exorcist* that the monolith has to *2001*.

In *2001*, the omnipresent monolith is not a stylistic flourish or a deliberate mystification; it is germane to the plot and theme of the film—however abstruse that plot and theme may be. The monolith is also part of the dramatic framework. While its appearances at the start and end of *2001* are somewhat oblique, its existence is central to the action throughout: a group of scientists visit the TMA-1 monolith on the moon, where it emits a shattering noise signal that triggers the next act; years later, David Bowman, the last remaining astronaut of the *Discovery One*, pursues a monolith floating in space that leads him to the Star Gate and the astonishing finale of the film.

By contrast, the ubiquitous Saint Joseph medal is an attempt to infuse a metaphysical dimension into straightforward material. Of course, the supernatural is not de facto straightforward, per se, but the structure and plot of *The Exorcist* are elementary. Once Linda Blair is strapped to the bed, the film becomes a chamber play, of sorts, with a small cast and a limited range of action. Other occult films of the 1970s are packed with incidents and set pieces. There is the elaborate Black Mass in *Beyond the Door*; there is, among a variety of other graphic atrocities, the baboon-attack scene in *The Omen*; there are the burnings, lashings, decapitations, rapes, and assaults found in everything from *Blood on Satan's Claw* to *Mark of the Witch* to *The Possession of Joel Delaney.*

For Friedkin, the medal was a way to enliven the proceedings by adding an extra helping of the uncanny, with mixed results. Despite his early admiration for filmmakers such as Antonioni, Bergman, and Kubrick, along with a few members of the nouvelle vague, Friedkin was never an intellectual director, and his open commitment to visceral phenomena made him the butt of jokes to a range of critics who saw in his philosophy naked commercialism, of the kind the New Hollywood was supposed to eradicate.

During his peak creative years, 1971–1985, Friedkin often inserted puzzling shots into his films to give them an air of profundity. Usually, these were the last sequences of the film, designed to leave audiences confused on their way out of the theater.

The French Connection ended with the infamous off-screen gunshot—Popeye Doyle possibly having caught up with Frog One somewhere beyond the boundaries of celluloid—befuddling observers for decades. Indeed, Friedkin acknowledged that he intended to produce such confusion; he even acknowledged his inspiration: Stanley Kubrick. "If they're talking about what something means in a movie, usually you've got a movie that people will want to see," Friedkin said in 1974. "Example: the obelisk in *2001.* People went around for years sitting around McDonald's, cocktail parties in Bel Air, saying, 'What the hell is the obelisk?' And that's why I put the gunshot at the end of *The French Connection.*"

Before the enigmatic closing sequence of Al Pacino staring at himself in a mirror (and then shifting his gaze to the camera itself), *Cruising* features a scene with a shadowy figure crossing a dimly lit street to a club that a serial killer, presumed to have been captured by authorities, has used as a pickup spot. This indeterminate finale adds doubt to an already muddled narrative about a series of slayings that may or may not have been solved.

Finally, in *To Live and Die in L.A.*, a stinger featuring the image of a character who had died earlier in the film might have been just as confusing as the gunshot in *The French Connection*—if anyone had actually seen it. Closing credits in the 1980s were far too long to linger for surprise extras.

Like Kubrick using the notion of a haunted house in *The Shining* as a justification for inscrutable plotting and even for continuity lapses, Friedkin would rationalize the Saint Joseph medal by asserting the supernatural essence of *The Exorcist.* "I have never liked that," Blatty told McCabe. "It doesn't make any sense, but nobody ever noticed. Once you do a motion picture with a supernatural background and supernatural events occur, you might be able to expect something like the Saint Joseph's medal. But what I do not expect is for a noted paleontologist-archeologist like Father Merrin looking at the medal to say, 'This is strange, not of the same period.'"

▲ ▲ ▲

The main narrative begins with Chris McNeil, an actress shooting a new film ominously titled *Crash Course*, hearing noises in the attic, the first sign of demonic infestation. When Chris checks in on a sleeping Regan, she notices that the bedroom window is open, on a chilly, breezy morning, hinting that Pazuzu has arrived. It is Halloween day (another element added by Friedkin to reinforce eeriness) and Georgetown will never be the same again.

With economical strokes Friedkin establishes the parallel plots that will ultimately converge halfway through the film. There is the story of Chris and Regan, playful and seemingly happy despite being a broken family, just before their ordeal begins. Then, as a counterpoint, there is the narrative of Father Karras, struggling with his faith, guilt-ridden because he has neglected his sickly mother. Chris and Karras lead lives that could not be more dissimilar, and Friedkin stresses this by intercutting between the affluence and lightheartedness of the McNeil residence and the poverty and gloom of Karras and his mother in her Hell's Kitchen apartment.

These two plots will neatly dovetail when Chris turns to Father Karras for an exorcism: Regan needs Karras to save her, and, after his mother dies, Karras needs someone to save.

When Chris finds a Ouija board in the basement and asks Regan about it, the unearthly elements of the film begin to cohere, with Regan at their center. Regan tells her mother she plays with the game "all the time" (hinting at her loneliness and establishing that repeated contact with the spirit world has occurred before Pazuzu arrived). The Ouija board has been left behind by the previous tenants, the sort of iffy detail that can be viewed as either a plot contrivance or as an unpredictable manifestation of the supernatural world. When the planchette slides away from Chris, Regan blames it on a being she calls Captain Howdy, a name that echoes Howard MacNeil—her negligent father.

Regan begins undergoing phenomena the morning after Chris is unable to reach Howard via telephone in Italy. Howard McNeil ignores Regan on her thirteenth birthday, seemingly precipitating her first disturbing episode. (It is a testimony to just how appealing Linda Blair is as Regan that the audience can identify with her future torments. The sketchy shorthand Friedkin used to develop her character was possible only because he had stumbled upon an unusually talented teenage performer.)

When Regan begins seeing doctors and specialists, the thematic setup is clear: the ineffectuality of modern science is no contest against the overwhelming power of faith. To demonstrate this point in the broadest terms, every authority in the film is not just ineffectual but a howling failure. Various doctors are depicted as both hapless and helpless. Each of them retains a smugness that emphasizes secular omniscience and clueless pedantry. (In the novel, Blatty works tirelessly to make clowns out of the medical professionals, but Friedkin, naturally, had less time to work with.) Dr. Klein, for example, has an office adorned by several framed photographs of sports cars, as if to hint at luxurious frivolity. He is the first authority figure to get clobbered by Regan, with Shaw Brothers sound effects accompanying the blow.

A psychiatrist (played by Arthur Storch) hypnotizes Regan only to get his balls squeezed and wind up being filmed by Friedkin in a gratuitous, over-the-top stunt shot primarily designed to jolt the audience. (It may also reinforce the sexual subtext that runs throughout *The Exorcist*.) Medical science is so inadequate that a roundtable suggestive of an emergency White House meeting convenes to tell Chris that her daughter should probably undergo an exorcism, citing the "power of suggestion," of course. Even a look at X-rays, as anodyne a procedure as can be found in a hospital, inspired an eardrum-shattering scene. (Eventually, law enforcement also takes its lumps, with the figure of Lt. Kinderman, who cracks silly jokes throughout the film, solves nothing, and arrives on the scene a few moments after Karras has plunged through the window. All of this suggests that Blatty not only had Columbo in mind when he sketched out Kinderman, but also Inspector Clouseau. Blatty had adapted the Harry Kurnitz play *A Shot in the Dark* for the screen in 1964 as a *Pink Panther* film.)

▲ ▲ ▲

The turning point of *The Exorcist* is the dream sequence, suffused with strange juxtapositions and filled with what Mark Kermode might call "reverberations." In the dream sequence, Karras fails to save his mother, setting up the theme of redemption in the finale. Alone on a traffic island, Karras watches, agitated, as his mother descends the stairs. Then he chases after her, too late, she has already disappeared. Karras has lost her.

Interspersed throughout the dream are images taken from the narrative (that is the film itself) as a whole. Because Karras cannot possibly have some of these elements in his subconscious, the dream sequence suggests some sort of mystic simultaneity, adding to the supernatural atmosphere of the film, or, thematically, hinting that evil is an omnipresent force. (Another interpretation, of course, is that Friedkin indulged in his penchant for deliberate obfuscation.) In the novel, Karras has a far less dramatic dream. From a window, he sees his mother emerge from a subway station before wandering, confused, on a teeming New York City street. When she turns back to the station, Karras bounds after her, unsuccessfully. For the film version, Friedkin overloaded the dream sequence to amplify the supernatural. Past, present, and future converge in the dream: the dog might be from the Iraq prologue, and the falling medal presages the moment when Karras loses his own medal in the struggle with Regan. The pendulum clock is also from the Iraq scene (clocks play no role at all in the novel) and the flash cut—sometimes inaccurately referred to as a subliminal image—of the demon (called Captain Howdy by *Exorcist* devotees) portends the future battle between Karras and Pazuzu.

Friedkin extrapolated, none too convincingly, on this sequence for a DVD commentary: "I was trying to show how symbiosis can occur between two different people whose lives are inextricably tied together in ways that are not clear to them as yet. It occurred to me to examine: what are dreams made of in a symbiotic situation? So moments from Karras's dream about his mother's death and images of the demon mixed together with images that we saw in Iraq sort of tie together the two disparate worlds of Karras and Merrin in ways that are going to indicate that they later come together, that they're united in this exorcism."

A few years earlier, Friedkin offered a slightly different interpretation to Mark Kermode: "The notion occurred to me that we have a finite understanding of time and space that may not be the way it actually is, may not be as organized as we made it. And so I played with that idea by having images that Father Merrin observed occur in Father Karras's dream. Because these two men were one day going to unite on this sort of battlefield."

In addition to setting a mood of dread and mystery, the gloomy opening third of the film serves a practical purpose: it repeatedly cues audience anticipation. This is a concept Friedkin borrowed from Alfred Hitchcock and *Psycho*. "I figured because of *Psycho*, I could get away with a lot in this *Exorcist*," he told the AFI. "I figured [Hitchcock] had about forty-five minutes in *Psycho* where absolutely nothing happened. It's a dull sort of story, but the audience is so expectant. The audience knows that they're coming in to see this horrific suspense film and they're not getting it. They're getting edgy and then suddenly, he whacks them with it and boom, you've got them in your back pocket. So, I figured what I'm going to try and do is make this *Exorcist* go on for about an hour with nothing happening and then see how long I could pull the string."

As if to compensate for its slow start, *The Exorcist* shifts into high gear after the dream sequence: the bed-thrashing, the assaults, the self-mutilation, the head-spinning, the vomiting, the baroque profanity, and, finally, the over-the-top exorcism scene.

▲ ▲ ▲

Visually, *The Exorcist* stuns, revealing the talent of cinematographer Owen Roizman, working on his second—and last—feature with Friedkin (the first was *The French Connection*). While recent horror films such as *The Mephisto Waltz* (1971) resembled an ABC Movie of the Week and *The Possession of Joel Delaney* (1972) was only a slight improvement, *The Exorcist* had a rich, textured look, simultaneously natural and eerie.

In an interview with *American Cinematographer*, Roizman described how he and William Friedkin settled on the aesthetic of *The Exorcist*. "When we first discussed the picture we naturally discussed style and he said that he would like this film to have a realistic, available-light look—very natural. But he said that he would like to take it a step above what we did the last time [on *The French Connection*] and not go for such a raw documentary feeling. It was to have a little bit slicker, more controlled look to it—and that's what we attempted to get. The sets were very normal. We didn't go for a *Psycho* type of house. All the rooms were basically designed to be elegant and well-furnished—a warm and moody house. What we tried to do, by means of the lighting, was to give it a kind of ominous feeling—as if some lurking, mysterious thing were hanging over it. That's about as far as we went with photographic style."

The brooding naturalism Roizman brought to *The Exorcist* seemed partly modeled on *The Conformist* (1970), a film whose look and compositions inspired countless New Hollywood productions. Directed by Bernardo Bertolucci, *The Conformist* made a star out of thirty-year-old Vittorio Storaro, the nonpareil cinematographer who would go on to win three academy awards. From *Last Tango in Paris* to *Apocalypse Now*, from *Reds* to *The Last Emperor*, Storaro produced an exquisite body of work notable for its expressiveness and virtuosity. (Bizarrely, Storaro would also shoot both versions of the snakebitten prequels of *The Exorcist*, *Dominion* and *The Beginning*.) For *Post Script*, Roizman recalled seeing *The Conformist* for the first time: "I'd just finished shooting *The French Connection* and went with my wife to see *The Conformist*. When the film was over, I turned to her and said, 'I'll never be able to do work like this. I better get out of the business right now.' I was totally intimidated. It just blew me away. . . . I just remember the designs of the shots were very interesting and that the lighting was natural yet completely stylized, which is kind of symbolic of everything Vittorio's ever done, a naturalistic but stylized look at the same time."

That combination—naturalistic but stylized—is precisely what Roizman achieved in *The Exorcist*, which earned him an Academy Award nomination. To put that in perspective, Gordon Willis failed to earn even a nomination for his work on both *Godfather* films (1972 and 1974, respectively), and it took until 1979 for Storaro to earn a nomination.

▲ ▲ ▲

One of the most memorable scenes in *The Exorcist* (which eventually became the image for the film poster) is the night Father Merrin finally arrives for the spiritual battle foretold in the Iraq prologue. Its action is almost quotidian—a man emerges from a taxi, pauses on the sidewalk, and looks up at a house. Yet this short sequence—fog-shrouded, shadowy, and with Merrin reduced to a silhouette—is suffused with a sinister visual poetry. What would have been a throwaway scene in one of the earlier 1970s horror films becomes a quiet showstopper, textured and atmospheric, with composition and lighting enhancing the otherworldly quality of the image.

It was also one of the most difficult setups for Owen Roizman to execute. "We shot night exteriors in Georgetown and the trickiest one was the scene where the exorcist himself arrives at the house," he told Dennis

Schaefer for his book *Masters of Light: Conversations with Contemporary Cinematographers.* "It's late at night and the shot starts with the camera pointing down the desolate, foggy street. Two headlights appear out of the fog and we see that they're coming from a taxicab that swings around in front of the house. The priest gets out and stands in the bright glow coming from the little girl's bedroom window. It was difficult to get that bright of a glow from a shaded window and we also had to hold a fog effect all the way down the street. Of course—wouldn't you know—just as we were ready to shoot, the wind came up, which made it more difficult to keep the fog settled in."

Inspired by *Empire of Light II*, a painting by the Belgian artist Rene Magritte, Friedkin composed a scene that reminded him of how the Surrealists "juxtaposed realistic but unrelated objects."

Such a layered approach to a seemingly minor scene bordered on incongruous to some critics. Richard Combs, for example, in *Sight and Sound*, who accuses Friedkin of "the overdirection of mood-setting sequences," thought the arrival scene was little more than hokum and reflected the essential hollowness of *The Exorcist*. "The shot looks like a cheap horror tactic," he wrote, "and the film continually struggles to suggest through atmosphere what it promises but fails to provide in substance." As a critique, this observation falls short in two ways. First, complaining about the distinguished look of a sequence minimizes the visual aspect of *The Exorcist*, and, perhaps, film in general. Second, the "overdirection" is a deliberate technique imposed from the opening shot of the film. The consistent heightening of both incident and non-incident in *The Exorcist* functions as a cinematic variation of the classical literary device of deinosis. J. A. Cuddon, whose *Dictionary of Literary Terms and Literary Theory* is standard, described *deinosis* as follows: "It was brought into use for bloody deeds, battles, storms, and so forth; in short, where something extra was called for. It was a way of raising the emotional temperature and charging certain passages with additional force and vigor in order to impinge on audiences more effectively."

For Friedkin, that "something extra" applied to nearly every frame of *The Exorcist*. In seeking to render even mundane expository scenes lively, Friedkin works overtime to elevate shot after shot. When Chris MacNeil heads home after completing her scenes in *Crash Course*, the film she is working on, Friedkin visually overloads what would be an otherwise innocuous sequence. Tracking shots of MacNeil walking are given an off-kilter quality: children in Halloween costumes remind us that it is a ghostly day, nuns with billowing habits walk by, and Chris spots Father Karras in intense conversation with another priest. Of course, adding the eerie "Tubular Bells" to the proceedings also gives the scene an unexpected frisson.

Another instance of this kind of dynamism occurs when Kinderman and Father Karras meet for the first time at an athletic field. After Karras completes his run, he and Kinderman discuss the strange death of Burke Dennings and the possibility of a murderous cult on the loose in Georgetown against the backdrop of a tennis match. This is one of several scenes that link Karras to competition, hinting at the battle to come and, possibly, his training for it. When he returns to New York City to visit his ailing mother, Karras glances at his boxing photos and Golden Gloves trophies. Later, he works out in a gym, taking out his frustrations on a heavy bag. His meeting with Kinderman has him jogging at a brisk clip around the track with gray sweats on, like Carlos Monzon preparing for an upcoming title defense.

Run-of-the-mill directors almost certainly would have approached utilitarian material with less adventure than Friedkin did in *The Exorcist*. In general, since *Rosemary's Baby* was released in 1968, American horror films had been largely undistinguished. Contemporary examples include *The Mephisto Waltz* (1971) and *The Possession of Joel Delaney* (1972), two productions whose far-out material might have been expected to produce more shrieks from the audience. Instead, they are strangely muted despite a few gruesome set pieces.

▲ ▲ ▲

Few narrative aspects of *The Exorcist*, not even the weak red herring involving Karl and Dennings, were as troubling as the climax, when Karras commits suicide. This poorly edited sequence left audiences bewildered and Blatty sour.

In the kind of gratuitous move Friedkin was never able to resist (although it was, reportedly, Jason Miller who came up with the idea), Karras goes into full combat mode after failing to resuscitate Merrin. He grabs Regan, throws her to the floor, and begins pummeling her, in what MMA aficionados would know today as ground-and-pound. After landing several overhand rights, Karras begins choking Regan, who shows no sign of the superhuman strength previously attributed to her and that had allowed her to disfigure Burke Dennings and heave him through the window. When Karras implores the demon to "Come into me!" Regan rips away the enigmatic Saint Joseph medal from Karras during their struggle, seemingly precipitating a demonic transfer.

Halfway through this strangling session, Karras, in a close-up, raises his head, looks at the billowing curtains, and is bowled over like a tumbler. When he regains his feet, his features have been altered—an accommodating Pazuzu has, as requested, taken possession of Karras. Next, a fleeting subjective shot shows Karras approaching Regan, hands outstretched, moving in for the kill, like the Mummy or Frankenstein from the old Universal days. On the floor, Regan, released from the spell of Pazuzu, is now a little girl terrified at what is happening. But before he can murder Regan, Karras regains his true self long enough to assume that his own destruction would also mean the destruction of the demon. He crashes through the window and to his death.

Not everyone understood what had transpired. While Blatty would insist that Karras found redemption by saving Regan and defeated the demon by tumbling to his death down the Hitchcock steps, reaction to the scene included mass confusion. To most filmgoers, Karras had been compelled to jump. In that interpretation, one that would flabbergast Blatty for years, the demon had won the archetypal showdown between good and evil—exactly the opposite of what Blatty had intended.

Troubled that viewers misinterpreted the grand finale, Blatty became even more incensed that his preferred cut, including his theological messaging, had been sabotaged. But the climax left both Blatty *and* Friedkin bewildered. So mystifying was this scene that Friedkin still doubted its logic in 2019 when he deliberated over it at length in the documentary *Leap of Faith*:

And I said, 'Bill—what happened there? He went out the window, obviously. How? Was he possessed?' 'No,' Bill said. 'No, he wasn't possessed. No, he made the conscious decision to take himself out the window and killing himself with the demon inside him.' I said, 'But Bill, that's suicide; it's a sin in the Catholic Church. Suicide is a sin.' It was confusing then; it's confusing now. First of all, I find it improbable that a character could call upon the devil to enter him or her. The devil does what the devil wants to do.

And at that moment, you see, for a split-second, his features change and become demonic . . . and then they unchange. The demon is not in him. That's specifically at Blatty's request. And most people don't see or even get we go back to Karras as Karras.

But it isn't even clear to me as I sit here why in the hell that happens. I defy anybody watching this to tell me what they make of that scene if they really look at it and study it.

I think if there's a weakness in *The Exorcist*, it's the end. I had no alternative, so I shot it the way he explained it to me. The moment is a compromise. It's not often as a director that I've had to film something that I didn't completely understand. In fact, that's the only instance I can give you. To me, it's a flaw. I can't defend that scene.

(In the 2000 version of *The Exorcist*, Friedkin tinkered with the problematic scene, even adding CGI elements in hopes of making it clearer, but it remains both theologically and narratively muddled.)

▲ ▲ ▲

While horror films generally require high-grade suspension of disbelief, the occult subgenre is particularly susceptible to gaps in logic. During the filming of *The Shining*, for example, Stanley Kubrick dismissed objections or confusion from his cast and crew on the grounds that not much mattered in the parallel universe of the supernatural. And while fandom has obsessed over *The Shining* for forty years, there is a more-than-likely chance that Kubrick, having shot multiple takes of every scene and produced endless reels of footage, simply overlooked continuity errors during the editing process, reasoning that the irrationality of the Fortean world of the film would justify them.

Despite all the talk of verisimilitude, *The Exorcist* is overloaded with improbabilities and inspires several practical questions (the kind that drive filmmakers and certain uber fans crazy) throughout. Alfred Hitchcock derisively called viewers who demanded a certain amount of logic "The Plausibles."

A "Plausible" might object to the scene where Sharon calls Karras over in the middle of the night to witness Regan materializing letters on her skin. When Karras arrives, Sharon, brandishing a flashlight in the unlit house, encourages silence and whispers: "I don't want Chris to see this." By that time, Chris MacNeil had already heard the demon voice emerge from her daughter; she had already seen Regan mutilate herself with a crucifix; she had already been forced to go down on a bloody Regan; she had already been knocked loopy by a blow to the face; she had already witnessed Regan turn her head around 180 degrees. As a plot point, Sharon calling Karras in the middle of the night and sneaking him into the house so that Chris can avoid some distress is both silly and meretricious. It is a pretext to insert a sense of suspense and to have somebody—anybody—in motion in a film whose critical moments are largely static and are confined to a bedroom. The "Help me" scene is the pivotal moment when Karrass is finally stripped of his doubts concerning possession, but its dramatization is absurd.

Another example that would trouble a "Plausible" involves the disappearance of the real world beyond the walls of 3600 Prospect Street. Eventually, secular authorities—including Lt. Kinderman, reduced to staking out the MacNeil residence in a fleeting scene—vanish completely from *The Exorcist*, replaced by ecclesiastical forces who will reestablish the natural order of things. And while the absence of any authority other than that of the Catholic Church can be justified as a thematic point, the fact that a disturbed child, on Thorazine, with a history of medical visits, who has just mutilated herself with a foreign object, could be left without professional oversight is the sort of common-sense lapse routine in horror films.

CHAPTER 24

The Fear Factor

espite advances in technique, technology, and special effects since 1973, *The Exorcist* is invariably declared the most frightening movie ever made, yet, in some ways, *The Exorcist* works against the prevailing notions of what makes a horror film effective. Traditional methods of building suspense, notably putting someone in danger or dramatically at risk (such as a spy coming close to having his cover blown), simply do not exist in *The Exorcist*. Think of Rosemary Woodhouse fleeing panic-stricken at the thought of being pursued by a cabal of Satanists; or Damien making a lethal beeline for his vulnerable mother while riding his tricycle in *The Omen*; or the thunderous, unearthly pounding at the door while Claire Bloom and Julie Harris cringe in bed in *The Haunting*; or Trish Van De Vere chased by a malevolent wheelchair in *The Changeling*; or Oliver Reed trying to drown his son in *Burnt Offerings* (and being attacked by trees and shrubbery when trying to escape the haunted house). In *The Exorcist*, the demon opens some drawers, projectile vomits, hurls profanities at Karras and Merrin, tries to manipulate them psychologically, and rattles the house with the strength of a forequake. After the initial flurry of power games—assaulting the psychiatrist, the doctor, and Chris—no one in *The Exorcist* is ever jeopardized again. At least—not openly. Even the murder of Dennings takes place off-camera. (Similarly, Father Merrin dies, presumably of a heart attack, while Karras is downstairs talking to Chris.)

Another issue in the fear department concerns Regan and her fate. While the audience is horrified by the torments she undergoes, and the central conceit of the film—young girl suffers unspeakable cruelties—immediately makes her an object of sympathy, the question of her survival seems predetermined. Even by permissive New Hollywood standards, killing a child was unimaginable (with the exception at the time being *The Mephisto Waltz*, a possession film with a satanic slant, in which an eleven-year-old girl dies off-screen, and a few years later in *Assault on Precinct 13*, a low-budget action thriller directed by John Carpenter), meaning that traditional audience expectations were in play during screenings. Only the most gullible filmgoer would believe that Regan would die before the credits rolled.

In addition, most of the characters have no relation to each other, presumably hindering audience identification. Karras and Merrin meet for the first time with only twenty minutes left in the film. Kinderman and Karras share one scene. Chris is acquainted with Merrin for all of a few seconds. Before she is possessed, Regan interacts only with Chris. The household staff, composed of Winnie, Sharon, and Karl rarely exchange dialogue with each other and disappear on the night of the exorcism.

Of all the characters in the film, only Father Karras has an inner life. Jason Miller outlined what it meant to develop Karras as the sole knotty protagonist of *The Exorcist*. "I think Father Karras is a man whose faith is beginning to crumble. He has a great deal of guilt concerning the circumstances of his mother's death since he chose to be a priest instead of supporting his family," he told Travers and Reiff. "I think he is finally on the edge of despair. His foundation is no longer there, the church has changed. The most difficult part about playing this character, that I can see now, is to remember that he is a human being first and a priest second. You can always play the priest, but it is finding that particular human being who happens to be the priest that is important. Otherwise, you have *The Bells of St Mary's*. It's too easy to play priests as perfect. You have to see beyond their broad outlines and find the less appealing qualities that provide humanity."

A young priest already doubting his faith, Karras begins to see the world—its omnipresent suffering—the same way that combative atheists and the lapsed often do: the ugliness of existence seems to undercut the notion of a just and loving God. The vagrant in the train station who pleads for money from Karras (while emphasizing their shared Catholicism) leaves Karras visibly shaken. When Karras rushes to the ward to see his mother, he seems almost repulsed by the disturbed and downtrodden who impede his path. Worse, as a psychiatrist, Karras must face the same doubts from his fellow Jesuits, who unburden themselves to him during official sessions. During the filming of *Crash Course* at Georgetown University, Karras laughs and enjoys himself, a respite from his troubles. When Karras leaves the scene, he lingers, looking back at the lively crowd, a crane shot seemingly highlighting his loneliness. Only later—when Chris, on the way home from the shoot, spots him with a solemn expression on his face—does the viewer understand that Karras has been reluctant to face his obligations as a psychiatrist. Until the exorcism scene, however, Karras struggles internally, without raising concern from the audience about his fate.

To overcome the lack of a dynamic identifiable character, *The Exorcist* offers ensemble torment instead. For most of the film, every major character is in agony. Father Merrin is immediately discombobulated by his realization that Pazuzu has returned as his archenemy. This understanding sends Merrin staggering through a landscape full of portents and in need of his nitroglycerin tablets. Regan and Chris share a handful of natural scenes before they descend into their nightmare ordeal. With less than five minutes on-screen, Father Karras is depicted as anguished by his religious doubts and overcome by guilt about his mother. Burke Dennings, who is more of a cameo, dies after last being seen in a drunken affray. Sharon, Karl, and Winnie all suffer vicariously along with Chris and Regan. Only Kinderman, played for laughs like most secular authorities in the film, is spared torment.

Plunging the entire main cast into despair sparks a kind of collective identification with the audience. And the free fall into diabolic agony culminates in the exorcism, a tour de force of white-knuckle filmmaking. It is this twenty-minute sequence, full of cinematic exclamation points, that truly earns *The Exorcist* its standing as an unforgettable fright machine.

The overwhelming key of the exorcism scene—loud, hectic, garish, with frenzied editing—is deliberate for two reasons: first, to shred the last remaining nerves of an audience that had already been intermittently under assault for more than ninety minutes, and, second, to avoid unintentional laughs. According to reports, *The Exorcist* got its share of giggles from audiences in 1974, but Friedkin understood that a measured pace would encourage reflection that might lead to wholesale laughter. (Think of most of the leisurely terrors of *The Amityville Horror*, whose astonishing box-office success belies its inadvertent comedy.)

To ensure a spellbound audience, Friedkin accelerated. The exorcism features more vomit, more head-spinning, more sexually loaded profanities, a few hellish visions produced by the demon, cracking ceilings, splinter-ing doors, feverish incantations chanted by Merrin and Karras, and more bed-shaking. And, finally, as a pièce de résistance, the levitation scene, which should not be decontextualized: in late 1973 and early 1974, this effect was simply astonishing. Brilliantly staged, the levitation, despite the piano wire being visible during the initial theater run, is completely unexpected, giving the audience a novel thrill, along with the collective thought, "What next?" Objects had levitated on film in the past, particularly during séances, and *The Hypnotic Eye*, a 1960 mystery thriller, featured a levitation scene in the context of a magic act, but only *The Exorcist* offered a graphic, expertly mounted rendition.

As the exorcism nears its tragic and redemptive end, Friedkin introduces one of the most successful ambiguities of a film overloaded with ellipses and confusion: the death of Father Merrin. When it comes to their pasts, both Karras and Merrin are vulnerable, and the demon exploits their psy-chic weaknesses ruthlessly. When Pazuzu appears during the exorcism—in a nightmare tableau shot with an exquisite shadows-and-fog look—it is clearly meant to be a hallucination, or a bespoke phantasmagoria conjured by the demon specifically for Merrin. A reminder, perhaps, of his draining battle against Pazuzu years earlier and a hint that Merrin is no longer a young man in his prime. In the short sequence, Regan is not bound, and the demon materializes behind her, almost like an actor waiting in the wings. A reaction shot of Merrin is followed by another cut to Regan, again laying on the bed this time, with her hands tied, reestablishing "reality" in the narrative.

For Karras, it is an eerily solid projection of his mother, sitting in the middle of Regan's bed, wearing the same gown she wore in her early hospital scene. This image externalizes the guilt Karras feels for having neglected his mother and nearly sends him over the edge. As he tends to Regan, placing a damp cloth on her forehead and checking her heart rate with a stetho-scope, Karras struggles to control his emotions. After taking his nitroglyc-erin tablets in the bathroom, a shaky Merrin returns and senses Karras is at his breaking point. Karras shouts at the possessed Regan, now speaking in Greek, "You're not my mother!"

But the most interesting aspect of this scene is that Karras believes Regan is near death, telling Merrin that sedatives will leave her in a coma. With her heart racing, her face sweating, and her chest heaving, Regan (or is it the demon?) reminds the priests that she is still a child. Her symptoms mirror those of Merrin, who, unbeknownst to Karras, has just returned from taking his nitroglycerin pills. A concerned Merrin orders Karras out of the room and prepares to begin the exorcism once more, this time, alone. Merrin kneels by the side of the bed and, after a moment of hesitation, opens his volume of the Roman Ritual. "Our Father, who art in heaven," he begins. Then, in a moment of weakness, he reaches out to Regan and takes her hand, the first time he has acknowledged her underlying humanity. (One of the most obvious contradictions, or continuity lapses, occurs in these post-levitation scenes: Karras binds Regan after she descends, but her hands are free when Karras checks her heart rate and Merrin resumes the exorcism.) The next time we see Merrin, he is dead, lying face down on the bed, with Regan leaning up against one of the posts. Karras sets Merrin on the floor, where the bottle of holy water (foregrounded in a low-angle shot) drips beside him, and feverishly but futilely attempts to resuscitate him.

In one of the creepiest shots ever filmed, Regan, in the bluish hell-light, a wisp of breath fogging the air, begins to chortle with malevolent aplomb while Karras struggles.

The question surrounding this scene is whether the demon somehow transferred her heart ailment to Merrin when he made physical contact with her, in a kind of complete-circuit reaction, like someone accidentally touching the third rail. Because Friedkin overused foreshadowing as a device in the film, it is more than possible that Merrin died via transference, of sorts, prefiguring how Damien will ultimately provoke the demon to pass into him.

If there are any twists in *The Exorcist*, which is a fairly straightforward narrative, they materialize when Merrin arrived at his predestined appointment. That the hero swoops in and dies within twenty minutes is the first surprise—a motif later repeated with a certain mock elan by Stanley Kubrick in *The Shining*—and that the exorcism is a complete failure is the second unexpected happening. After all, it is not the Roman Ritual that cures Regan, it is not the holy water, nor the brandishing of crucifixes; it is the cosmic vendetta between Karras and the demon, which, in effect, is extracurricular to the Catholic rites. But Merrin dying puts the spotlight on the real savior—Karras—and allows the audience to identify with the only fully drawn character in the film. Father Karras now carries the fear expectations of every spectator in the theater: Will Karras win this life-and-death battle? Or will he lose?

With minimal character development, a vulnerable protagonist (Regan) who is likely to survive, and little on-screen action (and even less dramatized peril), *The Exorcist* seems like a poor candidate for shivers. But *The Exorcist* regularly tops "Scariest of All Time" polls. This long-standing opinion is a testimony to its powerful technique, the universal sympathetic/sentimental appeal of its surface action (a child in jeopardy), its quality cast, and certain overt psychological contrivances. "I mean, I'm not interested in an interesting movie," Friedkin said about his strategy. "I am interested in a gut-level reaction."

▲ ▲ ▲

CHAPTER 25

The Age of Anxiety: Backgrounds
of *The Exorcist*

Since its release in 1973, *The Exorcist* has inspired endless interpretations and commentary from religious scholars, psychologists, cultural theorists, newspaper columnists, and film critics. Except for *The Shining*, no other American film of the last fifty years has generated so much exegesis. Unlike *The Shining*, however, which launched a cottage industry of readings, one that borders on madness and includes theories revolving around the Holocaust, the NASA moon landings, gematria, the Federal Reserve, and the genocide against Native Americans, *The Exorcist* is not a formalist puzzle.

In keeping with his egoism, William Peter Blatty took an unusual step concerning interpretations of his novel and, by extension, the film: he denied that *The Exorcist* was as complex or as interesting as its misguided explicators believed it was. Its blunt messaging—only God can save us from our degradation—is exactly what it appears to be. That uncommon admission mirrors one of the earliest critiques lobbed at the film by Vincent Canby of the *New York Times*, who wrote: "Unlike a lot of extremely dumb vampire movies, [*The Exorcist* is] about nothing else but what it says, demonic possession and exorcism."

Blatty, apparently, agreed. The post-modernists, the deconstructionists, the post-structuralists, the Queer theorists, the Marxists, the post-colonialists—to Blatty, these textual analysts were on the literary wild goose chase of a lifetime. And while most of the abstruse readings inspired by *The Exorcist* do, indeed, give Blatty too much credit, they consistently discount his declared literary process: Blatty repeatedly claimed that *The Exorcist* is a narrative that sprang from his subconscious. Written at white heat in what Blatty called "dream time" (between midnight and dawn), *The Exorcist* is a compendium of his political, theological, and personal obsessions. More than once, Blatty attributed *The Exorcist*, in part, to his psyche. "I believe that my subconscious, once it has the necessary raw material (data and research) and sufficient prodding (sweat), does most of my plotting; and that it knew, by the time I had made that notation, almost the entire plot of *The Exorcist*, slipping portions to my conscious mind a little bit at a time."

To admirers of the film, *The Exorcist* is about "the generation gap" and "the mystery of faith," relatively benign descriptions for what Blatty called a sermon. And the preacher at the pulpit always has his enemy: demon rum, infidelity, sloth, lust, vice. For Blatty, the subject of his sermon (or apostolic work, as he also called it), seems to have been inspired by a single throwaway scene from *Rosemary's Baby*: when Mia Farrow picks up an issue of *Time* magazine with the words "Is God Dead?" emblazoned on the cover.

The Exorcist is not a metaphor for the breakdown of family values or the loss of a national moral compass. Nor is it a meditation on the moral decay of an increasingly secular America during the free love, LSD, psychedelic rock, urban riots, and Charles Manson 1960s. No, *The Exorcist* is an open conservative reaction to those sociological changes and a modern jeremiad on the loss of religion. It is a scolding, hectoring work whose subtext cannot remain buried past the prologue in Iraq.

The loss of faith during the upheavals of the '60s would eventually trigger a backlash in the early 1970s (producing the derisively named "Jesus freaks"), but for now, Blatty seized on spiritual malaise, rectifiable by belief in the Catholic Church, as his theme. "First, the film is designed to have a powerful emotional impact," Blatty told *People*. "A sermon that people sleep through is utterly useless."

In his 1992 book *Horror*, Mark Jancovich pans the film while also noting its orthodox leanings: "However, not only is *The Exorcist* a pretentious and rather dull horror film, it displays a remarkably crude conservatism which distinguishes itself from more general developments in the genre. It does present the forces of order and chaos as being indistinguishable from one another within the modern world, but it does so specifically to establish the need for traditional forms of religious authority."

Some might argue for a more liberal reading of the film, especially when considering how Friedkin minimized the overarching message, but the novel is unmistakably open about its traditional values. As much as Friedkin worked to make a more enigmatic narrative, the film remains informed by the novel and its overdetermined construction as a harsh theological lesson. "I'm the interpreter of another man's vision," Friedkin told Travers and Reiff, "in this case, Bill Blatty's. But I have to have total control over how that vision is interpreted on film."

Consciously modeling *The Exorcist* on *Rosemary's Baby* led Blatty to emphasize topicality, and this fusing of contemporary themes into *The Exorcist* gives the novel its historical resonance. After all, the late Sixties were so chaotic that addressing them openly could succeed in two ways: as a hook to familiarize contemporary readers (thereby making it more accessible) and as an omnipresent device to reinforce the theme of moral decay in need of spiritual uplift. In addition, New Age pastimes, a drug sub-plot, occult allusions, and current slang and cultural references make *The Exorcist* a grab bag of early Seventies concerns.

In a 1974 cover story titled "The Exorcism Frenzy," *Newsweek* offered a neat explanation for why *The Exorcist* became such a cultural firestorm: "*The Exorcist* has captured the popular imagination and—if only for one Gothic moment—brought into frenzied focus the widespread anxiety, fantasies, and fears that have lately broken through contemporary American society. Like an image whose time has arrived, *The Exorcist* dramatically orchestrates current interests in the occult, psychic phenomena, Satanism and man's more fundamental yearning for some kind of reckoning with his destructive inclinations."

And many of those destructive inclinations reflected the challenges and shifting values of youth in an accelerated era that seemed to border apocalypse. "It was a film about explosive social change; a finely honed focusing point for that entire youth explosion that took place in the late '60s and early '70s," Stephen King wrote in *Danse Macabre*. "It was a movie for all those parents who felt, in a kind of agony and terror, that they were losing their children. And could not understand why or how it was happening."

Beginning in the 1950s, with the establishment of the hitherto unknown "teen" market, the arrival of rock 'n' roll, the juvenile delinquency scare (as seen in pulp novels such as *Hot Rod Gang Rumble*, *The Torrid Teens*, *The*

Cry Baby Killer, and so on), and the comic-book panic that led to Senate hearings, children became perpetual objects of anxiety in America.

Then the rebellious Sixties produced the hippie generation, the revolutionary generation, and the LSD generation—simultaneously. As early as 1963, Bob Dylan hinted at the future when he sang, "Your sons and your daughters are beyond your command," but it was Charles Manson, after the Tate-LaBianca massacres, who summed up the new American jitters: "These children that come at you with knives—they are your children. You taught them."

In 1968, Dr. Ray E. Helford and Dr. C. Henry Young published *The Battered Child*, a shocking exposé that sparked a full-blown panic about the ubiquity of child abuse. Five years later, Senator Walter Mondale introduced the Child Abuse Prevention and Treatment Act, which became law in January 1974.

At a time when divorce rates skyrocketed, when runaways became a quantifiable nightmare (eventually leading to the federal Runaway Youth Act in 1974), when drug use exploded, particularly in cities, teenagers became a vulnerable group. To top off the national youth nightmare, the Vietnam War proffered up a draft lottery system that promised to maim and kill thousands of young people a year.

David J. Skal, in his book *The Monster Show: A Cultural History of Horror*, also noted how *The Exorcist* reflected contemporary fears about kids. "The film became a highly publicized cultural ritual exorcizing not the devil, but rather the confused parental feelings of guilt and responsibility in the Vietnam era, when—at least from a certain conservative perspective—filthy-mouth children were taking personality-transforming drugs, violently acting out, and generally making life unpleasant for their elders."

Part of the new concern over children revolved around reproduction, with The Pill being introduced in 1960, only a few years before the Thalidomide scandal broke, panicking the entire Western world about the possibility of millions of deformed and mutated babies. In addition, activist groups such as the Redstockings and the liberalization of state laws propelled abortion through the news cycles and ultimately into national legalization in 1973.

The Exorcist also mirrors the widespread anxiety of collapsing morals and the effect of godless decadence on the Baby Boom generation. Blatty hinted at his underlying theme of domestic breakdown by using *King Lear* as his literary touchstone. (In 1965, Blatty, who wrote his thesis on Shakespeare, published a novella *I, Billy Shakespeare!* which drew little attention but received a handful of positive reviews.) *King Lear* is not only a tragedy about daughters betraying and deceiving their father but about the destruction of an entire family—dysfunction, Renaissance-style. *The Exorcist* abounds in *Lear* references. A film version of *Lear*, playing in theaters in DC, is mentioned by both Karl and Kinderman. (The film starred Paul Scofield, whom Blatty had considered for the role of Father Merrin before settling on Max Von Sydow.) Blatty named Regan after one of Lear's two treacherous daughters: "Chris shook her head; rueful; recalling: she had almost named her Goneril. Sure. Right on. Get ready for the worst." Goneril is the second of Lear's scheming daughters; the third, Cordelia, is morally sound.

As a reactionary novel, *The Exorcist* (over)dramatizes the threat modern values pose to the family unit. Chris MacNeil embodies the new permissive culture of the Equal Rights Amendment and the Sexual Revolution. The velocity of the feminist movement, sparked by Betty Friedan and *The Feminine Mystique* and the founding of the National Organization for Women, would, in a few years, bring about no-fault divorces and the legalization of abortion.

Chris is seen in action during *Crash Course*, confident, talented, and in control of the fictional scene, where, with the help of a bullhorn, she rallies dozens of protesting students, an ironic contrast to her future powerlessness against the hellish presence that eventually overtakes Regan. Her profession (she is not just an actress but a star) underscores a lifestyle that contributes to instability. The MacNeils, when on location, take temporary lodgings for the duration of the shoot. That picturesque house on Prospect Street, set in a prosperous Georgetown neighborhood, is not where Chris and Regan live. They are constantly in flux because of her professional commitments. Indeed, when Chris returns home from her shoot, she chats with Regan, who fills her in on her day, spent picnicking with Sharon. When Regan asks Chris if she can have a horse, Chris responds, "Maybe when we get back home."

But Blatty, in pursuing his stringent vision of moral comeuppance, loaded the dice. Although Chris is divorced, she is independent, successful, rich, stylish, and enjoys a close relationship with Regan. Her material circumstances (openly contrasted with how impoverished Karras and his mother are) allow her to have a small staff at her command. She is invited to White House lunches and holds soirées at her home with senators, astronauts, and Georgetown faculty in attendance. At the time the supernatural events take place, she is pondering an opportunity to direct her first feature film. In other words, the MacNeil household is not the typical target for demonic possession.

In a 2018 article in *The Atlantic* focusing on the recent explosion of demonic possession claims, Mike Mariani, speaking to several priests, describes the revealing facts about those seeking exorcisms. Most petitioners, for example, have had previous psychiatric troubles or, in some cases, have suffered sexual trauma in their past. Substance abuse is another common denominator. Finally, a supernatural element often preexists the possession, that is, a devout or evangelical victim already primed to believe in otherworldly happenings. Even the Hunkeler case featured an aunt devoted to Spiritualism who introduced Ronald Hunkeler to occult hokum, including the ever-present Ouija board (not a Parker Brothers production, most likely one manufactured by William Fuld from Baltimore, Maryland). The Hunkeler family also had links to Braucherei.

To qualify for demonic affliction in *The Exorcist*, however, all Regan has is a broken home and a nonresponsive father. Of course, she also has a divorcée for a mother, and, more important, from the point of view of a conservative writer looking to sermonize with gusto, Regan has a *nonbeliever* for a mother. These themes are more obvious in the novel, where Blatty makes Chris openly atheistic and, especially, materialistic.

When she visits her business manager (after taking Regan to the doctor for the first time), she is primarily concerned about purchasing a Ferrari. "Ben," she says, "I made eight hundred thou last year and you're saying I can't get a freaking car! Don't you think that's ridiculous? Where did it go?" The following pages focus on her finances and the particulars of her forthcoming high-society party.

Although Blatty depicts Chris with a homespun wit, he also suggests that she is something of an airhead. More than once, he underscores, at times via interior monologue and at times in his heavy-handed omniscient voice, the fact that Chris is not intellectually inclined:

For almost an hour, she probed to the barricades of minutiae. The data were easily found in texts, but reading tended to fray her patience.

Instead, she read people. Naturally inquisitive, she juiced them; wrung them out. But books were unwringable. Books were glib. They said "therefore" and "clearly" when it wasn't clear at all, and their circumlocutions could never be challenged. They could never be stopped for a shrewdly disarming, "Hold it, I'm dumb. Could I have that again?"

"Yes, I know," said Chris, "but I'm dumb. I mean, what's a Black Mass?"

"God, I'm dumb. You're a priest. You have to go where they send you."

"Well, maybe I'm dumb," she retorted, "but telling me an unknown gizmo in somebody's head throws dishes at a ceiling tells me nothing at all!"

"What the hell's a split personality, Father? You say it; I hear it. What is it? Am I really that stupid? Will you tell me what it is in a way I can finally get it through my head?"

In the film, Chris speaks far less foolish dialogue, and Friedkin has sketched her as irritable instead of ditzy. Just before shooting her scene in *Crash Course*, Chris twice expresses annoyance at last-second makeup applications. She dismisses her driver (telling him to drop off her bag) and walks home, where Sharon, her secretary, informs her that she has received an invitation to the White House. Chris is nonchalant about the invite, suggesting haughtiness. Then she angrily berates the operator when she fails to reach her ex-husband on the phone, an outburst accompanied by flouncing and the kind of blue language Regan will later bark and screech as her possession symptoms worsen.

Tellingly, as the film progresses, Chris slips increasingly into a domestic role. She serves coffee to Kinderman, washes and irons the shirt Karras wore when Regan vomited on him, makes Karras a drink in another scene, and sits downstairs knitting while her daughter undergoes an arcane ritual. Burstyn is deglamorized roughly forty-five minutes into the film, first with a black eye and then with a progressive haggardness. Her chic party dress (and a new hairdo) worn early in the film seem like an aberration by the time the exorcism begins. Symbolically, Chris is returning to her proper function in a male-dominated society, one where God is in the foreground and nuclear families are the norm.

The disintegration of the family unit and the effect of a lost father is personified by Regan, who is lonely, whiling away her days with a Ouija board in the basement of her temporary home, communicating with "Captain Howdy," an imaginary friend who is far less imaginary than Chris realizes. Indeed, Regan lives a strikingly isolated and claustrophobic existence within the parameters of the film. She has no friends, is never shown going to school, speaks to no one on the telephone, and spends the entire film indoors—except for the final scene, when she kisses Father Dyer after her ordeal is over and drives away from Prospect Street with her mother. (In addition, Regan never speaks a rational word to anyone but Chris. There is not a single line of dialogue between the unpossessed Regan and Sharon or Karl or Willie.) Two of her outings occur off-screen. When we first see Regan, she describes going to the park with Sharon, where she rides a horse (she is unsure if the horse is a gelding or a mare, the first sign of the sexual subtext that reveals itself later). A birthday outing (which would have included a solemn if off-kilter visit to the Tomb of the Unknown Soldier) stayed on the cutting-room floor, with only its aftermath remaining: Regan overhearing an apoplectic Chris, trying to reach her estranged husband, yelling on the telephone.

Her loneliness is accentuated, somewhat improbably, by the fact that she has no contact whatsoever with her father, Howard, who makes only a few oblique appearances in *The Exorcist*: first as the unreachable figure in Italy whom an irate Chris tries to telephone, as a reference on the cover of *Photoplay* magazine, which Regan reads in bed, and as a static black-and-white presence in several framed photographs placed around the house. (Howard may also be the other person on the line when Chris has a short phone conversation with an unidentified party. To this party, Chris claims that Regan is fine, as if unable to admit her failure as an independent mother.) Howard is not just an absentee father, he is a symbol of absentee fathers, and Blatty sets up a daisy chain of substitute fathers in the novel: Karl, Kinderman, Karras, and Merrin, as well as one spectacularly unfit replacement, Burke Dennings.

Our first glimpse of Dennings, as he directs *Crash Course*, reveals him to be obnoxious, yes, but also lecherous—and clearly smitten with Chris—two points that Friedkin establishes immediately. Of all the figures in *The Exorcist*, Dennings is the most enigmatic, and this initial scene sets the tone of his character. Nearly every moment of every frame Dennings appears in marks him as perverse, impish, drunk, or crude. Given the fact that Dennings is the only person killed by Pazuzu (Father Merrin, already frail, apparently succumbs to the strain of the exorcism ritual, but Friedkin allows for an alternative interpretation of his death), it is worth noting his brief but pivotal role in the film. The *Crash Course* shoot reveals him to be a foul-mouthed joker, but Chris appears charmed by his antics. But his drunken behavior at the party—where he antagonizes Karl, accusing him of being a Nazi, and then violently grapples with him—reveals him to be more than just a cut-up. (From a pragmatic point of view, Dennings draws Kinderman into the narrative, allowing for the red herring of a police investigation. But Kinderman, his role drastically reduced from the novel, ultimately serves little purpose and, like Chris, essentially disappears from the last third of the film. Karl is meant to be the main suspect in a subplot Friedkin never bothers developing.)

The question remains: Why is Burke Dennings the only victim of a demon who views opening a drawer telekinetically as a "vulgar display of power"?

In an earlier scene, before she undergoes possession, Regan seems preoccupied with Burke and the possibility that her mother is seeing him. Her bedtime conversation with Chris, filmed without either Burstyn or Blair aware that the cameras were rolling, shows how Regan has been brooding over the rupture of her family. Regan asks Chris if she is going to marry Burke Dennings. Chris denies it, adding, "Burke just comes around here a lot because . . . well, he's lonely. He don't got nothin' to do." To that, a puckish Regan gives an intriguing response: "Well, I heard differently. . . . ."

The implication is that Captain Howdy has been alarming Regan with stories about Dennings possibly replacing her father. Reynold Humphries, in *American Horror Film: An Introduction*, speculates, "If the Devil that possesses her kills Burke, it is because Regan cannot bear the idea of a second man behaving like her father, which is understandable, given the world in which Burke moves."

This reading—that Burke dies because he presents a further threat to family values—opens the possibility that Regan and the demon have, at least initially, some sort of symbiotic relationship, with the demon externalizing her anxieties. When Regan teases her mother about Burke, she simultaneously expresses her unconscious distress and effectively marks Burke for death.

It was against this roiling cultural background that *The Exorcist* tapped into the collective fears and anxieties of the American psyche—with help from the Warner Bros. publicity department and the cynical creators.

Marketed by Friedkin and Blatty as "more than just a movie," and as potentially cursed, *The Exorcist* found several willing media collaborators, including Rex Reed, who composed a lengthy syndicated feature about the bogus supernatural happenings on the set. Incredibly, Reed would write, "At some point, everyone connected with the film was possessed."

CHAPTER 26

▲ ▲ ▲

The Shock of the New:
Sex and Taboo

f all the sociological and cultural explanations put forth for *The Exorcist* phenomenon, few, if any, focus on film itself, circa 1973, as a changing medium or as an industry. Perhaps more than anything, *The Exorcist* flourished because of serendipity: the right cultural product at the right cultural time.

When discussing the overpowering effect of New Hollywood films, one must account for how shocking it must have been to go from a medium still dominated by musicals and costume dramas to one overrun by exploding blood squibs, profanity, and sexual frankness. Only a few years before *The Exorcist* opened, the Production Code still dictated what directors filmed, and consumers saw, and the average moviegoer had yet to acclimatize to the brave new cinematic world of "Suggested for Mature Audiences—" and beyond.

Nudity found in the cheap works of Russ Meyer, Doris Wishman, and Herschell Gordon Lewis (before he turned to gore) existed only on the fringes; Mr. and Mrs. Middle America were unlikely to seek out *Bad Girls Go to Hell* or *The Adventures of Lucky Pierre* in their local red-light districts. And, except for *The Pawnbroker*, the skin shown in more mainstream fare came from Europe, such as *The Collector*, *Darling*, and *Blow-Up* (with a rare entry from Canada, *The Fox*).

In 1967, *Bonnie and Clyde* (with *The Graduate* following a few months later) defied and then dismantled the status quo, leading to a rapid succession of adult material that challenged ingrained American notions of popular entertainment. From 1968 to late 1973, just before *The Exorcist* arrived, Hollywood produced one film after another intended for an enlightened market that did not exist a few years earlier, including *Rosemary's Baby, 2001: A Space Odyssey, Midnight Cowboy, Easy Rider, The Wild Bunch, M*A*S*H, Joe, Five Easy Pieces, Little Big Man, Wanda, Carnal Knowledge, The Last Picture Show, A Clockwork Orange, Klute, Harold and Maude, Cabaret, Straw Dogs, King of Marvin Gardens, The Last Detail, Badlands, The Godfather*, and *Mean Streets*. Except for *Rosemary's Baby*, which was more of a black comedy, none of these titles were horror films.

Seemingly marginal productions also broke through at the box office, including *Yellow: I Am Curious*, a Swedish experimental mockudrama whose nudity shocked US Customs officials; *Last Tango in Paris*, an intense European import slapped with an X rating; and the mafia-financed *Deep Throat*, first of the porno chic megahits. America found itself spellbound by the unusual sights and sounds of this new permissive era.

With sex, nudity, and violence sorted out, audiences still maintained hang-ups about taboos, particularly anything involving children, as witnessed by the dustup *Paper Moon* caused in 1973, when Tatum O'Neal said the word "shit." (By comparison, Regan shouting "Fuck me!" and "Let Jesus fuck you!" is Richter-scale material.)

And *The Exorcist* went much further than vulgarity with a sexual subtext that is, in a sort of oxymoron, as clear as some of the religious iconography in the film. This, ultimately, is established by the figure of Pazuzu.

Although the demon that possesses Regan in the film is never named, Blatty coyly revealed it in his book on *The Exorcist*: "I strongly doubt that he is Satan; and he is certainly none of the spirits of the dead whose identity he sometimes assumes. If I had to guess, I would say he is Pazuzu, the Assyrian demon of the southwest wind." (This association with wind may have determined many of the images of open windows and even the wide shot of the MacNeil home that kick-starts the main narrative. The long zoom to the house at dawn implies that Pazuzu may have arrived, on the winds, to afflict Regan. Later on, of course, the film hints that Regan inadvertently summoned Pazuzu by tinkering with a Ouija board.)

In the novel, there are a few references to Pazuzu, and the amulet that Merrin finds in the Iraqi prologue clearly depicts Pazuzu. (To the funny bone of almost everyone who saw it, the disastrous 1977 sequel *Heretic* invoked "Pazuzu" repeatedly, in nearly every possible vocal range and with nearly every possible emotional inflection.) But the damage Pazuzu causes in Washington, DC, and the fear his likeness generates in Merrin, leaves no doubt that he is cast as the villain in the umpteenth good-versus-evil paradigm. Contrary to his depiction in *The Exorcist*, however, Pazuzu was not representative of malevolence during the height of his renown.

How Blatty came to select an obscure Assyrian/Babylonian demon as the personification of darkness is a question he never answered. But as a symbolic figure, Pazuzu has a few elements that might have struck Blatty as appropriate for his themes. Most notably, Pazuzu, a patchwork of animals, including a dog, a bird, and a scorpion, had an erect penis with a snake-head tip. This last detail made Pazuzu the perfect candidate for the low-grade sex fever that runs throughout *The Exorcist*. (Of course, Friedkin being Friedkin, the statue created for the film had to have a porn-sized cock, Pazuzu transformed into the John Holmes of demonology.) Not only did Pazuzu manifest lechery, but its snake-head phallus links him to Regan through a confluence of associations. In *King Lear*, Shakespeare describes Regan as "sharper than a serpent's tooth." In the novel, William Peter Blatty describes Regan's spider-walk movements, when she is on the floor chasing after Sharon, as "serpentine."

Without the lewd implications of the snake-head phallus, it is less clear why Blatty would choose Pazuzu for his embodiment of evil. Pazuzu, after all, is pre-Christian, and the Bible overflows with promising demons, from Abaddon to Ziminiar. In fact, Pazuzu was at his peak Q score between five thousand and eight thousand years before Christianity. During the first millennium BC, however, Pazuzu made a comeback, becoming a popular amulet and a protective ornament across Mesopotamia. Women commonly wore amulets of Pazuzu to ward off the demon Lamashtu, a mortal threat to infants and children. "A woman in labor wore the image of the demon Pazuzu to counteract the evil of Lamashtu for herself, her unborn children, and her newborn child," wrote Karen R. Nemet-Nejat in *Daily Life in Ancient Mesopotamia*. This explains the "evil against evil" phrase spoken in the antiquities office as Merrin examines the unearthed amulet of Pazuzu. At a time when mythic figures avoided reductive labels, concepts such as good and evil were rarely defaults, and Pazuzu had the moral duality of many supernatural beings. As Dr. Nils P. HeeBel notes, these Pazuzu figurines were so popular and considered such powerful talismans, that some believed they would aid them in the Beyond: "Further indication for the usage of smaller Pazuzu representations as personal protective amulets can be seen in the fact that many small Pazuzu heads were found in graves, where they constitute part of the personal belongings of the dead."

That the protector of children and what Dr. HeeBel calls the "expeller of demons," would become the destroyer of Regan seems to reveal what Blatty had in mind when he selected Pazuzu as his malevolent force. Poetic license, driven by the presence of a conspicuous penis linked to serpent imagery, gave Blatty the sexual undercurrent that he was looking for. Of the hundreds of demons found in folklore, myth, and pre-Christian texts, Blatty selected one with a giant phallus. Thus, Blatty ensured prurient overtones that were later crudely emphasized by Friedkin on-screen.

To a critic such as Barbara Creed, who views the film through the lens of gender, *The Exorcist* has a conservative sexual subtext. "Connections drawn in the film between feminine desire, sexuality and abjection suggest that more is at stake than a simple case of demonic possession," she wrote. "Possession becomes the excuse for legitimizing a display of aberrant feminine behavior which is depicted as depraved, monstrous, abject—and perversely appealing."

No longer the playful teen who grabs sweets from the cookie jar and sculpts clay figurines, Regan has become what Creed called the "monstrous feminine—" a nightmare version of tainted innocence and a grotesque caricature of the modern liberated woman.

Her actions while fully possessed are overtly sexual: she tries to castrate the psychiatrist who hypnotizes her, masturbates with the crucifix, forces her mother to go down on her, shouts sexual obscenities, and mocks Karras and Merrin with gay slurs. On the surface level, *The Exorcist* may have been pop theology, but Blatty constructed a narrative whose underlying message of teen rebellion and sexuality as a threat to the natural order of things is clear.

▲ ▲ ▲

Just as the nudie subgenres of the early 1960s flourished out of sight in grindhouses and drive-ins, graphic horror films, such as *Night of the Living Dead* and *The Last House on the Left*, played off the beaten path. *The Exorcist*, by contrast, premiered in first-run theaters backed by a major studio and enough marketing clout to appear in weighty features from the *New York Times* to the *Chicago Tribune*.

Novelty, then, is one of the main reasons *The Exorcist* shocked America. The mind-blowing special effects of *2001* were passive, almost decorative, compared to the aggressive outrages of Friedkin and Co.

Even William Peter Blatty, who often downplayed *The Exorcist* as a "roller-coaster ride," conceded that part of the appeal of his religious harangue was prurient: "A large section of the audience probably came because something that shocking and vulgar could be seen on the American screen," he told Mark Kermode. "Bill Friedkin always said that would be the case; that they would come to see the little girl masturbate with the crucifix."

Horror-film critic Kim Newman also noted how the lurid crucifix scene would read to an overlapping audience during the early 1970s: "It attracted the attention of a huge audience of sensation seekers and amateur theologists who would have given *Werewolves on Wheels* a miss."

What Friedkin understood, that Blatty did not, was that no film with such over-the-top elements had ever been given such a widespread platform before. And, as what David Thomson once called a "chronic sensationalist," Friedkin realized that he had an opportunity to capitalize on virgin territory. The "mystery of faith"? That was for the suckers.

According to Blatty, Friedkin once stepped out of a particularly raucous showing of *The Exorcist* to phone him and mock any hope of spiritual uplift. Blatty related this anecdote to Adam Lechmere of the *London Observer*: "He said, 'There's your religious audience, Bill, waiting for your message. They're all stoned on marijuana, they're going crazy, can you hear them? They're having a party.'"

One aspect of the film that many critics seemed to overlook was that *The Exorcist*, despite haughty denials from both Friedkin and Blatty, was an exercise in horror. As such, its success is rooted in its effectiveness as a genre exercise. With nothing to compare it to in Hollywood, *The Exorcist* stood out alone in the mainstream, its intensity and excesses far superseding the tame-by-comparison *Rosemary's Baby*.

None of the wide-release horror films produced in the wake of *Rosemary* (including *The Mephisto Waltz*, *The Possession of Joel Delaney*, and *The Other*) could match the unique mix of over-the-top action chills with superior production values.

Directed by Peter Wendkos, *The Mephisto Waltz* has a made-for-TV quality ingrained in nearly every frame. Except for two glimpses of Jacqueline Bissett and Barbara Parkins nude, the film could air on CBS without a single cut. This tale of satanic hocus-pocus and possession also carries with it a hint of the campiness that undermined so much of the genre in the 1950s and 1960s.

Casting, which was a strength for *The Exorcist*, is also haywire in *Mephisto*. Just a little over a year away from achieving television stardom in *M*A*S*H*, Alan Alda seems out of place as the music journalist corrupted by the soul of a satanic pianist. Not only does Alda become a narcissistic elitist, but he also transforms into an unlikely sex machine. As one of the most beautiful women in Hollywood during the 1960s and 1970s, Bissett practically illuminates the screen; her portrayal of a quirky wife threatened by the forces of evil arrayed against her, however, is underwhelming. Only Barbara Parkins, still hot from *Valley of the Dolls* and a pair of *Playboy* pictorials, stands out in a witchy role that calls for her to be cold, scheming, and faintly aristocratic. Even the usually reliable Bradford Dillman seems flat. But the entire cast is compromised by kitschy material filmed in pedestrian style.

Similarly, *The Possession of Joel Delaney*, directed by Waris Hussein, lacks visual flair, although it is far more graphic and includes a genuinely disturbing Santeria exorcism scene. Like *The Mephisto Waltz*, which failed to generate much word of mouth during its run, *Delaney* understated most of its shocks while its subtext sometimes predominated. Unlike *Mephisto*, however, *Delaney* has a class lead in Shirley MacLaine. It also has gritty on-location shooting that gives the film a granular feel lacking in the generic California backdrops of *Mephisto*.

Both films operated as cultural metaphors: *Mephisto* is a parable about marriage and thwarted female agency, and *Delaney* aims to skewer class and privilege in a decaying New York City. Neither film, however, distinguishes itself with what makes *The Exorcist* stand out: camerawork, montage, pace, sound design, cinematography, editing. And, of course, neither *Waltz* nor *Delaney* specifically sought to break taboos (although *Delaney* culminates in an uncomfortable and objectionable scene involving children), which *The Exorcist* did with a ferocious, in-your-face zeal.

In 1972, Robert Mulligan, who directed the beloved object lesson *To Kill a Mockingbird*, joined the spook trend with *The Other*, an adaptation of the second-best-selling horror novel of 1971 (written by former B-actor Thomas Tryon). A far better filmmaker than Wendkos or Hussein, Mulligan infused *The Other* with occasional stylistic flourishes and made the most out of the high-gloss production values at his disposal. Its look—idyllic horror—reflects the enviable talent of cinematographer Bruce Surtees and one of its gimmicks (actual twin brothers never seen in the same shot) intrigues as well as occasionally frustrates.

One of the earliest of the evil-children fad that would take off in the '70s and would extend well into the 1990s (Macaulay Culkin, for example, in *The Good Son*) and beyond, *The Other* has several conventional scenes interspersed with visionary images and a few quiet shock moments. As a whole, *The Other* is unsatisfactory (it includes an overwrought performance by Uta Hagen), but its theme of a traumatic childhood is by turns poignant and disturbing.

None of the early 1970s horror films compared to *The Exorcist* when it came to staging. Friedkin had an eye for framing, despite eschewing blocking on *The French Connection* and often encouraging actors to move as they saw fit. This sense was magnified by his editing instincts, when he often juxtaposed startling images, usually with a sense of rhythm involved, sometimes, as Friedkin has stated, letting scenes play out longer than expected and sometimes cutting them before they concluded. That particular talent abandoned him as the years passed, but *The Exorcist* represents its peak.

Writing in *Castle of Frankenstein* in 1974, Joe Dante, the future director of *The Howling* and *Gremlins*, instantly recognized the watershed moment that *The Exorcist* represented: "Suffice it to say, there has never been anything like this on the screen before."

Just as the demon invaded the MacNeil household to terrorize Regan, *The Exorcist* invaded general movie theaters to terrorize the masses.

CHAPTER 27

Never-Ending Controversy

ithin weeks of its release, the *Exorcist* began sparking new controversies related not to the film itself but to its production. Just as *The Exorcist* was essentially critic-proof, negative publicity stemming from insider squabbles would have little effect on box-office performance. But the possibility that the film would suffer from industry backlash over a personnel ruckus was all too real. In the case of *The Exorcist*, potential Academy Awards were at stake, something that William Friedkin recognized the instant Mercedes McCambridge rocketed off the reservation.

In a January 24, 1974, interview with the *New York Times*, McCambridge, enraged by the fact that she had not received acknowledgement—either on the poster or during the end credits—lambasted Warner Bros. and Friedkin for their betrayal. "Just before you called," she told writer Charles Higham, "I was thinking, 'Does God want to punish me for playing the voice of the Devil?' I gave the most difficult performance of my life—and then Warners didn't give me a single credit on the picture or in the advertising. The man who supplied the jewels got a credit! I cried. Billy Friedkin promised me a special credit—'And Mercedes McCambridge.' He broke his promise—it's heartbreaking when someone you thought was a friend does that."

Years later, the still-feisty McCambridge elaborated on her complaints in her scrappy memoir *The Quality of Mercy*. "Warner Brothers and Billy Friedkin, the director, were determined that the whole endeavor be kept secret," she wrote of her participation in *The Exorcist*. "Nobody on the lot was to know I was there! Nobody! Billy Friedkin said it would spoil the mystery surrounding the movie if people knew how we were doing it. I believed him, like a fool. Thanks to Billy Friedkin, there was so much mystery surrounding my work in the movie that he gave me no screen credit at all! The furrier got credit, the jeweler got credit. I got nothing!"

To make matters worse, McCambridge undermined Linda Blair, which incensed Friedkin, who thought Blair could win a Best Supporting Actress Oscar. "Maybe," McCambridge growled to the *Times*, "people will think the sound-effects people simply fixed her voice up—that it was her vocal performance. But her vocal performance was laughable! I have nothing against the child. I've never even met her. But if people had heard her saying some of those obscenities, they would have fallen over laughing. Of course, she spoke every word. But much too fast. I said to Billy Friedkin, my director, 'Why did you have her gabble her words? It's impossible to fit my words to her lip movements!' No, it's not true that some of her words were blended with mine on the final track. All of the devilish vocality is mine—all of it. Every word."

Such was her fury that Warner Bros. added her name to the end credits of every subsequent print struck of the film when it went into wide release.

According to Friedkin, who may or may not have been acting selfishly in hopes of improving the Academy Award haul for *The Exorcist*, it was McCambridge who kept Blair from winning an Oscar. Years later, Blair would recall the McCambridge affair for the BBC. "All of a sudden, it was everything about Mercedes McCambridge," she said. "She did the voice, so they tried to pull my nomination for an Academy Award. It was an awful time after the film was released because everything was 'Did Linda Blair really do the film?'"

Would Blair have been considered for the Best Supporting Actress honor if it had been common knowledge that most of her lines during the last two reels of the film had been dubbed by McCambridge? Did the producers deliberately try to conceal this fact? Or was the dubbing so clear to viewers that the lack of pretense about Blair and her performance was strictly self-evident?

By keeping McCambridge under wraps, the producers seemed more than just press-shy. Surely, billing McCambridge would have been an asset for the film; the fact that she was overlooked remains a mystery. Although her star had waned since the 1950s, McCambridge was still an Academy Award winner (in 1949 for her Hollywood debut, no less, *All the King's Men*) and a subsequent nominee seven years later (in *Giant*, where she more than held her own against James Dean). Moreover, she remained in the public consciousness as a stage and radio presence. And everyone on the production side should have realized McCambridge was a loose cannon. She proved that to Friedkin and Warner Bros. by publicly obliterating the filmmakers and filing a grievance with the Screen Actors Guild. But McCambridge had been making the gossip pages as far back as 1954, when her feud with the imperial Joan Crawford on the set of *Johnny Guitar* boiled over into full public view.

Less than a month after McCambridge shot her double-barrel load, Friedkin responded. In a letter to the *Times* published on February 24, 1974, Friedkin explained his side of the story. "When I asked Miss McCambridge to do the demon voice, she accepted with enthusiasm, stating that she felt the film would be a spiritual experience for audiences as it was for her," Friedkin wrote. "She assured me and my associate producer, David Salven, that screen credit was of no importance to her and indeed her contract, which she signed without dispute, does not call for credit. This is common practice in the film industry. The best compliment an actress can receive for dubbing a voice is that audiences are unaware of the dubbing, and, for obvious reasons, studios don't go around publicizing what was dubbed or by whom any more than a magician makes it a practice to publish the tricks of his trade."

This comment ignores the fact that Friedkin had insisted a line for McCambridge had been mistakenly omitted from the closing credits. In later versions of this story, Friedkin would blame Warner Bros., saying that the studio had overruled his promise to McCambridge. To McCambridge, that promise of a screen credit was an acknowledgment not only of her performance but also of the intense effort it had required.

With an expressiveness that emphasized her talent for the dramatic, McCambridge went into vivid detail about her struggles voicing the demon as well as the psychic and physical toll the role took on her. "I had to imagine Lucifer. I had to imagine the incredible, bottomless agony—the eternal agony of a lost soul. I drew on memory for that. I've been an alcoholic, saved by AA, and I've seen people in state hospitals, vegetables in straitjackets, the hopeless, abysmal, bottomless groaning and screaming. I used imitations of those hellish cries. I've been through hell, and I thought, 'Who better than I would know how the Devil feels?' I'm out of hell, he's there forever. To be on death row for eternity has got to be some kind of sentence."

McCambridge had indeed struggled with alcoholism. More than once, she had been hospitalized after a binge, and at least twice, in despair, she had tried to commit suicide. That her fragile emotional well-being was at risk in taking her part so seriously was not a case of histrionics. "So I cried out from my remembered hell," she said, recalling her ordeal in the service of art. "And when I spoke the scene in which the little girl spits out green vomit, when I made the ugly sounds of violent expectoration, I swallowed eighteen raw eggs, with a pulpy apple. To convey the feeling of the Devil being trapped, I had the crew tear up a sheet and bind me, hand and foot. Sometimes I was so exhausted, and my circulation was so sluggish that I wasn't able to drive home; I stayed in a motel near the Burbank Studios. My voice was ruined. For weeks, I couldn't talk above a whisper. So you see after all I went through why I'm mad at Billy Friedkin for not getting me on those credits. Any child could have wiggled on the bed. If there was any horror in the exorcism, it was me!"

In his letter to the *New York Times*, Friedkin summed up the entire affair with fury and indignation. "The success of the film has brought out the best and the worst in a lot of people, but Miss McCambridge's outrageous attempt to detract from Linda Blair's portrayal and push herself into the spotlight is the most unjustifiable and unprofessional action I have ever encountered as a filmmaker."

The first clause in that statement might also have been alluding to a young woman named Eileen Dietz.

▲ ▲ ▲

On February 2, 1974, news broke of Dietz, a hitherto unknown stage actress from Bayside, Queens, petitioning the Screen Actors Guild in hopes of challenging the legality of a contractual clause she had accepted in order to participate in *The Exorcist*.

In her filing, Dietz claimed that a gag order (what is today essentially a nondisclosure agreement) prevented her from publicizing her role as a double for Blair, which harmed her career prospects. She also noted that her standard contract (reportedly for a salary of $16,000) ultimately negated supplemental agreements. The Screen Actors Guild ruled in her favor. But her subsequent comments vexed nearly everyone involved in producing *The Exorcist.*

With her last bit part in films occurring in 1966, Dietz had been virtually anonymous in Hollywood. Her decidedly limited claims to fame were a recurring role in *The Doctors* (the soap opera that had once featured Ellen Burstyn) and a few stage appearances in New York City. Ultimately, her physique got her onto the set of *The Exorcist.* At just over five feet, Dietz made a plausible body double for Blair, who would be replaced for the scenes that required physical potency, such as the walloping of doctors, and for the notorious crucifixion sequence, deemed too obscene for a thirteen-year-old girl to enact.

Dietz appears in the dream sequence—she is the unnamed demon inserted via what Friedkin would call a subliminal cut into a montage of surreal images. Years later, Friedkin would say that dream demon (whom fans have nicknamed Captain Howdy) was a makeup test saved from the trash bin and repurposed for the segment.

Before Dietz came out publicly with her story, she met with Friedkin in his office to discuss how she could use her experience on *The Exorcist* to earn more roles in Hollywood. The conversation went poorly. "He said I would never work again and that he would personally blacklist me and report me to SAG," Dietz told the *Los Angeles Times.* "My husband asked if this was a threat and when Friedkin said yes, we left."

As usual, the no-holds-barred Friedkin was both succinct and savage. "An absolutely disgusting, outright lie by a desperate person," Friedkin said. "All kinds of people have made outlandish claims regarding this picture."

A few days later, Dietz issued a contentious statement, responding to the vicious comments from Friedkin. "*The Exorcist* has turned into a kind of Watergate in that they are trying to cover up who really acted the demon," she wrote. "As everyone knows, hell hath no fury like Mercedes McCambridge denied billing. She performed the demon in the girl's voice. I performed the demon in the girl's body."

Whatever her role in the film, Dietz was within her rights to protest her anonymity clause. To deny her the opportunity simply to tell future casting agents and directors that she had been a part of *The Exorcist* crew was an unusual step, most likely a by-product of Friedkin enshrouding Blair in secrecy to improve her chances of winning an Academy Award. It was one thing to keep Dietz out of the end credits; it was another to insist that her résumé reflect a blank spot of nearly a year. But had Friedkin thought that far ahead when he hired Dietz? It was clear that Friedkin was protecting Blair when he insisted Mercedes McCambridge remain clandestine, but the voice recording was done in postproduction. Dietz, on the other hand, was there from the beginning.

If a wide-ranging profile featured in the *Chicago Tribune* just a few days before *The Exorcist* opened is any indication, Friedkin was obsessed with accolades. "All I can think of is to win again what I've already won," he said. "Winning the Academy Award isn't everything; it's the only thing. It's as important to me as being President." Could that competitive, combative attitude be applied across the board? Not just Best Picture but Best Cinematography, Best Sound Design, Best Editing, and Best Actress?

Instead of retracting her statement, Dietz decided to double down. "I've never been treated like that and called a liar," she told Robert Taylor of the *Oakland Tribune*. "I know what I did. I did every possession scene in the film." That doubtful claim can be disproven by watching the film, where Blair is front and center during most of the demonic mayhem.

But Dietz added professional pride to the equation as well, saying: "When you draw on years of acting experience in order to shake, shriek, spit, vomit, and masturbate with a crucifix without even an honorable mention, you begin to feel a little sorry for yourself."

On the *Barry Gray Show*, a popular radio program aired on WMCA in New York, Friedkin atomized Dietz at the same time as he outlined her (limited) role in the film. "Linda Blair's stand-in, Eileen Dietz, following Mercedes McCambridge's lead, decided to try and build a career on the false claim that she played some of the demonic scenes in the picture. She was a stand-in and a photo double in a handful of scenes that last a few seconds on-screen. Her contribution, ten shots, totaled twenty-eight seconds in a film that runs two hours. It's like when you see a film in which the guys are playing poker and there's a close up of the hands. You use a double for the hands. It's a common practice. Gene Hackman's double was used to a greater extent in *The French Connection* than this girl was used as a double for Linda Blair."

As with most disagreements in Hollywood, lawyers soon arrived on the scene, documents in hand. In this case, they represented Blair, who demanded that the Screen Actors Guild hold an arbitration hearing to determine who deserved credit for what in *The Exorcist*. Dietz demurred, saying that her only goal—to have the gag order lifted—had been achieved. In refusing arbitration, Dietz appeared to be retreating. But the damage had been done. Blair, who believed that an Academy Award had slipped from her grasp, had been undermined by both Dietz and McCambridge, and, to an extent, Friedkin, whose insistence on secrecy was initially inspired by the showbiz ideals of Hitchcock and William Castle but had morphed into deception.

Dietz would go on to rack up over one hundred credits in bit roles ranging from sitcoms (*Happy Days*) to television movies (including *Helter Skelter*) to undistinguished low-budget horror outings. Blair would win a Golden Globe—not an Oscar—for her performance in *The Exorcist*, and, ironically, she would wind up in the same tacky career loop as Dietz in the 1980s and 1990s.

▲ ▲ ▲

There was another figure who fell out with the filmmakers after *The Exorcist* became a sensation. After completing *The Exorcist* in 1970, Blatty took a copy of it to his next-door neighbor Shirley MacLaine. Like Blatty, MacLaine had a hankering for the supernatural, and had regularly conducted séances in her Los Angeles house with Blatty being one of the attendees. They had become friends on the set of *John Goldfarb, Please Come Home*. The quirky MacLaine was a permanent fixture in gossip columns and entertainment magazines, a celebrity whose fame transcended her acting career, which, after more than fifteen years—she debuted in the offbeat Hitchcock comedy *The Trouble with Harry* in 1955—was as eccentric as her personal life, which included an open marriage.

She recognized herself instantly as the inspiration for Chris MacNeil, the independent, carefree, outspoken actress with a salty tongue. "He patterned the protagonist, Chris MacNeil, after me—using my yellow jaguar, the French couple who worked for me, J. Lee Thompson, the director who directed me in *Goldfarb* and *What a Way to Go*, and who had a habit of shredding his scripts and eating them," MacLaine wrote in *Dance While You Can*, her first best-selling memoir.

Apparently, she was not just an inspiration, but a research subject as well. "I remember Bill Friedkin, who directed *The Exorcist*, coming to my apartment in New York while he was shooting with Ellen Burstyn, watching me as I made blueberry pancakes for breakfast," MacLaine wrote. "He checked how I moved, sat, rushed around, even how I cursed with Southern 'eloquency.'"

When Blatty showed MacLaine the completed manuscript, she was intrigued enough to take it to Lew Grade, head of ITC. Grade and MacLaine had a production agreement and were soon to embark on their first feature together, *Desperate Characters*. As an Englishman in his mid-sixties, Grade may not have been attuned to the satanic chic taking over America at the time; he saw limited potential in *The Exorcist* and made a lowball offer to Blatty, who promptly declined. Although MacLaine was now out of *The Exorcist* orbit, she was still fascinated by the supernatural theme and went on to star in *The Possession of Joel Delaney*, an adaptation of another hit occult novel.

A globe-trotting individualist with a liberal streak and zero interest in Catholicism (she was far more attuned to Eastern mysticism), MacLaine soon grew weary of hearing Blatty repeat that he had based Chris MacNeil on her. "Shirley is a good friend of mine," Blatty told the *Philadelphia Inquirer* after MacLaine had already distanced herself from him. "Was a good friend of mine. I always found myself weak at female characterizations. I don't know why, but I always found it a little difficult to put myself inside a woman's head. I mean let's face it, there's a great deal of enigma there. Either through man's ignorance or the complexities of a woman's mind. They're infinitely more complex than I can grasp. At least if I model a female character on a living female, I know that all of her exterior actions, her speech will be authentic. I knew her well, so I thought, 'Why not Shirley?' Shirley even said some of the things I have the mother say in the book."

By dropping her name wherever he went, Blatty, whose waking hours seemed equally devoted to publicizing his film and flaunting his supernatural adventures, was likely trying to raise the profile of *The Exorcist*. MacLaine was a far bigger celebrity than anyone involved in the film (including Friedkin) and piggybacking on her unique fame meant piquing the interest of a much broader audience. "He says he did pattern it after me," MacLaine said. He went around the country saying it. I sort of brought Blatty into the business with *John Goldfarb, Please Come Home*, then he does something like this."

Although MacLaine tolerated her own link to *The Exorcist*, Blatty crossed the line by mentioning her daughter, Satchi, as well. "I don't think he realized what this meant to me and my daughter. They started teasing her in school about having the devil in her."

According to some reports, MacLaine had her lawyers send Blatty a cease-and-desist to keep him from promoting *The Exorcist* franchise, in part, by using her name. Given the marketing strategy devised by the production (playing up the occult, exaggerating tales of possession, etc.), Blatty was probably happier that MacLaine went to the press with her grievances: that was the kind of publicity *The Exorcist* team prized above all.

Her claim, however, that Blatty used a photo of her daughter as the cover image of the original hardback is, to say the least, improbable. A publisher as large as Harper & Row has an entire graphic design department on hand for book covers and interior layouts. Rarely are impromptu photos from amateur shutterbugs used for dust jackets.

Still, MacLaine felt that Blatty had taken advantage of their friendship. "My only experience with the devil," she said, "is Bill Blatty!"

CHAPTER 28

Backlash

hen *The Exorcist* earned ten Academy Award nominations in January 1974, it seemed inevitable that some sort of snafu would ensue: the shifty cast of characters involved in the production, the cloak-and-dagger routines common to Hollywood, and the controversial nature of the film itself all but guaranteed trouble.

Except for *Midnight Cowboy* in 1969, the Academy had rarely been adventurous in its selections. A year before *Midnight* triumphed—a nightmare twelve months in which Martin Luther King Jr. and Robert F. Kennedy were assassinated, riots broke out across America, the Vietnam War continued to rage, and the live-feed mayhem of the Chicago Democratic Convention left television viewers aghast—the Academy selected *Oliver!*, a period musical imported from the UK as Best Picture of 1968.

To make it even more difficult for *The Exorcist*, horror movies had never been an Academy favorite. No horror film had ever won an Oscar for Best Picture, and only a handful produced winners in any other category. Not since the early 1940s, when *Dr. Jekyll and Mr. Hyde* (1941) and *The Phantom of the Opera* (1943) earned multiple Oscar nominations, had the Academy treated horror films with anything close to respect. Even *Psycho*, despite four nominations, failed to win an Academy Award, and *Rosemary's Baby* received two nominations, with only Ruth Gordon winning for Best Supporting Actress.

On April 2, 1974, the 46th Academy Awards ceremony took place at the Dorothy Chandler Pavilion in Los Angeles, California. Of its ten nominations, *The Exorcist* won two: Best Sound (Robert Knudson and Chris Newman) and Best Screenplay Based on Material from Another Medium (Blatty). These muted results sparked a predictably noisy response from William Peter Blatty. "Why don't they wrap it up and pack it in—forget it!" he grumbled to the *Los Angeles Times.* "The Academy should fold its tent and go back to baking apple strudel or whatever they can do well."

Almost immediately, Blatty hinted at a conspiracy, suggesting that aging director George Cukor had spearheaded a backlash against *The Exorcist.* At his self-important best, Blatty speculated as to why Cukor was resistant to the charms of his production. "I think the film has such an emotional impact and is touching a nerve at the same time," he said. "Sometimes that nerve is very raw and we don't want it disturbed. Perhaps Mr. Cukor misunderstood or his nerve was too rawly disturbed, and he didn't appreciate the intrusion forced on him, perhaps, to think about things he doesn't want to contemplate."

Years later, Blatty would explain his outbursts to Bob McCabe. "I was quite crushed, frustrated by it," he said. "The bloom was off the rose when it didn't win Best Picture. And I was a young man and I was foolishly intemperate in my comments about all that right afterwards, which I regret. But I really felt that we were robbed. I mean look at the directorial work— therefore the achievement. How can you compare the winning film that year with what Bill Friedkin did? It was a job every heavyweight director in the country was afraid to tackle, too tough for them. I felt awful."

At the time Blatty made his intemperate comments, he was forty-six years old, inadvertently revealing one of the reasons *The Exorcist* was not a favorite to win in any of the prominent categories: He was insufferable. Blatty and Friedkin, as a duo, had alienated their share of those inside and outside the film industry with an act rarely seen before in a major production. Over and over, Friedkin and Blatty insisted on the transcendent message of their film, displayed their arrogance openly, like war standards on the battlefield, spoke about occult mumbo jumbo with clear commercial motives, and had a cast and crew that insisted the film was cursed. In an essay published in late 1974, Mark Falonga, one of the few enthusiastic critics attached to a film journal (*The Velvet Light Trap*), explained why some of his contemporaries detested *The Exorcist*: "Another entrenched misunderstanding which seems to prevent *The Exorcist* from getting its devilish due involves an overreaction to the obnoxious personality of its original author, William Peter Blatty." This statement applies just as well to the Academy Awards process—even more so, perhaps, considering that Blatty had a tag-team partner (Friedkin) who was loud and abrasive, two characteristics that did not apply to the soft-spoken novelist.

Other reasons for the backlash had to do with the film itself. Despite its Oscar nominations, despite its box-office performance, despite its claims of profundity from its producer and director, *The Exorcist* was still a film that half of the critical establishment found revolting. And, contrary to what Blatty claimed, *The Exorcist* did not meet unanimous approval from religious quarters, either, as if such approval carried cinematic merit. (One of the strangest rationales for peacocking about a film is that ecclesiastical authorities approve of it, yet even at the awards ceremony, before the disappointing results were announced, Friedkin proclaimed: "I've been told by sources in the Vatican that they have seen it and liked it.")

In other words, the chances that some members of the Academy dismissed the film based on a consideration of its virtues were solid. Somehow, Blatty and Co. never thought that the revulsion by half the critical establishment would cross over into the Academy voters. They were wrong. If the Academy members were divided down the middle about *The Exorcist* (as Nat Segaloff reported in *Hurricane Billy: The Stormy Life and Films of William Friedkin*), the possibility of splitting votes among the remaining nominees was automatic. And while you can find many *Exorcist* devotees (including critics) who felt that *The Sting*, a lightweight caper film with overwhelming star power, was an unworthy Best Picture winner in 1973, they rarely mention that *Cries and Whispers* might have earned top honors if the Academy was interested in rewarding artistic merit and not just escapism or special effects.

Such a prospect, one rooted in taste, seemed inconceivable to Blatty. "There's no doubt in my mind that *The Exorcist* is head and shoulders the finest film made this year and in many other years," he said a few days after the ceremony.

(Although it *was* peculiar that the Academy scotched the visual-effects category for 1974; such an unusual move might have simply triggered Blatty, a man who believed he had the supernatural gift of precognition, a man who believed extraterrestrials were responsible for evil, a man who believed that he was some sort of conduit for the spirit world beyond the reach of mere mortals.)

Never to be outdone, Friedkin, decades later, would still bemoan the plot against *The Exorcist*. In a conversation with *Rolling Stone* in 2018, he added Robert Aldrich to the short list of conspirators. "There was a campaign against *The Exorcist* led by Robert Aldrich and George Cukor. The guy who produced the award show that year told me they were going around saying, 'If *The Exorcist* wins Best Picture, it's the end of Hollywood as we know it.' Fuck them. I think there was a lot of resentment and jealousy. Robert Aldrich wanted to direct *The Exorcist*. And I think what bothered Cukor was that the film was disturbing and blasphemous, as well as the fact I had recently won it for a little fucking documentary about two cops."

Imagine George Cukor, who collected Oscar nominations as if they were stamps and whose *My Fair Lady* grossed more than *The Exorcist* (when adjusted for inflation), being jealous of William Friedkin. Similarly, despite an up-and-down career, Aldrich also had more hits than Friedkin, and hits were all that mattered to Friedkin—until he stopped making them. (Unlike Friedkin, neither Cukor nor Aldrich ever suffered a dry spell of nearly thirty years.)

As to Aldrich being named by Friedkin as part of a conspiracy, the public record seems to refute that. "Everyone in Hollywood was disturbed about *The Sting*," Aldrich said in an interview, "because it won the Academy Award over *The Exorcist*, but they shouldn't have been, because if they had any brains they wouldn't take the Academy seriously. The two films are not even in the same league."

As in any industry, particularly one as treacherous as Hollywood, politicking for awards is standard. Just a few years earlier, in 1968, the wretched *Dr. Dolittle* received a Best Picture nomination seemingly based on 20th Century Fox indirectly bribing Academy members. Mark Harris, in his book *Pictures at a Revolution*, described the low-rent process: "In January and February, Fox booked sixteen straight nights of free *Dolittle* screenings at its theater on the lot, and promised dinner and champagne to any voter who showed up." That, apparently, was all it took to sway some Academy members, not necessarily some bitter vendetta waged by a pair of veteran filmmakers.

What irked Friedkin and Blatty, it seemed, was that the politicking in 1974 was not completely in their favor. But Warner Bros. mounted an overwhelming campaign on behalf of Linda Blair in hopes of winning an Oscar. This tactic backfired when entertainment reporter Charles Higham, having heard the whispers about voiceovers, published his explosive interview with Mercedes McCambridge in the *New York Times*. "The studio's infamous attempt to obtain [Blair] the award by denying Mercedes' crucial contribution to her performance was a main reason for my writing the piece," Higham wrote in his book *Celebrity Circus*.

More blunt about the McCambridge controversy were Peter Brown and Jim Pinkston in *Oscar Dearest: Six Decades of Scandal, Politics and Greed Behind Hollywood's Academy Awards, 1927–1986*: "Flaks at Warner Brothers quickly began figuring the box-office draw of an Oscar for Linda and went wild with greed. To ensure its success, the studio carefully erased the identity of a potent though secret ingredient in her performance—the 'voice' of the devil—furnished magnificently by former Oscar winner Mercedes McCambridge."

Whether or not Blair deserved an Oscar is debatable, but the fact remains that contemporary observers doubted her chances of winning, believing that a performance hidden behind effects and makeup, along with a voice-over job by Mercedes McCambridge and confusion about what Eileen Dietz did or did not do, was enough to dash her prospects. "As a result, the members of the Academy may have a devil of a time trying to decide which part of Miss Blair deserves the award, although director Friedkin angrily insists that she earned her nomination," wrote Kathleen Carroll of the New York *Daily News* before the ceremonies took place.

Normally unpretentious and levelheaded, Blair added to the messy record in a 1998 interview with Mark Kermode. "I won the People's Choice; I won the Golden Globe," she said. "Nobody can take that away from me. I was nominated for an Academy Award. But then, all of a sudden, Hollywood's like, wait a minute, we don't want this movie here. And this is what I have read and researched over the years because I really, as an adult, wanted to know what happened. I'm the victim of it, I want to know what happened. Some very prominent directors, with a lot of power, felt that this was a trash film. It shouldn't be here, and if she didn't do the voice, then take away her nomination. I didn't know any of this—I was protected, thank God. But I'm glad as an adult I know the truth behind it because I didn't know why we weren't winning Academy Awards when it was such a brilliant film." The implied upshot—that some Academy members should have voted for a film they thought was trash—is illogical. But little surrounding *The Exorcist* had ever been rational.

A few years after *The Exorcist* flopped at the Oscars, Friedkin would get revenge, of sorts. In a bizarre move, the Academy of Motion Picture Arts and Sciences picked Friedkin to direct its 49th annual ceremonies for ABC. On March 29, 1977, the Academy Awards broadcast foreshadowed his decline: the production was a bomb. "I made a lot of mistakes during the show," Friedkin told Nat Segaloff, "and I think, ultimately, it was not a good show. It was a debacle."

PART IV

THE NIGHT-MARE CONTINUES

CHAPTER 29

The Downward Spiral of
William Friedkin

I n the mid-1990s, as the twenty-fifth anniversary of *The Exorcist* approached, William Friedkin was at his nadir. After a string of disasters, the former New Hollywood holy terror, who had won an Oscar for Best Director when he was thirty-six, had been driven to music videos (Laura Branigan, Wang Chung, Barbara Streisand) and the wasteland of television. This was before the era of Peak TV, and calling "Action!" on *The Twilight Zone, C.A.T. Squad*, and *Rebel Highway* could hardly compare to working on *The Sopranos* or *Breaking Bad*.

A streak of flops going back to *Sorcerer* (1977) even included a turn at a straight horror movie (Friedkin had always denied that *The Exorcist* was a lowly genre film), *The Guardian*, a ludicrous 1990 potboiler about a nanny who sacrifices babies to a killer tree. *The Guardian* was excoriated when it was released, drawing keywords no director ever wants to see in type: inept, absurd, stupid, cheap, et cetera.

But mixed reviews had greeted most of his films since the dawn of the 1980s, with only *Cruising* and *To Live and Die in L.A.* inspiring more than just reflex dismissal. In fact, *Cruising* inspired outrage from gay activists for its seedy depiction of the long-since-vanished leather scene, and *To Live and Die in L.A.* produced its share of admirers awed by a 1980s aesthetic so hyperreal it had to be deliberate.

A glossy, raucous MTV take on *The French Connection, To Live and Die in L.A.* inadvertently highlighted, via unflattering comparison, just how far Friedkin had fallen from his peak. Where *The French Connection* reveled in raw, ad-libbed dialogue, *TLDLA* bursts with television-cop banalities; where the car chase in *The French Connection* was an exhilarating one-man show with a few other vehicles involved as collateral damage, *TLDLA* featured a chase that included several guns, a train, multiple vehicles in pursuit, forklifts, pallets, 18-wheelers, and a packed freeway that ultimately hosts an impromptu demolition derby. In some ways, *To Live and Die in L.A.* doubled as a case study on the differences between 1970s film principles and those of the gaudy 1980s, when everything was bigger, faster, louder.

And yet, between the seemingly endless stock scenes found in nearly every vigilante-cop film, *TLDLA* is bursting with vivid sequences and ideas that often short-circuit in execution but nonetheless linger long after the closing credits. The enigmatic Eric Masters (played by an eerily magnetic Willem Defoe), a painter who moonlights as a counterfeiter (or is it the other way around?), is an unforgettable villain. Masters sets fire to his canvases after completing them—a nod to the Auto-Destructive Art movement of Gustav Metzger, perhaps, or the Cremation Project of L.A.–based painter John Baldessari—while his nihilistic demeanor gives Masters a gravitas most celluloid criminals lack.

A procedural montage of Defoe in action as a counterfeiter is spellbinding and suggests the wordless, bravura sequences of criminal operations staged by Robert Bresson (*A Man Escaped*), Jean-Pierre Melville (*The Red Circle*), and Jules Dassin (*Rififi*).

The wrong-side-of-the-tracks location shooting, exposing tumbledown areas of a sprawling city depicted as a glitter zone throughout the 1980s, is both inspired and determined. This is not the sparkling dream-factory Los Angeles of the Sunset Strip or Hollywood Boulevard, but the marginal edges, rarely seen on a $6 million dollar budget, the kind of desolate spots where Richard Ramirez, The Night Stalker, might have mainlined, or where The Hillside Stranglers might have plotted their next atrocity.

While *The Exorcist* is a cynically made film—with audience manipulation baked into every frame—*TLDLA* is cynicism personified. Without a single admirable character (except for Sam Elliot, whose screen time is curtailed by the plot), and with a sprawling body count, *TLDLA* remains, along with *Sorcerer*, the bleak personal signature of a filmmaker who has steadfastly denied the notion of the auteur.

Ultimately, it is his commercial instinct that leads Friedkin astray. Full of overblown incidents, foot chases, confrontations, beatings, wisecracks, and explosions, *TLDLA* sags beneath the cliché scenes of the rebel cop that go back at least to *Dirty Harry* and, of course, *The French Connection*.

A middling critical response notwithstanding, *TLDLA* was one of the few post-*Exorcist* films Friedkin directed that did not lose money. His next project, *Rampage*, was shot in 1986, but when its producer (and distributor) De Laurentiis Entertainment Group went bankrupt, the film remained in limbo for nearly six years.

His big-budget comeback began after his wife, Sherry Lansing, became head of Paramount Pictures. For Paramount, Friedkin directed *Blue Chips* in 1994, a basketball film that failed to match *Hoosiers* by any metric, and, a year later, *Jade*, a debacle that would stain his reputation in more ways than one.

An erotic thriller scripted by Joe Eszterhas, at the time the hottest, if tawdriest, screenwriter in Hollywood, *Jade* failed even by the lewd and lowdown standards of its genre. Sparked by the VHS revolution and the explosion of cable channels, the erotic thriller filled a niche for racy content far more respectable than the offerings of sleazy porno theaters, hard-core video cassettes, and issues of *Hustler* or *Penthouse*. Cinemax, Showtime, the direct-to-video market, and the ubiquitous TV movies released by everyone from ABC to the Lifetime Channel all produced glossy mysteries, thrillers, and suspense films with a healthy quota of steamy sex scenes. The hazy cinematography came from Brian De Palma, the pulpy plots from tabloid headlines, and the actors from the D-list. In 1987, *Fatal Attraction*, a stylish celluloid warning against adultery and bipolar women, kick-started the market for criminal titillation, but it was *Basic Instinct* (1992)—garish, convoluted, self-aware, and also scripted by Eszterhas—that spawned clones at every level of the industry.

When Paramount announced that they had signed Friedkin to helm *Jade*, they simultaneously issued what amounted to anticipatory denials about nepotism. Producer Robert Evans and Eszterhas insisted that Friedkin was the perfect choice for *Jade*.

Even in Hollywood, where underhanded deals were a way of life, this convenient arrangement raised heretofore cynical eyebrows throughout Tinseltown. For someone who had embodied the New Hollywood ethos of defiance and risk, a man who had dared studios to fire him, being a coddled member of the industry elite was a bizarre time-warp moment. Other filmmakers from that era had burned out (Rafelson, Cimino, Bogdanovich,

Penn), died (Ashby), vanished (Terence Malick), hit rough patches (Pakula, De Palma, Altman, Schatzberg, Coppola), or found continued success (Mazursky, Scorsese, Spielberg), but none became de facto cogs of the studio machine they had tried to overthrow just twenty years earlier.

To lessen negative publicity, Lansing decided she would have to do some preemptive damage control. So she approached Eszterhas, whose *Jade* screenplay had reportedly cost her $4 million. "I was flattered but I smelled what was coming," Eszterhas wrote in his scorched-earth memoir *Hollywood Animal*. "Sherry was married to Billy Friedkin, who desperately needed a hit movie—*The Exorcist* and *The French Connection* were so very many years ago." Lansing convinced Eszterhas to supply trade reporters with adulatory boilerplate about Friedkin in exchange for what a baseball general manager would call "future considerations."

And how did Billy Friedkin repay Eszterhas for such kindness? He mutilated the screenplay.

This brazen double-cross so incensed Eszterhas that he told Lansing he would expose their informal agreement about publicly glad-handing Friedkin a year earlier. "Blackmail" is not a word used among the smart set in Hollywood, at least not as recently as the 1990s, but a leveraged position often pays off. On August 26, 1995, the *Los Angeles Times* reported: "Paramount Pictures has agreed to pay Hollywood screenwriter Joe Eszterhas $2 million for a blind script commitment. If the movie is actually made, Eszterhas can potentially earn $4 million, sources said." Most likely, that blind script was for something called "Male Pattern Baldness," a property that was never developed.

As for the movie itself, *Jade* was a fiasco, earning less than one-fifth of its $50 million budget during its theatrical run. VHS sales and rentals were also negligible, and the DVD version went out of print almost instantaneously. Despite two hot names headlining (the sultry Linda Fiorentino and David Caruso, fresh off *NYPD Blue*), and the promise of serious kink, *Jade* could not overcome its ham-fisted direction. Disjointed, confusing, and cliché-ridden—it was as if Friedkin had lost the ability to create a streamlined narrative. Coherence had never been a strong suit for him, but *Jade* was so convoluted that it was recut after a screening for critics. Finding a kind review of *Jade* in 1995 was like finding a Picasso in the Museum of Bad Art.

Jade seemed like the end of the road for Friedkin, only sixty years old but steadily declining since the early 1980s. In *Easy Riders, Raging Bull*,

Friedkin made a stark confession of his failures. "I never set out to make a bad film," he said. "I thought in each case they were going to be as good or better than anything I had done. I went through this long period of wondering why I wasn't being received in the same way. Now I've reached the point where I know why. These films just weren't any fucking good. They have no soul, no heart. They don't even have any technical expertise. It's as though someone reached up inside an animal and pulled the guts out. The thing that drove me and still keeps me going is *Citizen Kane*. I hope to one day make a film to rank with that. I haven't yet."

Two years after *Jade*, Friedkin staged a made-for-television reboot of *Twelve Angry Men* for the cable network Showtime. And then—

In 1998, *The Exorcist* was rereleased in England.

CHAPTER 30

Pazuzu Returns

In 1974, when it opened in England, *The Exorcist* received an X rating from the British Board of Film Classification (BBFC, with the "C" originally standing for Censors), which was unsurprising. What was surprising, however, was the fact that it passed into theaters without a single excision.

The notoriously squeamish British censors had been banning and mutilating horror imports since the heyday of Universal. Indeed, in response to the influx of vampires, mountebanks, werewolves, ghouls, and mad scientists, the BBFC established an H rating—specifically targeting horror films. That was in 1932. During World War II, horror films were banned outright in the UK because of their potential to lower morale.

More than thirty years after the initial Universal cycle, the BBFC apparently found *The Exorcist* less objectionable than *The Island of Lost Souls*. Secretary of the BBFC Stephen Murphy justified the clean X at the time: "It is a powerful horror movie. Some people may dislike it, but that is not a sufficient reason for refusing certification."

For *The Exorcist*, censorship troubles would come a decade later, when the Video Recording Act (VRA) became law in England and introduced oversight of films for home viewing. This brief puritan era that targeted material deemed obscene even saw police raiding video stores to clear the shelves of objectionable films. In 1988, after a lengthy review process, *The Exorcist* was essentially banned from the VHS market in England.

Despite years of appeals from Warner Bros., the BBFC refused to grant *The Exorcist* a reprieve. Speaking to film critic Mark Kermode, BBFC secretary James Ferman said: "The problem with *The Exorcist* is not that it's a bad film but that it's a very good film. It's one of the most powerful films ever made, and it is its power that's the problem on video. The fact is that you're importing it into children's homes, and probably into children's bedrooms, because now more than 50 per cent of children in Britain have TVs in their bedrooms and many of them have a video player as well."

Occasional midnight shows and revivals played throughout England, but *The Exorcist* was becoming a distant memory when the BBC released a twenty-fifth-anniversary documentary called *Fear of God*. Presented by Mark Kermode, *Fear of God* reintroduced the raw eeriness of *The Exorcist* and the tribulations (both real and imagined) behind the scenes. Once again, in more depth than ever, the stories of curses, misfortunes, ingenuity, and conflict (as well as the same spiritual pseudo-profundities) aired to a receptive public.

As she would in her 2006 memoir *Lessons in Becoming Myself*, Ellen Burstyn insisted that malevolent powers had invaded the set and had targeted the entire crew. "It deals with very heavy forces," she said about *The Exorcist*. "And I was a little worried about what that would mean to work with those forces."

Linda Blair recounted some of her ordeals during the production, including a matter-of-fact retelling of her painful bed-thrashing scene. "That's the footage they used in the movie," she said, "where I'm crying my eyes out because they are brutally damaging my back."

Despite knowing that the Hunkeler case had earned its notoriety through his misinformation campaign, Blatty continued lying about its veracity in his usual theological word salad: "My exploration, looking back on it now—it didn't occur to me at the time—but my exploration of this subject matter, digging and digging and digging to find proof that, yes, this happened; this wasn't made up. This occurred, and we have no explanation for it. No one has yet to offer an explanation for it based upon the material universe. And that was all grounded in the terror of total obliteration, of death. That's what that was all about. I mean, it was a personal pilgrimage of my own."

The irascible Friedkin, whose chaotic 1970s peak had just been chronicled by Peter Biskind in the book *Easy Riders, Raging Bulls*, reappears, a glint of mischief in his eye as he recounts the adventures (some of them even true) of directing one of the most controversial films in American history.

Outtakes and reconstructed scenes from the film, locked away for a quarter of a century, might have given Friedkin a spark. These scenes included the spider walk that had long tantalized fans via rumors and the sit-down between Karras and Merrin to illustrate thematic points.

It was what followed the release of *Fear of God*, however, that set the stage for a new version of *The Exorcist*.

When *The Exorcist* was given a wide rerelease in England in October 1998, it shocked everyone by shooting to the top of the box office, even surpassing the opening grosses of big-budget Hollywood pabulum such as *Lethal Weapon 4*, *Deep Impact*, and *Rush Hour*. This unexpected success gave an opening for Warner Bros. to exploit a dormant property further, for William Friedkin to vault back into center stage, and for William Peter Blatty to see his moralism, at last, on the silver screen, where he always knew it belonged.

CHAPTER 31

▲ ▲ ▲

Millennium: Restoring
The Exorcist

Thanks to the stunning box-office performance of *The Exorcist* in
England and the lost footage Warner Bros. had unearthed for *Fear of
God*, all the creative and commercial parties involved in the original
film convened to plot an alternate version. Finally, after more than
twenty years of bitterness, William Peter Blatty persuaded Friedkin to allow
him into the editing room.

Despite his open disdain for the theological messaging Blatty obsessed
over, Friedkin agreed to reassemble, as best he could, *The Exorcist* according to the original cut, which had come in at two hours and eleven minutes.
"I was quite willing to let the film stand," he told the *Los Angeles Times*.
"What I originally cut out was strictly for length and pacing and because I
didn't think the spirituality needed to be spelled out. I thought the audience
got it. Blatty insisted they didn't."

When Friedkin finally agreed to revisit the film, he reversed course on
nearly everything he had said since 1973, not only about *The Exorcist* but
about several of his cinematic principles. "But again, I believe that *The
Exorcist* is a kind of masterpiece and it's defined in a way as much by what's
left out as what is included," he told Bob McCabe, explaining why he had no
interest in reliving the past.

To justify this new version of his "masterpiece," Friedkin claimed that
his aesthetic viewpoint had evolved since 1973, but his cinematic vision
from 1995 to 2003, just before and just after the rerelease of *The Exorcist*,
hardly seemed any different than his outlook of the previous two decades.

Jade is full of inanities and has the requisite car chase. In addition, with its senseless plot, *Jade* saw Friedkin once again mistake confusion for ambiguity. *The Hunted*, his 2003 bomb, was pure sensation, with less character development or backstory than an episode of *The A-Team*. Only *Rules of Engagement* (a tepid courtroom drama described by film critic Elvis Mitchell "as a movie that is basically like the world's most expensive episode of the television show *JAG*") might qualify as a change of pace for Friedkin—and not for the better. Meant to be a crowd-pleaser, *Rules of Engagement* was pure popcorn fare, its flagrant messaging bordering on jingoism. If it had not been clear before, scale was a problem for Friedkin, whose inability to assemble a coherent narrative seemed linked to the size of the film budget. Essentially, Friedkin had not changed aesthetically or emotionally, so what led him to revisit *The Exorcist*, his last hit?

On September 22, 2002, *The Exorcist: The Version You've Never Seen* opened to generous, if not wide, release nationwide. Along with its ungainly title, the film featured an extra eleven minutes of restored footage. More than a quarter of a century after its debut, *The Exorcist* would once again prove its box-office staying power, ultimately grossing more than $100 million globally.

Among his many distinctions, William Friedkin is also one of only a few directors to oversee a revised version of a film that is inferior to the original. After all, Friedkin had final cut over *The Exorcist* in 1973 (when Blatty complained to studio heads about his beloved theological scenes remaining on the cutting-room floor, they declined to intervene), and he had not suffered from the kind of heavy-handed corporate interference that had mutilated films by Erich Von Stroheim, Fritz Lang, Orson Welles, Arthur Penn, Sam Peckinpah, nearly everyone who directed under Howard Hughes at RKO, and countless others. A film such as *Blade Runner*, with its seemingly endless iterations, differs from *The Exorcist* because producers butchered what Ridley Scott had originally delivered. Subsequent revisions of *Blade Runner* left Scott out of the equation, for the most part, until 2007, when he personally assembled the definitive version. By contrast, the original *Exorcist* was repeatedly deemed a masterpiece by Friedkin, who also clarified that he felt what Blatty wanted verged on sermonizing. "Some of the scenes, I felt, were simply overstated and preachy when I looked at them, specifically the scene where Father Merrin tells Father Karras what this all means," Friedkin told Bob McCabe. "There were other scenes where Blatty had the characters telling each other what the meaning was. And it seemed to me, when I made the film, that the meaning was inherent in every frame. I didn't want some guy explaining it in the picture to some other character in the film and ultimately to the audience. I felt it needed no explanation. Like magic realism—there it is."

In the 2000 version of *The Exorcist*, the change in tone is immediately apparent. Instead of opening on the entrancing image of the shimmering sun and the voice of a muezzin singing the Muslim call to prayer, we see the exterior of the MacNeil residence at night, an establishing shot straight out of an episode of *Seinfeld* or *Friends*. The subsequent boom shot glides from the bedroom window down to the street (mimicking the future plunges of Burke Dennings and Father Karras) before halting with the blazing streetlamp in the frame. What follows is a cut to the Virgin Mary statue, impassive and not yet defiled, and then the title cards.

With this prologue before the prologue, Friedkin could not make his intentions any clearer: instead of beginning with the challenging use of film grammar—including the symbolism of the sun, an oblique reference to the theme of the film ("God is great," sings the muezzin), and the electrifying montage sequence of the Iraq scene—he has kicked off *The Exorcist* with conventional tropes and hopes. This gratuitous prologue seems to announce: You Are About to Witness Very Important Things.

In addition to reinserting some of the weakest Blatty dogma, Friedkin also abused technological advances to bludgeon viewers over the head with images meant to reinforce themes so obvious they made Blatty look subtle by comparison. Several CGI images of demons superimposed (sometimes obtrusively, sometimes unobtrusively) in various scenes are often close to comical.

Not only are the CGI projections hokey, but they also completely undercut any reading of possible ambiguity—an element that Friedkin insisted he had deliberately crafted in keeping with his stated philosophy of open-ended narratives. In the earlier version, the head-spinning scenes were enough to dispel most thoughts of ambiguity—at that point, Regan is clearly not suffering from some form of conversion disorder—but Friedkin insisted on the possibility of multiple readings.

"I made the film in a way that it could very definitely not be possession," he told *Cinefantastique*. "There are very clear-cut things in the movie that indicate that what you are seeing is always from someone's point of view and from someone in an extremely heightened state of mind. There is a shot, for example, of the apparition of the demon Pazuzu appearing in the room that both priests, or one or the other, may be seeing. Now I don't say that the demon Pazuzu was in the room, I'm saying that it's possible, given the background, the training, and the upbringing of these priests, that they may be victims of momentary insanity. The mother in a heightened condition may be contributing to what they are seeing and calling it supernatural. There are several explanations which the film leaves open."

These claims of ambiguity are iffy at best, especially since the head-spinning and skin branding are viewed by multiple characters. In 2000, however, any kind of hallucinatory reading was impossible. There is no mistaking that a supernatural agency controls events once flash cuts of "Captain Howdy" are introduced while Dr. Klein is examining Regan or images of Pazuzu are shot onto range hoods in the kitchen and on doorways, like the film projections at an *Exploding Plastic Inevitable* happening.

One of the worst instances of Friedkin overdoing CGI involved the sequence in which Karras commits suicide. In the original cut, when the demon possesses Karras, he hurls himself through the window to a violent death on the steps below. The 2000 version, however, not only uses CGI to make Karras look more fiendish but it also gives us a billowy, superimposed image of Mrs. Karras hovering over the window, seeming to suggest a panoply of interpretations—all of them maudlin. Is the ghostly presence of Mrs. Karras advising Karras on what to do? Is she promising Karras that they will meet in the afterlife (an idea Friedkin might have picked up from Blatty, who was forever contacting spirits from the Beyond)? Is it a hint of mercy for his impending suicide, which is, after all, a mortal sin in the eyes of the Catholic Church?

Even Blatty, ecstatic over the updated version of *The Exorcist*, seemed unsure about the effect. "Billy added a quasi-subliminal flash, a near-subliminal, into that scene. When the bedroom curtains billow out, there's a face flashed, and it's Karras's mother. I was very worried that the audience would think that Father Karras then commits suicide over his guilt about his mother, but Billy insisted, and it's still in the revised version."

Using CGI liberally also meant undermining his original insistence, more than twenty-five years earlier, of avoiding camera tricks and optics. In 1973, Friedkin had already used a matte shot for the projectile-vomit scene and a dissolve for Karras falling prey to Pazuzu, so his claims of eschewing optical effects never withstood scrutiny. Rudimentary effects such as super-impositions had existed as far back as the Lumiere Brothers and were comparable in quality to the kitschy projections Friedkin inserted ad hoc into *TVYNS*. Yet Friedkin limited these optical effects in the original version of *The Exorcist*. More than twenty-five years later, why would he resort to CGI masks on Regan and several spotlight appearances of Captain Howdy? There is the distinct possibility that Friedkin thought he needed to supercharge the shocks for a new generation already accustomed to the outrages of *I Spit on Your Grave*, *Friday the 13th*, *Maniac*, *Evil Dead*, and *Pieces*, along with the technical advances of special effects reflected by *The Howling*, *The Thing*, *A Nightmare on Elm Street*, and *The Fly*. By 2000, horror films were largely CGI affairs with casts composed of nondescript (but photogenic) twenty-somethings. Only a year or two later, the genre spawned frenetic light shows based on video games, and the sensory overload of the early aughts may have forced Friedkin to modernize. As a result, the 2000 version of *The Exorcist* occasionally veers into direct-to-video territory. (Friedkin seemed to acknowledge this when an Extended Director's Cut hit the market in 2010—some of the ludicrous demon imagery had been removed.)

Of the material inserted into the revision, the sequence of Regan undergoing her first medical examination and meeting Dr. Klein is most justified. It returns continuity and logic to a narrative that veered abruptly from Regan having fun at the party to her urinating on the carpet just before offering a cryptic warning to a guest. The next time we see Regan, her appearance presents a major hole in the plot. Nobody, including critics as harsh as John Simon and Pauline Kael, pointed out what William Peter Blatty did—repeatedly—about this continuity blunder. "Any craftsman seeing that picture has got to get a case of the giggles when you go to the party scene and there's Regan, laughing," Blatty told Thomas D. Clagett. "She's happy. She urinates on the rug. A minute later, she says, 'Mother, what's wrong with me?' And Chris says, 'It's nerves like the doctor said'—what doctor?—'You keep taking your pills.' What pills? Movies are magical, and you don't have to do exposition on everything, but this was just unacceptable."

With his insistence on a relentless pace and a two-hour running time, Friedkin was willing to sacrifice logic to meet his ends, and he later acknowledged that a slower tempo might have helped. "Overall, I think that the gradual evolution of Regan's 'disease' is handled a lot better in this new cut," Friedkin told Mark Kermode. "You get much more of a sense of the slow onslaught of whatever is affecting this girl. The stuff we've put back in provides a better foundation for the concern of her mother and of the doctors, but it also says something about the medical establishment's willingness to resort to prescription drugs." (It should be noted that this is the kind of sociological comment that both Friedkin and Blatty previously denied being interested in conveying.)

The famous "spider walk" scene was the centerpiece of the rerelease and the marketing strategy for Warner Bros.—all new chills promised to viewers who may not have gotten enough shocks from the original. Glimpsed publicly for the first time as an outtake in *The Fear of God*, the spider walk existed in two versions. In one, Regan scuttles down the stairs backward, flicks out an elongated tongue, and begins chasing Sharon around the house, nipping at her ankles. The second version depicts Regan stopping at the bottom steps and opening her mouth for an outpouring of blood.

While there is some confusion as to why the spider-walk scene never appeared in the first cut, with Friedkin finally settling on the practical flaw of the wire rigging being visible on-screen, special-effects man Marcel Vercoutere told *Fangoria* that the shock set piece might have been considered overkill: "I think it was too much. Friedkin didn't know how far to take it. He didn't want a film people would laugh at. Besides, that scene was kinda bloody, when she bites someone. Blood was running down all over her face because she was upside down at the time."

Friedkin also cited the gratuitousness of the scene. "I just didn't think it worked for a lot of different reasons," Friedkin told Bob McCabe in 1998. "One, it was one more visual effect that we didn't need, one that really stretched credulity. For example, why is she walking like a spider? In all of the other scenes Reagan is basically a victim of the attack by the demon. And in that scene she is flaunting her demon-ness and I thought we were dealing with a story here that was stretching credulity enough at every turn. Why ask for more?"

The real problem with the spider-walk scene, however, is how out of place it feels, highlighting its patched-in nature. There is no follow-up to the spider walk, and its sudden end, via smash to black, stresses the cut-and-paste impression the sequence gives. Worse, the spider walk jars the narrative and introduces one of those incongruities often found in B-films when the money has run out, or a can of film has been misplaced. After showing superhuman agility to scuttle down the stairs in a physically impossible way and then gushing blood from her mouth, Regan is next seen, almost laughably, sitting in a chair for a hypnosis session with a therapist. Not even in Hollywood fantasyland could such a chronology exist.

During the therapy hypnotism scene, Friedkin uses a demonic CGI flash to alter her features, clumsily alerting the viewer that Regan is now, like the Incredible Hulk, transforming into full-possession mode. Apparently, the spider walk and the stream of blood from her mouth were not enough of a clue that whatever ailed Regan was not of this earth.

Further additions should have remained in the vaults. For example, a scene in which Sharon puts on earphones to block out the sounds of Regan screaming adds little to the narrative, either thematically or visually. Thankfully, no one could find the sound reel for the scene where, in front of the Tomb of the Unknown Soldier, Linda Blair asks her mother to explain why people die, a cringeworthy bit straight out of an *ABC Afterschool Special* and an example of just how trite Blatty could be. A similarly mawkish scene occurred in the novel, when Chris and Burke Dennings have an earnest discussion about God and mortality that would embarrass most YA readers.

As with the 1979 rerelease of *The Exorcist*, which featured Dolby (nonexistent in 1973), Friedkin primarily concerned himself with sound design, an acknowledgment, of sorts, that what makes *The Exorcist* most nerve-racking is the carefully selected clamor emerging from the speaker systems. The new version of the film underwent yet another sonic overhaul, this one a digital upgrade in Surround EX, with the help of Steve Boeddeker of Skywalker Sound.

In his mixed review of *TVYNS*, Roger Ebert suggested that Friedkin had rereleased *The Exorcist* for one reason only: money. "While these scenes may have various rationales in the minds of Friedkin and Blatty, they have one obvious rationale in the thinking at the studio: They provide an excuse for the theatrical rerelease, and will help sell the video, even to those who already own the earlier version," Ebert wrote.

An angry Friedkin phoned Ebert and responded with his usual mix of bombast and embellishment, claiming that Warner Bros. was against the rerelease. Whether Friedkin said this with a straight face is unknown, but Warner Bros. refusing to exploit an existing property is almost laughable. Warner Bros. had released *The Exorcist* in various remunerative iterations over the years: at least two theatrical encores (in 1976 and 1979), licensing to HBO, CBS, local stations, basic cable and other pay channels such as Showtime, releases on VHS, Betamax, and Laserdisc, including two different VHS and DVD editions for the twenty-fifth anniversary of the film.

A new version of *The Exorcist*, a film that opened as the top money-maker in the United Kingdom in October 1998—without a single altered frame—would only add to the bottom line.

In 1979, Warner Bros. had forked over at least $150,000 for a rerelease of *The Exorcist*, and this decision was based solely on a Dolby remix of the soundtrack. Yet Friedkin would have the public believe that Warner Bros. was uninterested in tapping the VHS and DVD market again after seeing—and benefiting from—the surprise windfall from the United Kingdom in 1998.

That spark of interest seemed to spur Friedkin into altering a film he once said could not be improved. At that time, late 1998, Friedkin had directed three films in the 1990s; all were flops, and two were full-fledged critical disasters. But the successful rerelease of *The Exorcist* served as a springboard back into big-budget filmmaking. Even as *The Rules of Engagement*—a $60 million production once again released under the watchful eye of his wife at Paramount—sputtered at the box office, Friedkin was sifting through scripts.

In 2003, Friedkin directed his last major Hollywood film. Top-lined by Tommy Lee Jones and Benicio Del Toro, *The Hunt* crashed and burned as well, earning such epithets as "stupid," "brain-dead," and "schlock" along the way. Warner Bros. fared much better. Less than two years after releasing multiple versions of *The Exorcist* (regular and deluxe editions on both VHS and DVD), Warner Home Video cleaned up on a DVD (and other ancillary licensing deals) of the 2000 version.

▲ ▲ ▲

If Ebert decided to retreat from his claim of commercial motivation, he never retracted his opinion about what made *TVYNS* an inferior version of *The Exorcist*: its schmaltzy end, tacked on seemingly to comply with some sort of unspoken quota for "extra" material. "An ending that struck the perfect closing now has been replaced by one that jars and clangs and thumbs its nose at the film," Ebert wrote.

Friedkin had despised the original finale in the shooting script: Father Dyer and Lt. Kinderman walking off together, à la Casablanca, to begin a beautiful friendship. "I thought it was a lame way to end this movie," he said. "It's the ending in the book and it's very good, but the whole scene was nothing but a pastiche on the last scene of *Casablanca*. I filmed it and I cut it. But I said, 'Bill, why do we want to end our movie like *Casablanca*, using the dialogue of *Casablanca*? This is an original movie. Why hang the reference out there like that?" That quote, spoken to Bob McCabe, was only a few years before *The Version You've Never Seen* was released.

Ultimately, "lame" was not enough of a descriptor for Friedkin. "I shot that ending, and it was no fucking good at all," he said. "It was so anticlimactic for this picture. It worked very well in the novel as a sort of nostalgic and upbeat ending, but I didn't like it in the film, so I cut it."

In his 2011 book *Shock Value*, Jason Zinoman describes how up-and-coming horror filmmakers viewed the ending of *Psycho* as a letdown and a cop-out. "The most serious grudge that horror directors hung onto was that Hitchcock ruined *Psycho* when he explained the madness of Norman Bates in the final scene," he writes. "Much of the movie attempted to see life through the eyes of a psychotic, but when the police caught Norman and locked him in a room for questioning, Hitchcock returned to a more comforting point of view—the safety of a diagnosis from the medical establishment."

One of the directors Zinoman quotes about the disappointing ending of *Psycho* is William Friedkin. "If you took the scene out and you end on just Norman Bates, with Bernard Herrmann's music, it would have iced people in a way that it did not. Most intelligent people do not want simple answers."

When an interviewer for *Cinefantastique* commented on how Alfred Hitchcock rarely explained events or motivations, Friedkin responded: "Except for *Psycho* at the end, with that lousy, gratuitous explanation directed at a ten-year-old mind."

But by inserting the explanatory scene between Father Merrin and Father Karras during an exorcism time-out, Friedkin offered the same simple answers; and in the new ending between Father Dyer and Lt. Kinderman, he went further—providing an insipid sequence meant only to reassure. A by-product of the *Casablanca* scene is that it undercuts the gravitas of the previous one hundred twenty minutes to introduce levity and hint at the artifice of the narrative.

Still, the allure of *The Exorcist* remained, based not only on its initial reputation for everything from blasphemy to causing freak-outs, but now with its mystique revitalized by recent twenty-fifth-anniversary retrospectives and the documentary *Fear of God*. In 2000, *The Exorcist* was once again a box-office success.

If possible, Blatty was even more arrogant than in 1973, when he at least acknowledged friction during the production and criticized the final cut as merely a mechanical effort. Now, in light of his original vision finally being released, his pronouncements were tinged with a pomposity surprising even coming from a man who believed his novel had been some sort of gift to believers and nonbelievers alike. "Behind all the cynicism of the young today, there is a hunger for spiritual truth," Blatty said. "They're out there, waiting for it. Well, it's here."

CHAPTER 32

▲ ▲ ▲

In the Wake: Imitations and Sequels

While Hollywood has traditionally been known as a dream factory, it is also an assembly line specializing in imitations. More than anything, this explains the genre cycles that come and go every few years. To Hollywood, a proven formula is worth repeating until the box-office receipts finally taper off.

When *Jaws* became a surprise blockbuster, every sea predator imaginable headlined its own film—as well as a few other animals (such as alligators and snakes) associated with aquatic environments—and *Star Wars* produced the dreaded space opera, reviving *Star Trek* and introducing the world to *Krull* and *The Ice Pirates*.

Gangster films, romances, musicals, melodramas, war epics, and Westerns—broader categories—were joined by, among dozens of others, science fiction, juvenile delinquents, motorcycles, LSD, rock 'n' roll, beach culture, spies, kung fu, nunsploitation, CB radio flicks, vigilante, skateploitation, slasher films, neo-noirs, erotic thrillers, and yuppies in peril outings. One of the longest cycles in Hollywood history lasted for over a decade: the celebrity-stacked disaster film, which kicked off, noisily, with *Airport* in 1970 and continued until it became a target for parody in *Airplane!* (1980).

Not long after *The Exorcist* opened, the satanic and occult imitations materialized like spirits from an unusually productive Ouija board. Most of them came from Europe, particularly Italy and Spain, two countries that had produced satanic melodramas years before *The Exorcist* appeared. A few titles released while *The Exorcist* still played in theaters included

Beyond the Door, *Demon Witch Child*, *The Antichrist*, *The Sexorcist*, and *Night Child*. One of the most infamous *Exorcist* carbon copies of all, a Blaxploitation knockoff called *Abby*, disappeared from theaters after Warner Bros. sued the producer for copyright infringement.

ITC rereleased *The Possession of Joel Delaney*, hoping to draw stragglers unable to score tickets to *The Exorcist*. Giallo virtuoso Mario Bava assented to having new cornball exorcism scenes featuring Elke Sommer spliced into his 1973 phantasmagoria *Lisa and the Devil*, retitled *The House of Exorcism* for the American market.

Although *The Exorcist* spawned a widespread subgenre, only *The Omen* succeeded as a major studio release in the mid-1970s, when the satanic/possession cycle still had legs. *The Amityville Horror*, more of a traditional, if unintentionally funny, ghost story, outgrossed *Alien*, *Rocky II*, and *Apocalypse Now* in 1979. But the demonic possession film became a rare sighting in the Eighties and Nineties. In *Nightmare Movies: Horror on Screen Since the 1960s*, Kim Newman noted how poorly *The Exorcist* fared in kick-starting a cycle. "Big-budget *Exorcist* followers, including *The Manitou*, *The Omen*, and *The Sentinel* (1977) find so little worth stealing from Friedkin's film that they return to *Rosemary's Baby* and pilfer its plot instead. *The Exorcist* subgenre burned out instantly. Recently, only *Amityville II: The Possession* and *Mausoleum* (1983) have bothered to lift any of its trappings."

It took until 2005, with the successful release of *The Exorcism of Emily Rose*, for a new cycle to begin and, with it, dependable returns. From 2005 to 2022, nearly two dozen exorcism films have hit the US market, produced by major studios, cable channels, and streaming platforms looking for cheap content for subscribers.

Despite being one of the most profitable films in history, *The Exorcist* never developed a successful franchise. What followed in its wake, sequels and prequels, were utter catastrophes. *Exorcist II: The Heretic* was dumbfounding in its awfulness, all the more so because a major talent directed it: John Boorman. A fiasco from conception to filming to wrap, *Heretic* inspired some opening-day theatergoers to hurl debris at the screen. "There is a very strong possibility," wrote the cantankerous John Simon, "that *The Exorcist II* is the stupidest major movie ever made." (Always the contrarian, Pauline Kael spitefully preferred *Heretic* over the original *Exorcist*.)

If any film had earned the right to be called "cursed," it was *Heretic*, whose behind-the-scenes backstory rivals that of the original 1973 production. Not only did John Boorman fall seriously ill with valley fever, contracted from sand on the set that had been shipped in from Africa, but his nine-year-old daughter, in line for a part in the film, dropped out after having a tumor removed from her leg. To add to the misery index of *Heretic*, both Louise Fletcher and Kitty Winn had to undergo gallbladder surgery during the production, and producer Richard Lederer underwent heart surgery not long after shooting began.

Richard Burton (second-billed after Linda Blair), sadly decaying after years of alcohol abuse and a permanent midnight lifestyle, played the part of Father Lamont with all the flair of a somnambulist. As for Blair (who, although only seventeen at the time of filming, had a lot in common with Burton), her long-standing indifference to acting as a craft betrayed her on the screen, and her after-hours habits made her regularly late to the set, in the process delaying the shoot.

Heretic might even have been pre-cursed: Lee J. Cobb, set to reprise his role as Lt. Kinderman, died before filming began, precipitating wholesale revisions of the script.

Ignoring the incoherence he had produced, Boorman blamed the furious reaction to *Heretic* on coarse audience tastes. "Millions of people had enjoyed watching a child being tortured in *The Exorcist*," he wrote in his memoir, *Adventures of a Suburban Boy*. "*The Heretic* would be the antidote, a film about goodness rather than evil. I should have known better. Kubrick told me the only way to do a sequel to *The Exorcist* is to give them even more gore and horror than before. No one is interested in goodness."

Thirteen years later, *The Exorcist III: Legion*, directed by William Peter Blatty, hardly fared any better. In response to his disgust over *Heretic*, which he mocked whenever he had a chance, Blatty also produced a DVD, only without a sense of visual flair or the far-out quality Boorman reached for. (Although having NBA Center Patrick Ewing appear in a bizarre dream sequence certainly counts as quirky.) The final product reflected not only his penchant for sermonizing, but it also allowed Blatty to indulge in his outmoded humor, a talent he had honed by imitating S. J. Perelman and, later, somewhat paradoxically, Joseph Heller. One-liners and zingers pepper the opening third of the film, and its incomprehensible plot verges on parody. And while Blatty is less concerned with over-the-top set pieces than the original *Exorcist* was, his pulpy imagination is actually more sensational-ized and, not surprisingly, far more pretentious. Here a clearly challenged George C. Scott, playing Lt. Kinderman, quotes Shakespeare to his fellow officers: "Macbeth is about the numbing of the moral sense." A remarkable actor (who even excelled at twisting, manic Paddy Chayefsky monologues in *The Hospital*), Scott is doomed to recite dialogue written by a man who would rather have been behind a pulpit than behind a camera.

In 1994, Friedkin commented on *Legion* in a syndicated feature. "I thought it was stupid," he said. "I thought it was just dreadful. It had no reason to be made."

Later, Blatty claimed that the studio had mangled his efforts, but no version of *Legion* would have succeeded with such a heavy-handed director behind the camera. Even so, Blatty, perpetually convinced of his genius, told Bob McCabe: "It's still a superior film. And in my opinion, and excuse me if I utter heresy here, but for me it's a more frightening film than *The Exorcist*."

With a franchise potentially hobbled, it took another fifteen years for a follow-up that proved just as catastrophic as the previous sequels. When John Frankenheimer dropped out of directing an *Exorcist* "prequel," New Hollywood veteran Paul Schrader stepped in, one of the oddest choices for a late substitute imaginable.

By far the most talented filmmaker ever involved in *The Exorcist* fran-chise, Schrader had remained at odds with major studios throughout the '80s and '90s, concentrating on independent features and nonetheless regu-larly suffering cinematic agonies. *Affliction* sat on the shelf for nearly a year before opening, and *Forever Mine* never made it to theaters.

But, for Schrader, *Dominion* was rock bottom. *Dominion* tells the story of a young Father Merrin (played by Stellan Skarsgard), a footloose arche-ologist working in Africa and suffering from a crisis of faith after traumatic events in World War II. In Kenya, he unearths a buried church that seem-ingly releases Pazuzu, wreaking supernatural havoc between metaphysical discussions among the characters.

A talky script and cost overruns immediately put Schrader in the hole, and a screening of the rough cut for studio executives triggered Morgan Creek Productions, panicked at the lack of action and violence, to demand reshoots. Eventually, the studio fired Schrader. Then, in a bizarre move that seems oddly appropriate for this chaotic franchise, Morgan Creek remade the film, with Renny Harlin (best known for *Die Hard 2* and *Cliffhanger*) directing, using some of the remaining sets from *Dominion* and pressing Skarsgard back into action only months after he had left the role of Father Merrin behind.

With Harlin in charge, *Exorcist: The Beginning* was guaranteed to have an MTV aesthetic, with frantic camerawork, kinetic action scenes, and a few gross-out set pieces. Transforming Father Merrin into some sort of Indiana Jones character makes explicit what had been implicit in 1973: that Jesuit priests are superheroes. By putting Merrin in constant motion, including a little gunplay, Harlin shot a film so far from the original conception of *The Exorcist* as to make it more suitable for a Sega Genesis console. Unfortunately, this haphazard approach may have been what Morgan Creek wanted, but *The Beginning* was already a familiar potpourri to contemporary audiences used to the recent occult adventure genre, which had in just a few years produced *Stigmata*, *The Mummy*, *The Ninth Gate*, *The Irrefutable Truth about Demons*, and *The Convent*.

Predictably, William Peter Blatty lambasted the latest variation of his novel (with a hint of his ever-present lack of self-awareness): "After a slam-bang opening sequence, Harlin's prequel deteriorated into what was surely the most humiliating professional experience of my life, particularly the finale," he told Dave Kehr of the *New York Times*. "I don't blame Renny Harlin, for he gave Morgan Creek, I promise you, precisely what Morgan Creek demanded: not shocking obscenity, but shocking vulgarity."

In an online interview with Erik Kristopher Myers, Schrader recalled going to a theater to compare *The Beginning* with his own as-yet-unreleased *Exorcist* prequel. "What I feared most was that it would be pretty good. If it was pretty good, good enough, it would be assumed that mine was worse, and any chance of my film being resurrected would be gone. So as I sat there and watched, I was rather sort of happy with it. I thought, 'This is really bad.'"

In 2005, after *Exorcist: The Beginning* had bombed, Morgan Creek brought Schrader back to complete *Dominion*, hoping to recoup some of its sunk costs via DVD sales and cable licensing. They gave Schrader a pittance (reportedly $35,000) for the renovation job and released the compromised result to the rapidly dwindling art-house circuit. *Dominion* earned less than the catering budget of most Hollywood productions but remains the best of *The Exorcist* sequels. The kind of meditation on faith and evil that William Peter Blatty had hoped to make, *Dominion* is brooding, gloomy, and fatally flawed by its makeshift construction. How Morgan Creek chose Paul Schrader—twenty years without a major studio gig or a budget in the double-digits—is just as big a mystery as the decision to release two versions of the same film within less than a year.

Three of the four *Exorcist* sequels share the same obvious conceptual gaffe: a global focus that upended the localized, everyday horror of the original. No longer a straightforward narrative confined to recognizable environments, the sequels are a mishmash of mystical and magical elements overloaded into outlandish plots. Of the four markedly different directors, only Harlin (by nature, of course) avoided excessive theological philosophizing, long stretches of which dominate *Heretic*, *Legion*, and *Dominion*, hindering momentum at every turn.

The Beginning wound up being the end of the franchise on the silver screen for almost two decades.

CHAPTER 33

Aftermaths

J ason Miller had always been ambivalent about Hollywood, if not outright disdainful. In a 1975 feature profile by Rex Reed, Miller spoke
about the pressures of success in the Broadway theater world. "The same
kind of thing happens in Hollywood," he said. "Soon as you're a success they want to package you. I sit in their offices and nod, but I never
sign anything. The big word out there is clout. I'd like to have enough of
it so I may never have to compromise in my choice of roles or execution
of them."

For a while, before the studio heads ("idiots") and the stars ("animals")
disheartened him, Miller made his bid for clout. Two months before *The
Exorcist* opened, Miller was already headlining for the first time—in *The
Nickel Ride*, an offbeat crime downer directed by the hot-and-cold Robert
Mulligan. To play the glum role of Cooper in *The Nickel Ride*, Miller reportedly rejected the part of Travis Bickle in *Taxi Driver*. It was an odd choice,
given that Miller, who had lived in New York, would be, temporarily, at
least, away from the Southern California milieu he found so alienating.
"Hollywood is a strange place," he told Reed. "A total youth fantasy, with
billboards for Forest Lawn. It's a death trip based on glamor and money.
When your fantasies don't work out, you get Charles Manson."

The Nickel Ride bombed, and Miller never topped a Hollywood pro-
duction again. His messy, meandering career led him to some strange places.
He starred opposite Stacey Keach—the man he replaced as Karras on
The Exorcist—in *The Ninth Configuration*, reuniting with William Peter

Blatty on a bizarre project in and out of theaters on separate occasions under different producers and different titles. Neither release drew an audience. By then, Miller had already become a regular on television, starring in movie-of-the-week fodder such as *A Home of Our Own* (in which he played a priest), *F. Scott Fitzgerald in Hollywood* (as the title character), and *The Dain Curse* (a miniseries based on the Dashiell Hammett novel about a cult). Things hardly improved for him in the 1980s. A tumultuous preproduction phase on a film version of *That Championship Season* (with George C. Scott quitting after clashing with William Friedkin, who himself would walk away from the project) led to Miller producing and directing the film himself. Hardly anyone saw it, despite Robert Mitchum joining the cast.

Finally, almost predictably, Miller returned to his hometown of Scranton, Pennsylvania, in 1986, where he became artistic director of the Scranton Public Theater. A few years later, William Peter Blatty tapped him to reprise his role as Father Karras (in ghostly fashion) for *Exorcist III*—at the insistence of Morgan Creek Productions, which squeezed William Peter Blatty into adding new scenes.

Along with Ellen Burstyn, Miller, who developed a drinking problem, was the last holdout regarding nonsense about a curse surrounding *The Exorcist*. As far as the cast and crew of *The Exorcist* went, Miller was second only to Blatty in the hocus-pocus department. Miller even made a photo-op visit to the Smurl residence in Pittston, Pennsylvania, one of the most transparent of supernatural hoaxes, on par with the shenanigans that produced *The Amityville Horror* in the late 1970s. Jack Smurl, who claimed that demonic forces overran his house, did not stop at mere hauntings; he also claimed to have been raped several times by a succubus in the middle of the night. "The family is terrified that the infestation of the home will go to the family," Miller told the *Times-Tribune*, sounding eerily like William Peter Blatty.

In the last fifteen years of his life, Miller appeared in the occasional B-film, but he seemed far happier working in theater, away from the spotlight. At the end of the Nineties, Miller mounted something of a comeback. He premiered a new play, "Barrymore's Ghost," in Seattle. In 1999, *That Championship Season* had a successful revival in New York City. And *Nobody Hears a Broken Drum*—an earlier Miller play—ran once again in Pennsylvania. Then, of course, *The Exorcist* returned in 2000, giving him more face time than he had received in decades.

Jason Miller died in 2001, aged fifty-three, of a heart attack.

▲ ▲ ▲

Coming off of the record-breaking success of *The Exorcist*, Ellen Burstyn continued her remarkable streak in *Alice Doesn't Live Here Anymore* (1974), winning an Academy Award for Best Actress with a dynamo performance that practically melts the screen. Directed by Martin Scorcese, *Alice* demonstrated just how far Burstyn had come from her days as a regular on *The Doctors* and *Iron Horse*.

Like several of her New Hollywood peers (Nicholson, De Niro, and Pacino, in particular), Burstyn carried the actor-as-auteur concept until the end of the decade, when personal cinema in America inched closer and closer to obsolescence. From *The Last Picture Show* (1971) up to *Same Time, Next Year* (1978), Burstyn worked with Peter Bogdonavich, Bob Rafelson, Friedkin, Martin Scorcese, Paul Mazursky, Alain Resnais, Jules Dassin, and Robert Mulligan. Wisely, she sidestepped *Heretic*—a sinkhole that swallowed up nearly everyone involved—but there were already hints that, as far as Tinseltown was concerned, Burstyn had passed her expiration date: her work for Resnais and Dassin took her overseas, to France and Greece, respectively.

The glitz, glamour, and gaudiness of the 1980s, where older women in particular found themselves waylaid by the frivolity of the times, left Burstyn at loose ends. Thanks to the new blockbuster mindset (sparked, in part, by *The Exorcist*, although *Star Wars* gets most of the retrospective blame) and the growing presence of studio executives in Brooks Brothers suits, Hollywood had become more soulless than ever.

Not even her collection of Academy-Award hardware made a difference. In fact, Oscar nominations for *Same Time, Next Year* and *Resurrection* (1981) seemed to hasten her vanishing act. Burstyn went from working with some of the top filmmakers of the 1970s to marginal talents such as J. Lee Thompson and Bud Yorkin. "In 1986 my career was at its nadir," she wrote in her memoir, without citing specifics, but that year Burstyn starred in her own sitcom for ABC, *The Ellen Burstyn Show*. The network pulled the plug after eight episodes.

When Burstyn accepted a part in a Menahem Golan film (*Hanna's War*, 1988), she hit rock bottom. After a patchy if sometimes surprising career in Israel, Golan arrived in America, where he settled into pure schlock for the next thirty years. Before hooking up with Burstyn in 1988, his previous directorial efforts included the ridiculous Sylvester Stallone arm-wrestling flick *Over the Top* and the noisy Chuck Norris blow 'em up *Delta Force*. Pecs, biceps, and rocket launchers were only part of the Golan formula. As co-head of Cannon Films (prolific low-budget trash masters of the 1980s), Golan produced, among other celluloid detritus, *Hospital Massacre*, *American Ninja*, *Hard Rock Zombies*, the *Death Wish* sequels, *Texas Chainsaw Massacre II*, and every form of machine-gun mayhem imaginable, from *Invasion U.S.A.* to *Cobra* to *Avenging Force*.

(In the mid-1980s, Cannon occasionally gambled on talent, including Roman Polanski, Robert Altman, Andrei Konchalovsky, Lina Wertmueller, and, incredibly, Jean-Luc Godard.)

"There are never many good film roles for women but what there were, I was not being offered," she explained in a syndicated feature published just before her ill-fated sitcom.

For most of the Nineties, Burstyn alternated between occasional small roles in Hollywood and in a slew of television movies—fifteen features and one miniseries. No matter what kind of role she played, Burstyn brought her customary intensity and emotional range to it.

In 2000, at the age of sixty-eight, she made a shock comeback, earning another Oscar nomination as an amphetamine-racked widow in the harrowing *Requiem for a Dream*.

▲ ▲ ▲

Of the many ready-made narratives circulated by guileless media outlets after he died in 2017, the most flatteringly inaccurate was that William Peter Blatty had seen his career as a comic novelist and screenwriter derailed by the potent horrors of *The Exorcist*, with the *New York Times* (mis)leading the way: "Before Mr. Blatty wrote 'The Exorcist,' he was a master of comedy."

As a journeyman humorist, Blatty received the occasional laudatory review, but most of his novels met with mixed notices and all of them with nonexistent sales. Even the egocentric Blatty noted this in his 1974 book *William Peter Blatty on The Exorcist: From Novel to Film*. Indeed, one of his most consistent stories about composing *The Exorcist* is that he was jobless when he began writing it. True, he alternated that unemployment tale with a few others, but in 2013, when he reminisced about *The Exorcist* for a

Blu-Ray edition feature, he still claimed that losing his livelihood had been the key motivating force behind his first serious novel.

Later complaints of having been pigeonholed in a genre category he disdained seem fanciful. "When Woody Allen writes something serious," he groused in 1980, apparently without a hint of self-awareness, "he's proclaimed a genius, but for me, nobody wanted to know."

Of course, nothing prevented Blatty from writing whatever he pleased. Stephen King, the most successful horror novelist in history, had little trouble diversifying when he had the urge. By the 1980s, when King was already a popular-culture icon, represented in film, television, and print, he began regularly writing in several genres: science-fiction, fantasy, suspense, and crime. He also produced several "straight" dramatic novellas such as *The Body* (later filmed as *Stand By Me*), *Rita Hayworth and Shawshank Redemption*, and *Hearts in Atlantis*.

One of the nonfiction books King wrote, *Danse Macabre* (1981), an overview of horror and the supernatural in pop culture, features an aside on Blatty. Writing about Ira Levin, whose wit he admired, King stated: "I am suggesting that the books [Levin] has written achieve suspense without turning into humorless thudding tracts (two novels of the Humorless, Thudding Tract School of horror writing are *Damon*, by C. Terry Cline, and *The Exorcist*, by William Peter Blatty—Cline has since improved as a writer, and Blatty has fallen silent ... forever, if we are lucky)."

By contrast, Blatty produced nothing not related to *The Exorcist* or his previous works for nearly forty years. The difference between King and Blatty (other than talent, of course) is that there was little demand for what Blatty wrote pre-*Exorcist*.

In 1978, Blatty released an altered version of his 1967 satire *Twinkle, Twinkle "Killer" Kane*, with a new title, *The Ninth Configuration*, continuing a pattern of repurposing work he had previously published. A year later, Blatty wrote and directed *The Ninth Configuration*, a film whose distribution woes reflected a lack of confidence in the final product. After United Film Distribution (until then known primarily for disseminating *Kentucky Fried Movie* and *Dawn of the Dead*) dropped it, *The Ninth Configuration* found a home at Warner Bros., which returned the rights to Blatty after minimal public interest greeted its opening. United Film Distribution picked it up again and, following the well-established protocol of B-film impresarios, rereleased it under a different title (*Twinkle, Twinkle "Killer" Kane*). It failed once more, despite Blatty making his usual grandiose sales pitches to the media. "In my opinion," he said, "*The Ninth Configuration* is like nothing ever seen on-screen before because of its effects on the emotions—shock, drama, comedy, horror."

As with *The Exorcist*, which he claimed had converted umpteen souls to Catholicism, Blatty insisted *The Ninth Configuration* transcended mere cinema. "The picture has a variety of levels," he said. "Woven through the mystery storyline is violence, suspense, and some comedy. It entertains. But there are a couple of other dimensions that members of the audience must contribute to the film. If people do contribute, this movie will certainly affect their emotions and perhaps change their lives."

Since its disastrous release, *The Ninth Configuration*, with its strange set pieces, ludicrous staging, and wild shifts in tone, has developed a cult following (there are no bad films anymore, just cult favorites and underrated gems waiting for rediscovery) led by his media cheerleaders and by his own claims of profundity.

When Blatty was contacted to work on a sequel to *The Exorcist*, he had no interest. "Warners did approach me," Blatty told Bob McCabe, "and at the time I thought: the story is over. Karras fell down the steps; he's dead—the story is over. There is no sequel possible. So I declined." But the failure of *The Ninth Configuration* drove Blatty back into *The Exorcist* orbit. *Legion*, published by Simon & Schuster in 1983, was a direct sequel to *The Exorcist*, and it encouraged Blatty to pontificate in his usual manner. "I come to a conclusion that permits good and an absolute God to exist. The answer is in *Legion*."

As a publicity gimmick, Blatty sued the *New York Times* for millions of dollars, arguing that the newspaper had deliberately left *Legion* off its bestseller list, causing him a fortune in royalties. He lost the suit but achieved his goal: meretricious coverage of a book that produced only a fraction of the buzz that *The Exorcist* had a decade earlier.

After *The Exorcist III* (an adaptation of *Legion*) underwhelmed at the box office in 1990, Blatty laid low until the twenty-fifth anniversary of the original *Exorcist* made him relevant again. When his preferred cut of the film opened in 2000, he was back in the limelight, praising himself, spinning the same untruths about the Hunkeler case, and philosophizing about God and evil in ways that make one question the value of a Georgetown University education.

In 2001, he rereleased *William Peter Blatty on The Exorcist: From Novel to Film* without his original screenplay and gave it a new title: *If There Were Demons Then Perhaps There Were Angels*, ensuring further monetization of his work. Similarly, Blatty revised *The Exorcist* for a new edition of the novel, published in 2013, reinforcing the Catholic message of the book as if it had not been clear enough forty years earlier.

For better or worse, Blatty single-handedly launched the horror-fiction boom with the success of *The Exorcist*. From the early 1970s on, hardly a horror/gothic paperback emerged from the printers without some sort of comparison or reference to *The Exorcist* emblazoned on its cover, in all the gaudy typefaces (Ringlet, Eckmann, Pretorian, Marschall, Rubens). This allusion to both the novel and the film was a surefire selling point for marginal publishing houses. Often, *The Exorcist* was one of three titles cited in the tagline hype, along with *Rosemary's Baby* and *The Other*. (In a few years, *The Omen* would become a fourth staple blurb.) *The Exorcist* also produced specialized subgenres well into the 1980s, among them Catholic horror, with priests or churches at the heart of the shivers. *The Search for Joseph Tully* by William Henry Hallahan, *The Sentinel* by Jeffrey Konvitz, *Dark Angel* by Sean Forestal, *Night Church* by Whitley Streiber, and *In the Name of the Father* by John Zodrow are just a few examples of this peculiar literary species. David Seltzer novelized his own screenplay for *The Omen*, scoring a surprise bestseller that produced several follow-ups. In 1983 James Herbert published *Shrine*, which lampoons publicity-mad priests, in what suggests a rebuke of the technical advisors and collared bit players in *The Exorcist*.

For the first time since 1971, Blatty published an original novel, *Dimiter*, which he had been working on since the 1980s. Released in 2010 by Forge Books, an imprint of Tor, *Dimiter* received the usual mixed reviews but barely caused a ripple in popular culture. In a welcome change of pace, however, Blatty produced no foolish lawsuits on its behalf.

From 1979 on, Blatty filed more lawsuits and petitions than he published novels: at least two against Warner Bros., one against the *New York Times*, and one against his alma mater Georgetown University, which he deemed insufficiently virtuous. His 198-page canon suit, written with the purpose of stripping Georgetown University of its Catholic designation, included 476 footnotes, 91 appendices, and 124 witness testimonials. Blatty had always been guilty of overwriting.

What did Blatty oppose in Georgetown? Tolerance of gay people, toler-ance of pro-choice advocates, and, especially, two speaking engagements outraged him: one featuring then-secretary of Health and Human Services Kathleen Sebelius and the other spotlighting then-Congresswoman Nancy Pelosi. (Both Sebelius and Pelosi were alumni of Trinity College, where they had enrolled before Georgetown was fully coed.) It was a campus produc-tion of *The Vagina Monologues*, however, that seemed to have been the breaking point. For Blatty, it was fine for Georgetown to tolerate his outré vagina scene (with a bloody crucifix as a prop), but an explicit play about female sexuality? That was far beyond the pale.

The *Georgetown Voice*, the student newspaper of GU, used its edito-rial page to rebuke Blatty and his antediluvian views: "The only intolerant orthodoxies at Georgetown are those Blatty himself is perpetuating with his misguided petition. We should be proud of our 'radical autonomy' and continue promoting diversity and inclusivity as the foundational principles of Catholic education."

With the release of his memoir *Finding Peter: A True Story of the Hand of Providence and Evidence of Life After Death* in 2015, Blatty solidified his standing as a true believer of supernatural forces far beyond Catholic dogma. Ghosts, parallel universes, UFOs, demons, Ouija boards as gateways to the other side—Blatty had been, for decades, the walking embodiment of the *Fortean Times*. In *Finding Peter*, Blatty details how he communicated with his dead son, Peter, who died from a heart ail-ment when he was nineteen. "For so many people of faith," Blatty told the *Washingtonian*, "our belief in life after death is often a very intense hope—more than a full knowledge of fact—and this book gives them some tangible evidence."

In a series of interviews, Blatty marketed *Finding Peter* by extrapolating his out-of-this-world beliefs. He offered this revelation to the *Washington Post* about one of his more peculiar convictions: "There is one person in my greater family who I'm convinced probably—let's make that very probably—is a case of reincarnation."

A year before he died, Blatty blurbed a book by Dinesh D'Souza. It was a tie-in to an unhinged right-wing documentary that D'Souza had produced about Republican bête noire Hilary Clinton. The blurb would also appear prominently on the film poster. "Utterly terrifying," Blatty wrote, "and based on a true story."

▲ ▲ ▲

Like most of his New Hollywood colleagues, William Friedkin self-destructed with egotistical gusto just when he should have reached his peak. In fact, Friedkin might have drawn up the blueprint for the crash-and-burn rebels who followed in his catastrophic wake.

Before Francis Ford Coppola mortgaged everything he owned to make *Apocalypse Now* (burning himself out for the next ten years) and Michael Cimino single-handedly bankrupted United Artists with *Heaven's Gate*, there was *Sorcerer*. A retelling of *The Wages of Fear* (not a remake, Friedkin would growl), *Sorcerer* was a $20 million boondoggle whose failure sent Friedkin into a spiral. "It was extremely difficult to shoot and the fact that the film was not a success is one of the most disappointing things that's ever happened to me," he told Robert J. Emery in 2002. "I thought, after it was finished, that I had finally made a film that really worked for me and I was very pleased with it, but it was really a failure. I have to say it was both a critical and a commercial failure and it hurt me very deeply. There was a deep wound from which I may have only recovered recently."

A dismal box-office washout when it was released, *Sorcerer* has since been reclaimed as a lost classic. Its bravura set piece—two trucks loaded with nitroglycerin attempting to cross a primitive suspension bridge during a rainstorm—is breathtakingly executed and functions as a correlative of the filmmaker taking chances with his art.

Friedkin had taken physical risks in *The French Connection* (and cultural risks in *The Exorcist*—little Regan masturbating and blaspheming), but *Sorcerer* saw him taking existential risks. Overbudget, subject to forces majeures, grueling location shoots, and a rotating crew, Friedkin joined German visionary Werner Herzog as an insurance gamble for bond companies. Just as Herzog oversaw productions in Peru and (later) Brazil and Ghana that verged on anarchy, Friedkin lost control of a shoot that saw him at his obnoxious, imperious worst.

In addition to spotlighting his daring approach to filmmaking and his gift for staging action, *Sorcerer* also exposed one of his worst flaws—a mania for gratuitous sensationalism. Tacky judgment calls have marred nearly every film Friedkin directed: the needless gunshot at the end of *The French Connection*, the confounding stinger in *To Live and Die in L.A.*, the absurd car chase in *Jade*, and the ridiculous brawl between

Tommy Lee Jones and Samuel L. Jackson in *Rules of Engagement*. In *The Guardian*, Friedkin added a supernatural element to the script that did not exist in the source novel by Dan Greenburg. (Worse, that supernatural element was a homicidal tree.) Even *The Exorcist* had a moment of gunplay when Merrin drives out to see the statue of Pazuzu. Suddenly, heavily armed guards stream through a doorway, rifles at the ready. And Karras pummeling Regan MacNeil also borders on being a cheap action bit.

But *Sorcerer* goes overboard with its quartet of prologues. Where *The Wages of Fear* gathered desperate, rough-hewn characters in an end-of-the-world locale without presenting overly detailed backstories for them (thereby keeping the mystery of how they wound up in such straits, to begin with), *Sorcerer* creates and dramatizes newly scripted histories of each doomed member before the main storyline begins. That allows Friedkin to pack more incidents, characters, violence, and sets into a film whose simple premise Henri-Georges Clouzot had masterfully heightened in 1953. The first twenty minutes of *Sorcerer* features machine guns, car crashes, explosions, murder, and suicide. This overkill action, which takes place in various locations, including Israel, France, and New Jersey, could barely titillate an audience already attuned to films specifically about incident and spectacle (*Jaws* and *Star Wars*, for example), and Friedkin nearly disintegrated after *Sorcerer* flopped.

"My sudden success in Hollywood after years of failure had convinced me that I was the center of the universe," Friedkin wrote in his memoir. "Many were waiting for me to crash, and I obliged them in spades. I had flown too close to the sun and my wings melted."

With *Cruising* (1980), Friedkin enraged the largest gay community in North America with his raw, if sometimes risible portrayal of the now-long-extinct BDSM leather scene in New York City, forcing him to loop dialogue on location shoots disrupted by raucous protesters. The sordid bars were real (they dotted the once notorious Meatpacking District, now home to a combination of swank retail and cultural hotspots, including the Whitney Museum), and so were the denizens in each scene. As a snapshot of a pre-AIDS gay subculture, *Cruising* has a shocking sociological power, and its seediness gives the film enough rude atmosphere to fascinate. As a crime thriller, however, *Cruising* is hopelessly disjointed and murky, its graphic violence and enigmatic conclusion alienating viewers from every demographic. Once again, Friedkin conflated incoherence with ambiguity, as much a trademark for him as car chases.

Not even the star power of Al Pacino, as a cop who goes undercover in the BDSM netherworld to find a serial killer who targets gay people, could help *Cruising* at the box office or with the critical establishment. Wrote Bruce Kirkland of the *Ottawa Journal*: "Operating under the guise of truth and art, a calculating filmmaker has dumped on the public a most deplorable travesty, a sickness, a tasteless madness, a film called *Cruising*."

By 1989, the William Friedkin story began generating cheerless sub-headlines. The *Los Angeles Times* wrote: "After 16 hitless years, *The French Connection* and *Exorcist* director seeks to turn heads again with *The Guardian*."

After *The Guardian* bombed, Friedkin concentrated on optimizing *Sorcerer* for the home market, first on VHS (in late 1990) and then on Laserdisc (in 1992). When *Blue Chips* and *Jade* also sputtered, Friedkin appeared finished at last. "I always feel that the film I'm working on is the best work I've ever done," he told Robert J. Emery for the book *The Directors: Take Two*. "Often, after it's released, I don't know what the hell I was thinking."

From 1980 until 2006, Friedkin directed only two films with anything resembling verve: *To Live and Die in L.A.* and *Rampage*, his disturbing if flawed treatise on capital punishment. (His made-for-cable remake of *Twelve Angry Men* is also notable for its staging and intense performances.) But Friedkin made a minor comeback in the late 1990s predicated on his glory days from the Nixon era, keeping his name afloat even as his filmmaking sank to miserable depths.

Although *Easy Riders, Raging Bulls* burnished his renegade legend, it left him miffed. "I never read it," Friedkin told the *San Francisco Chronicle*. "I've heard a lot about it, and friends and I have talked about it, and they all tell me it's completely inaccurate. I know what the guy did: He went to ex-wives and irate ex-girlfriends and boyfriends, and he just put in all the slag they could throw in. And he never really bothered to check any details. . . . It's a collection of truth, half-truths and rampant untruths."

In the United Kingdom, the mythologizing documentary *Fear of God* and the rerelease of *The Exorcist* spurred Friedkin into restoring the Blatty-approved version of *The Exorcist*, which became a hit and a hot topic for the media in 2000.

In *A Decade Under the Influence*, a 2003 documentary about the New Hollywood, Friedkin also stood out for his crankiness and bluntness, even among the cast of rowdy talking heads.

His entertaining 2013 memoir, *The Friedkin Connection*, is considered by some as candid and self-lacerating, but Friedkin avoids mentioning some of his biggest bombs and calls *Rules of Engagement* "a box-office hit," a designation that must have surprised the accountants at Paramount. A few of his attempts at self-introspection are undercut by arrogance, deflection, and just a hint of delusion. "Some of my films have been dismissed, others overpraised. But *Jade*, a critical and financial disaster, contained some of my best work. I felt I had let down the actors, the studio, and most of all, Sherry. I went into a deep funk. Was it the *Exorcist* curse, as many have suggested, a poor choice of material, or simply that whatever talent I had was ephemeral? Maybe all of the above."

A pair of low-budget productions scripted by playwright Billie Letts, *Bug* (2006) and *Killer Joe* (2011), gave Friedkin something close to general acclaim for the first time since the Reagan era. Yet both films combined could not generate the box office of his long-forgotten Chevy Chase dud *Deal of the Century* (1983). Still, *Bug* and *Killer Joe* showed a focus and a commitment to the bleak material at hand.

Overseeing a restoration and rerelease of *Sorcerer* in 2014 led to a critical reevaluation of the film that had all but ended Friedkin as a top director. Two more documentaries about Friedkin and *The Exorcist* (*Friedkin Uncut* and *Leap of Faith*) kept him in the public eye, and his ham-fisted documentary on a prolific exorcist named Father Amorth returned him to the supernatural milieu of his greatest success.

Friedkin may have been living off his past, but maybe, for him, at least, it was a past worth living off.

▲ ▲ ▲

Throughout the shooting of *The Exorcist* and into postproduction and publicity, a half-dozen crew members would insist that Linda Blair had emerged from the experience unscathed, but barely a year after the film wrapped, she was burning rubber in the Hollywood fast lane and, before the end of the decade, she would become a teenage alcoholic, bizarrely mirroring one of the dismal TV movies she starred in after establishing Regan MacNeil as an offbeat cultural touchstone. Her brief but lurid interval in the spotlight culminated with a notorious drug bust in 1977.

"*The Exorcist*, for me, lasted a lifetime," Blair told A&E.

Like Jason Miller, accosted in the streets by disturbed strangers looking for salvation, Blair suffered from her newfound fame. Wherever she went for a few years post-*Exorcist*, she drew attention for more than her celebrity status. "I scared thousands of people," she told *Fangoria*, "and they would look at me—they would see me in a supermarket, in a clothing store—and their reaction was unbelievable. I freaked people out."

While Blair may have inadvertently terrorized gullible shoppers, what she suffered far exceeded the average jump scare. Just as America produced thousands of lost souls convinced that they were in the grip of Satan after viewing *The Exorcist*, so, too, did it mass-produce ticket buyers delusional enough to believe that Linda Blair was truly some sort of diabolical entity. "The whole devil thing never hit me," she told *Fangoria*. "But because it was about the supernatural, demonology, et cetera, the types of people that were attracted to the film were pretty intense people. And I attracted a lot of weird people around me."

Unable to differentiate between fact and fiction, those weird people not only flinched when they saw Blair in person, but some of them also sent death threats to her. When she was only fifteen, Blair had a security detail shadowing her. Then, a few years after the height of *Exorcist*-mania, stalkers began harassing her. "When I was eighteen, it kind of happened again and the FBI was in on it, because the man called the police and said he was going to kill me. So I lived in a hideout from that and then the drug bust came on top of it, for something I really did not do. Because of that, the paper nicely enough published my address, so the guy had my address. I'd come home at night and be so horrified. It's just so unbelievable."

In 1974, the gossip pages also reported that Blair was dating twenty-five-year-old Australian rock singer Rick Springfield. A few months after they were first spotted as an item, Blair and Springfield began living together in Los Angeles. At the time, Blair was fifteen, not yet old enough to meet the minimum for the age of consent, but her mother had returned to Connecticut in 1974, leaving Blair under the watch of her older sister, Deborah. "When I lived with my friend in Hollywood, mother was a little upset at first because I was only fifteen," Blair told the New York *Daily News*. "But then she said there was no use trying to stand in the way of love.

I didn't feel precocious about living with a man at that age. It was great. I never dated much in school. You know, I didn't have boyfriends in the traditional sense. When I did date, it was in groups. So when I came to California, I went straight from living at home to living with a man."

In an episode of *Intimate Portrait* on the Lifetime network, the narrative voice-over bizarrely refers to the Springfield-Blair pairing as a May-December romance when it was clearly something else. In fact, it was illegal. Springfield put his own time-capsule spin on it for an episode of *Biography* on A&E. "Now, probably I would have been burned at the stake, you know. But back then, it was just, 'Oooh, that's kind of weird,' you know. But to us, it was very, very natural."

If her role as a demon-possessed child was not enough to distinguish Blair from the run-of-the-mill teen, her subsequent appearances gave her an even darker allure. The mid-1970s saw Blair develop enough negative connotations to make her a strange symbol of the prurient American id, and she achieved this unique distinction mostly in middle-class living rooms across the country.

The made-for-television movie had become a family tradition since *See How They Run* premiered in 1964, often bringing hot-button sociological issues to the masses, with a campy, moralistic, slapdash quality that would differentiate it, negatively, of course, from Hollywood releases. Early on, however, made-for-television productions had higher ambitions. The first film shot specifically for television had been *The Killers*, directed by action auteur Don Siegel and starring Lee Marvin, Ronald Reagan, Angie Dickinson, and John Cassavetes, but its high-octane violence sent executives scurrying despite the all-star cast and crew. Instead of airing on NBC as scheduled, *The Killers* received an unexpected theatrical run.

A decade later, Linda Blair starred in *Born Innocent*, a teen delinquency melodrama so coarse it lit up switchboards at NBC and launched sensitive newspaper columnists into overdrive. In her first screen appearance since *The Exorcist* (other than a guest spot on a game show), Blair plays Christine Parker, a serial runaway who winds up, at fourteen, sentenced to a juvenile detention center after her dysfunctional parents sign her over to the state.

In the notorious centerpiece of the film, made doubly uncomfortable because of its duration, Christine is held down by her cellmates and raped with a plunger handle. Subsequent outrage from viewers forced NBC to issue defensive statements as to the sociological value of the film; even so, it excised the scene completely for future airings. (NBC would be sued, unsuccessfully, by the parents of a nine-year-old girl who had been sexually assaulted by a group of kids with a Coca-Cola bottle in imitation of the rape scene in *Born Innocent*.)

Although Blair is sexualized throughout, with a pair of strip searches, two shower scenes, and the gruesome rape, *Born Innocent*, despite its undeniable salaciousness and a certain amount of implausibility, is remarkably effective. As the rare prime-time downer, *Born Innocent* also stood out from *The Wonderful World of Disney*, *Happy Days*, *The Mary Tyler Moore Show*, *Good Times*, and *The Waltons* the same way Charles Manson might have stood out at a debutante ball.

The documentary look solidifies the nightmare quality of *Born Innocent*, and the climax, which includes a scorched-earth riot and a closing scene of the now-hardened Blair joining her rapists and walking off into the distance just before the credits roll, feels almost revolutionary. No happy ending? No redemption? No mawkish speeches of the kind William Peter Blatty cherished? Nearly fifty years later, *Born Innocent* looks like some sort of terrible accident, one that completely blindsided a country watching the first season of *Little House on the Prairie* by the millions. *Born Innocent* seemed to say, to hell with the so-called "Family Hour."

A ratings bonanza for NBC, *Born Innocent* set the template for Blair as a teen martyr to whom not just bad things happen—but very, very bad things. After a small role in the disaster spectacular *Airport 1975*, Blair returned to the airwaves with *Sarah T.—Portrait of a Teenage Alcoholic* (directed by Richard Donner just before his breakthrough with *The Omen*), another grim problem film with a title that effectively functions as a spoiler. Unlike *Born Innocent*, *Sarah T.* is less objective and far more preachy; nonetheless, Blair spends a significant amount of on-screen time suffering, and, in keeping with her sexualization, at one point, her character offers to trade her body for a bottle of liquor.

When Blair headlined another made-for-television extravaganza a year later (this time for ABC), she became a national concern. As an illiterate farm girl kidnapped by an escaped mental patient (played by Martin Sheen) in *Sweet Hostage*, Blair, now sixteen, seemed less typecast than the subject of some sort of cultural experiment. At the *Buffalo News*, Jeff Simon seemed genuinely disturbed by the Linda Blair phenomenon. "How is it possible that a teenage actress can be making a busy career out of being violated, abused, and victimized, most often in kinky circumstances?" he asked.

Other media observers and critics also began hand-wringing. "Linda Blair has become a professional victim," wrote Bill Carter of the *Baltimore Sun*. The *Philadelphia Inquirer* referred to her as an "exhibitionist," and the *Los Angeles Times* imagined that Blair was probably asking herself, "Who do you have to know to get OUT of this business?"

Then came the announcement that Blair would star in the inevitable *Exorcist* sequel, slated for release in mid-1977. The assumption, of course, was that Blair, at some point, would be further tormented by the forces of evil along with the priests who battle to save her.

When shooting began for what became known as *Exorcist II: The Heretic*, however, Blair had serious life-imitating-art problems to confront. By then, her Lolita relationship with Springfield was over, but Blair had adopted certain hedonistic aspects of the rock 'n' roll outlook. This included, among other indulgences, liquor. In no time, Blair became a real-life *Sarah T.*, struggling with alcoholism and depression. She explained the extent of her dependency to *Lifetime*: "For me to drink whatever I could find—vodka, a quart or a bottle, whatever, I don't know, I can't remember— but it was enough for me to know that I could get to bed and that I would pass out."

Although Blair would deny it, to the extent of making statements that suggested reaction formation, drugs were also a problem. In fact, her insatiable appetite for drugs scared off her latest boyfriend, Glenn Hughes, ex-bass player for English proto-metal band Deep Purple and singer/multi-instrumentalist for hard-rock road warriors Trapeze, back in America for a reunion tour. Despite having lived out the excesses of the rock era in the early 1970s and having once told *NME*, "I spent a million dollars on cocaine," Hughes could not keep pace with Blair. "Like me, Linda was very addicted to cocaine," he told *Classic Rock* magazine in 2011. "I was going completely off the rails, and I'd found the perfect mate to stumble along with. We shacked up in LA together. It's incredible to tell you this, but I broke up with her because she was doing so much blow, it was getting too intense for me to be around. We'd be driving down Sunset Boulevard, she'd have an ounce of cocaine in a bag on her lap, and she'd be doing bumps through a straw. I'm thinking: 'Any minute now they're going to catch us; whoever they are.' I couldn't deal with it. A few weeks after we broke up she got busted."

On December 20, 1977, Linda Blair made global headlines when she was arrested on drug charges and linked to a nationwide cocaine ring. An army of DEA agents and local law enforcement descended on her small Cape Cod house in Wilton, Connecticut, to serve a fugitive warrant from Jacksonville, Florida. While there, officers discovered amphetamine (aka speed) on the premises, another setback for Blair, who now had a possession charge tacked onto a rap sheet that would soon include conspiracy to buy or sell cocaine.

Blair was whisked to the Court of Common Pleas in Stamford for arraignment, where she posted bail of $2,500, with a continuance date scheduled for January 18. In the meantime, Duval County (Florida) requested her extradition to Jacksonville, where the fugitive warrant had originated. In October 1977, Blair had traveled to Florida to attend the funeral of Ronnie Van Zant, lead singer of Lynyrd Skynyrd, who had died in an airplane crash. As part of the rock circuit (she had dated, among other musicians, Tommy Bolin of Deep Purple, Jim Dandy of Black Oak Arkansas, and Glenn Hughes of Trapeze and had even graced the cover of a recent issue of *Circus* magazine devoted to "Women in Rock"), Blair roamed through a netherworld of barbiturates, crank, coke, morphine, and quaaludes, with heroin still an occasional risk (Tim Buckley had overdosed in 1975 and Bolin in 1976, and the loss of Janis Joplin and Jim Morrison was still fresh). "At the funeral, someone suggested we do some cocaine," Blair told the *San Francisco Examiner*. "I felt horrible, and dope was not on my mind. But a senator's daughter convinced me, and we bought some coke from a couple who were also breeding Basenji dogs."

Unfortunately for Blair, it turned out the dog breeders were also part of a sprawling drug ring. "All I wanted to do was buy a dog," she would later claim. Instead, Blair purchased cocaine at least twice from George Edward Mangum, described by the press as a cocaine wholesaler from Jacksonville, Florida. Mangum even bragged to an undercover agent that business had picked up when Blair arrived in Florida. After years in the spotlight as a fictional object of morbid appeal, a rare selling point, Blair was now a nonfiction attraction. She was also facing serious jail time during an era when the DEA was ramping up the War on Drugs.

To some, her troubles were inevitable. "Linda Blair's drug bust (for cocaine) comes as no surprise to those of us who watched her two years ago—when she was sixteen—at a Black Oak Arkansas concert in Chicago," wrote Aaron Gold in his "Show People" column for the *Hartford Courant*.

The *Miami Herald* dug into her past and reported that Blair "was once asked by her trainer not to participate in a horse-riding event because he thought she was under the influence of drugs and was unable to function properly."

While Blair fought extradition to Florida, her case in Connecticut proceeded. On April 17, 1978, the state dropped charges when Blair agreed to enroll in a rehab program. She exited court laughing that day, but four months later she was busted again, this time carrying two joints in her purse at Calgary International Airport.

To save her already precarious career, Blair made public statements about drug use that were, on the surface, nothing short of preposterous. "Some people may not understand, but I really don't like them," she wrote in the *Bridgeport Telegram*. "When any of my friends get involved with drugs I get upset." If so, then her rock 'n' roll lifestyle, where nearly everyone she knew snorted, swallowed, or shot up, must have left her perpetually distressed. And the Jacksonville bust was no exception: while Blair would continue to maintain her innocence about drug use in general, her recent ex-boyfriend Teddy Hartlett and her bodyguard Steve Schiano were also part of the dragnet, charged with conspiracy to buy or sell cocaine. (Both would eventually plead guilty to lesser charges.)

After Connecticut and Florida both dropped state charges against Blair, a federal grand jury returned a sealed indictment in Jacksonville in March 1979. When grand jury testimony revealed that Blair had twice purchased cocaine in small amounts (each time one-quarter of an ounce), it was clear that what she was interested in was personal use.

Because Blair was already implicated, prosecutors might have viewed her as someone who could shine a spotlight on the drug scourge, which would only get exponentially worse in the 1980s and 1990s. Most likely, the federal charges against Blair were trumped-up: although it was established that she used drugs and had purchased cocaine from Mangum, the conspiracy angle suggested prosecutorial overreach. In the late 1970s, half the entertainment industry in America snorted cocaine. It was one of several adult fads produced by the "Me" decade, along with porno chic films, wife swapping, and primal scream therapy. "The whole town of Hollywood is coked out of its head," Robert Blake once said.

Eventually, after numerous court appearances, Blair would plead guilty to conspiracy to possess cocaine, a federal misdemeanor, and a significant downgrade from the original charge of intent to distribute. In June 1979, U.S. District Judge Howell W. Melton sentenced her to three years of probation and ordered her to perform community outreach. Blair was also fined $5,000.

At around the same time as her legal ordeal began, Blair saw *Exorcist II: The Heretic* bomb in theaters, damaging her hopes of a future beyond sensationalized TV appearances. Directed by John Boorman, who had distinguished himself with the modernist noir *Point Blank* (1967) and the harrowing blockbuster *Deliverance* (1972), *Exorcist II* was one of the great follies in Hollywood. Its initial reception from opening-weekend viewers (which included uproarious laughter and debris hurled at the screen) so disturbed Warner Bros. that Boorman raced back to Hollywood to re-edit the film and shoot new scenes in hopes of salvaging the international box office. Nothing, however, could be done to improve such absurdity.

After her plea deal, Blair returned to the screen in *Roller Boogie*, produced by Brooklyn huckster Irwin Yablans to exploit the twin fads of disco and roller skating. A minor hit, *Roller Boogie* was the last time Blair would star in anything even remotely resembling a mainstream release until 1990 when she spoofed her role as Regan MacNeil for the Carolco Pictures film *Repossessed*.

Her projects were notable for alternating between pure exploitation and sheer ineptitude, with a few films shelved before achieving delayed release and others so fringe that they were ignored when they opened. *Savage Island*, for example, was a grindhouse cheapie that almost defies description: It is three different films cobbled together to produce one seventy-nine-minute adventure in sleazoid trash. After cutting and pasting parts of two existing Italian torture fests (*Escape from Hell* and *Orinoco: Prison of Sex*, both from 1980), the producers asked Blair to appear, with a machine gun, for a prologue and a bloody ending that totaled one reel of screen time. "A job is a job," Blair told the *Los Angeles Times*, reflecting a pragmatic worldview that jibed with her general indifference toward acting.

Although Blair had become someone associated with a certain kind of disreputable entertainment, she had, in the past, drawn the line at nudity. More than once, Blair had stated that she would never show skin in a film. "I'll show my body to individuals of my choosing," she said in 1978. "Now, if I had a body like Raquel Welch. . . . My contracts say they cannot even simulate me in the nude."

That conviction apparently did not apply to print media; in 1982, Blair posed topless for *Oui* magazine. Her explanation for choosing a career step uncommon for serious actors in the early 1980s was that it would remove the child-star stigma from her public image—as if her cocaine bust and her permanent status in gossip columns had not been enough to separate her from a teenybopper aura. Topless spreads of Blair also appeared in *Playboy Italy* and *High Society*, adding to a lurid image that had developed since *Born Innocent* in 1974. In the wake of her nude snapshots, that image would flourish beyond the printed page.

By the mid-1980s, the drive-in market was vanishing, and so was the grindhouse circuit—two dependable outlets for marginal entertainment ranging from homegrown martial-arts flicks to zombie and cannibal shockers imported from Italy to women in prison escapades to first-wave slasher films saturated with Kensington gore to sleazy urban thrillers.

The arrival of VHS created the direct-to-video market, which fed the insatiable hunger for fringe trash. And Linda Blair would eventually star in several B vehicles throughout the decade. Often, she would appear nude in them, producers exploiting the on-screen notoriety she had developed as a teen in the 1970s. Blair was naked in fairly graphic scenes in *Chained Heat*, *Red Heat*, and *Savage Streets*, while partial nudity figures in both *Night Patrol* and *Bedroom Eyes II*.

In a 1987 interview with *Fangoria*, Blair, still only twenty-eight, looked back with acrimony—not professional detachment—over some of her roles. "I personally hate *Chained Heat*," she said, about the outré women-in-prison quickie co-starring Sybil Danning. "I've never even watched the whole thing. It made good money, but it was a piece of trash. To this day the problem with my career is that this film keeps playing and producers don't want to hire me because of it. *Chained Heat* has actually ruined my career. Plus, it was not the movie I signed to do. I signed to do a totally different movie that was made and it's a really big problem in my life. Wow, was I unprotected."

Forty years ago, the alternatives to mainstream Hollywood productions included scuzzy exploitation impresarios who would skirt ethics as often as they would bounce checks. Although grindhouse films of every sort have recently earned retroactive critical attention, they are hardly ever considered in their cold, transactional light as disposable products manufactured as cheaply and as cynically as possible, with a bare minimum of talent involved, for the sole purpose of extracting a grimy dollar from ramshackle theaters in urban wastelands.

That world, one where cinematic art is virtually nonexistent, is where Linda Blair spent most of the 1980s. In 1990, to publicize her flop spoof *Repossessed*, she made the media rounds and sounded bitter in a *Los Angeles Times* profile. She blamed her reps for the sleazy arc of her post–*Roller Boogie* career: "I was involved with a manager who put me in touch with an agent, and neither of them really protected my career. I did movies that didn't give me any script approval. They kept me working, but in what? Trash. It was the worst nightmare of my life. I did a topless scene in a shower in one picture. They promised they would shoot only from the shoulders up. I learned the hard way."

In an interview with *Deep Red* magazine, Blair expanded on her charges of exploitation. "The script they gave me for *Chained Heat* was nothing like the script that we ended shooting. The movie became a T & A film. I cried more than you'll ever know, but there was nothing I could do. I had already been paid. My managers weren't there to support me. It was awful; it was a case of either take my top off in the shower or get sued. I can't tell you that this is a great business. People can be really mean."

Over the years, Blair sometimes denied that she had been blacklisted because of her drug bust and sometimes insisted that she had. (For comparison, it should be noted that neither Anjelica Huston nor Jodie Foster suffered blowback from their cocaine scandals.) But her fringy career often seemed like a by-product of indifference. Again and again, she would repeat that acting was just a way to underwrite her horse-riding ventures. "I'm not a dedicated actress and show business is definitely not my entire life," she told the New York *Daily News* in 1975. When she hit the media circuit in 1981 to promote *Hell Night*, she mentioned still being too young for Jane Fonda–type roles and possibly doing some comedy in the future, but she seemed completely detached about film as a popular art form and as a creative medium with a scale of aesthetic values. "I never really cared about acting," she told UPI in 1981. "Maybe because I've been doing it since I was a kid."

Still, Blair was a survivor. She spent the next two decades or so as what might be uncharitably called a D-list celebrity, starring in direct-to-video foolishness, making guest appearances on countless television shows, popping up (somehow) a pair of Australian cheapies, becoming a regular on the *Hollywood Squares*, and then, finally, enjoying a steady gig as the host of *Scariest Places on Earth*, a ghost-hunting show that aired on cable for several years. But there has never been anything uncharitable about Blair, whose philanthropic pursuits (ranging from environmental causes to rescuing dogs) are a far cry from her early post-*Exorcist* life when she faced the strange results of a strange celebrity profile: "How would you like it," she once asked, "if every day, everywhere you go, someone would ask: Spin your head or throw up?"

CHAPTER 34

▲ ▲ ▲

Dark Legacy

I n 2003, more than thirty-five years after his second novel shocked the reading public, Ira Levin expressed guilt about his role in popularizing Satan as a cultural trope in America. "Lately, I've had a new worry," Levin wrote. "The success of *Rosemary's Baby* inspired *Exorcists* and *Omens* and lots of et ceteras. Two generations of youngsters have grown to adulthood watching depictions of Satan as a living reality. Here's what I worry about now: if I hadn't pursued an idea for a suspense novel almost forty years ago, would there be quite as many religious fundamentalists around today?"

On the other hand, despite inspiring a spike in exorcisms (and laying the groundwork for the Satanic Panic madness of the 1980s), William Peter Blatty never felt responsible for any of the negativity associated with his potent novel/film combination. Though his religious fervor spurred him to write a preachy novel intended to inspire readers, *The Exorcist* caused plenty of collateral damage.

Before *The Exorcist* kicked off one of the strangest and long-lasting fads in American history, there were barely a handful of documented cases of exorcism in the United States. In conducting thorough research for years, Blatty could only uncover two. One of them (the same story that had inspired Ray Russell for his novel *The Case Against Satan*) allegedly took place in Earling, Iowa, in 1928. "I found the material on the case in Iowa, but unfortunately, all of the participants were deceased," Blatty wrote. "And I was left with this account which struck me as having been written by an overly credulous person, so that was absolutely useless to me. But it was clear to me that something called possession was going on, and it was real."

That last sentence sums up Blatty, and his occult worldview, concisely. Without concrete evidence, and while citing the Iowa case as unlikely, he nevertheless asserts the existence of extraordinarily improbable events. Like many conspiracy theorists, whose delusions exclude contradictory facts, Blatty seemed predisposed to magical thinking. Overriding faith in God and Catholic tenets is one thing, but Blatty never stopped being at the center of uncanny phenomenon. Blatty claimed that a supernatural visit from his dead mother convinced him to continue writing *The Exorcist* when he was ready to give up; Blatty claimed that he had experienced paranormal contact through the use of a Ouija board (no doubt the one mass-produced by Parker Brothers); Blatty could be found in the audio room of the New York City studio, trying to reach his beloved mother in the great beyond; Blatty would eventually write a memoir about maintaining a ghostly relationship with his dead son.

Today, exorcisms are exploding across the United States (and other heavily Catholic countries) with priests, seemingly backtracking from the psychological advances made through the '50s and '60, going so far as to claim that demons have been texting their victims, bypassing human bodies as conduits. *The Exorcist* did not only spur a few cases of false possession but set in motion an entire satanic/exorcism industry. From the underground exorcism movement of the 1970s, documented by Malachy Martin in his best-selling book *Hostage to the Devil: The Possession and Exorcism of Five Contemporary Americans* (which was viciously panned by Blatty in a review so ironic only someone as self-regarding as Blatty could have written it), to the Satanic Panic in the 1980s, to the deliverance ministries of the 1990s and beyond—*The Exorcist* has been an inspiration to religious cranks and zealots as well as the mentally ill.

In 2018, *The Atlantic* published a story on the explosive rise of exorcisms in America, which now has over one hundred full-time exorcists among its Catholic dioceses despite the decline in actual churchgoing members. In early 2019, the *Catholic Herald* featured a cover story with the title "Driving Out the Devil: What's Behind the Exorcism Boom? by R. Andrew Chesnut, PhD, and Kate Kingsbury, PhD, an anthropology professor at University of Alberta. Chesnut elaborated on the widespread popularity of exorcisms to the *VCU News*. "Yes, I think most Americans and Europeans, in particular, would be very surprised to know how widespread the practice of exorcism has become over the past few decades. Many Americans and Europeans of my generation were influenced by the seminal film, *The Exorcist*, which presents demonic deliverance as an extraordinarily rare, almost covert, Catholic rite. As my co-author Dr. Kate Kingsbury and I point out in the article, exorcism has become so commonplace today that some exorcists even expel demons remotely, via cell phone."

Even some of the Catholic authorities that Blatty and Friedkin so smugly held up as defenders of *The Exorcist* faith seemed to regret their support. "I don't want to give the impression of knowing more than I really do," Father John Nicola told Michael Cuneo. "As Damien Karras said in the movie, 'There are no experts in this field.' This is one of the first things I told Blatty and Friedkin when they invited me up to New York for an interview. So I might be wrong, but I'm concerned about the direction things seem headed. The televised exorcism of that poor girl Gina on *20/20* some years back was utterly bizarre. [*A woman named Gina, described by her doctor as "actively psychotic," underwent an exorcism on ABC.*] She probably shouldn't have received an exorcism at all, let alone a televised one. From my vantage point, some of the priests doing exorcisms these days are too rash, too loose and easy with their investigations. Why do we have all these exorcisms? Are they absolutely necessary? Somehow I doubt they are."

Sources

Books

Allen, Thomas B. *Possessed*. iUniverse, 2000.

Batterberry, Ariane Ruskin. *Prehistoric Art and Ancient Art of the Near East*. New York: McGraw-Hill, 1971.

Biskind, Peter. *Easy Riders, Raging Bulls: How the Sex-Drugs-and-Rock-'n'-Roll Generation Saved Hollywood*. New York: Simon & Schuster, 1998.

Blatty, William Peter. *The Exorcist*. New York: Bantam Books, 1972.

Blatty, William Peter. *Which Way to Mecca, Jack?* New York: Bernard Geis, 1960.

Blatty, William Peter. *William Peter Blatty on The Exorcist: From Novel to Film*. New York: Bantam Books, 1974.

Boorman, John. *Adventures of a Suburban Boy*. London: Faber & Faber, 2003.

Boorman, John. *Conclusions*. London: Faber & Faber, 2022.

Brady, John Joseph. *The Craft of the Screenwriter: Interviews with Six Celebrated Screenwriters*. New York: Simon & Schuster, 1981.

Burstyn, Ellen. *Lessons in Becoming Myself*. New York: Riverhead Books, 2006.

Cagin, Seth, and Phillip Dray. *Hollywood Films of the Seventies: Sex, Drugs, Violence, Rock 'n' Roll and Politics*. New York: Harper & Row, 1984.

Carroll, Noel. *The Philosophy of Horror, Or, Paradoxes of the Heart*. New York: Routledge, 2003.

Case, George. *Here's to My Sweet Satan: How the Occult Haunted Music, Movies and Pop Culture, 1966–1980*. Fresno: Quill Driver Books, 2016.

Clagett, Thomas D. *William Friedkin: Films of Aberration, Obsession, and Reality*. West Hollywood: Silman-James Press, 2003.

Cowan, Douglas E. *Sacred Terror: Religion and Horror on the Silver Screen*. Waco, TX: Baylor University Press, 2008.

Culhane, John. *Special Effects in the Movies: How They Do It*. New York: Random House, 1981.

Cuneo, Michael. *American Exorcism*. New York: Doubleday, 2001.

Derry, Charles. *Dark Dreams 2.0: A Psychological History of the Modern Horror Film from the 1950s to the 21st Century*. Jefferson, NC: McFarland, 2009.

Elsaesser, Thomas. *The Last Great American Picture Show: New Hollywood Cinema in the 1970s*. Amsterdam University Press, 2004.

Emery, Robert J. *The Directors: Take Two*. New York: Allworth Press, 2002.

Eszterhas, Joe. *The Devil's Guide to Hollywood: The Screenwriter as God!* London: Duckworth, 2007

Eszterhas, Joe. *Hollywood Animal: A Memoir*. New York: Knopf, 2004.

Fernandez, Declan Neil. *Horrible and Fascinating—John Boorman's Exorcist II: The Heretic*. Albany, GA: BearManor Media, 2022.

Friedkin, William. *The Friedkin Connection: A Memoir*. New York: HarperCollins, 2013.

Gottlieb, Sidney. *Alfred Hitchcock: Interviews*. Jackson: University Press of Mississippi, 2003.

Harris, Mark. *Pictures at a Revolution: Five Movies and the Birth of the New Hollywood*. New York: Penguin, 2008.

Hendrix, Grady. *Paperbacks from Hell: The Twisted History of '70s and '80s Horror Fiction*. Philadelphia: Quirk Books, 2017.

Holland, Glenn Stanfield. *Gods in the Desert: Religions of the Ancient Near East*. Lanham, MD: Rowman & Littlefield, 2009.

Hubai, Gergely. *Torn Music: Rejected Film Scores, a Select History*. West Hollywood: Silman-James Press, 2012.

Jones, Alan. *The Rough Guide to Horror Movies*. London: Rough Guides, 2005.

Kawin, Bruce F. *Horror and the Horror Film*. London: Anthem Press, 2012.

Keach, Stacy. *All in All: An Actor's Life On and Off the Stage*. Lanham, MD: Rowman & Littlefield, 2013

Kermode, Mark. *The Exorcist (BFI Film Classics)*. London: British Film Institute, 2020

King, Stephen. *Danse Macabre*. New York: Everest House, 1980.

Konow, David. *Reel Terror: The Scary, Bloody, Gory, Hundred-Year History of Classic Horror Films*. New York: St. Martin's Griffin, 2012.

Lane, Christopher. *William Friedkin: Interviews*. Jackson: University Press of Mississippi, 2020.

Levin, Ira. *Rosemary's Baby*. New York: Random House, 1967.

MacLaine, Shirley. *Dance While You Can*. New York: Bantam, 1991.

Marasco, Robert. *Burnt Offerings*. Richmond, VA: Valancourt Books, 2015.

Matheson Richard. *Hell House*. New York: New York: Tor Books, 1999.

McCabe, Bob. *The Exorcist: Out of the Shadows*. London: Omnibus Press, 2000.

McCambridge, Mercedes. *The Quality of Mercy*. New York: Times Books, 1981.

Newman, Howard. *The Exorcist: The Strange Story Behind the Film*. New York: Pinnacle Books, 1974.

Newman, Kim. *Nightmare Movies: Horror on Screen Since the 1960s*. New York: New York: Bloomsbury Publishing, 1988.

Newman, Kim and Marriott, James. Horror: *The Definitive Companion to the Most Terrifying Movies Ever Made*. London: Carlton Books, 2013.

Oldfield, Mike. *Changeling: The Autobiography of Mike Oldfield*. London: Virgin Books, 2007.

Olson, Christopher J. *Possessed Women, Haunted States: Cultural Tensions in Exorcism Cinema*. Lanham, MD: Lexington Books, 2016.

Olson, Daniel, ed. *Studies in the Horror Film: The Exorcist*. Lakewood, CO: Centipede Press, 2011.

Pallenberg, Barbara. *The Making of Exorcist II: The Heretic*. New York: Warner Books, 1977.

Phillips, Kendall R. *Projected Fears: Horror Films and American Culture: Horror Films and American Culture*. Santa Barbara, CA: ABC-CLIO, 2005.

Pinteau, Pascal. *Special Effects: An Oral History: Interviews with 38 Masters Spanning 100 Years*. New York: Harry N. Abrams, 2004

Rebello, Steven. *Alfred Hitchcock and the Making of Psycho*. New York: Soft Skull Press, 2013.

Ringgren, Helmer. *Religions of the Ancient Near East*. Philadelphia: Westminster Press, 1973.

Rueda, Sergio A. *Diabolical Possession and the Case Behind The Exorcist: An Overview of Scientific Research with Interviews with Witnesses and Experts*. Jefferson, NC: McFarland, 2018.

Schreck, Nikolas. *The Satanic Screen: An Illustrated Guide to the Devil in Cinema*. London: Creation, 2001.

Schaefer, Dennis. *Masters of Light: Conversations with Contemporary Cinematographers*. Berkeley: University of California Press, 1986.

Segaloff, Nat. *Arthur Penn: American Director*. Lexington: University Press of Kentucky, 2011

Segaloff, Nat. *Hurricane Billy: The Stormy Life and Times of William Friedkin*. New York: Wiiliam Morrow, 1990.

Skal, David J. *The Monster Show: A Cultural History of Horror*. New York: Norton, 1993.

Stewart, Fred Mustard. *Mephisto Waltz*. New York: Coward McCann, 1969.

Stewart, Ramona. *Possession of Joel Delaney*. New York: Little, Brown, 1970

Sutherland, John. *Bestsellers: Popular Fiction of the 1970s*. New York: Routledge, 1981.

Timpone, Anthony. *Men, Makeup, and Monsters: Hollywood's Masters of Illusion and FX*. New York: MacMillan, 1996.

Travers, Peter and Stephanie Reiff. *The Story Behind The Exorcist*. New York: Crown Publishers, 1974.

Tryon, Thomas. *The Other*. New York Review Books Classics, 2012.

Turnock, Bryan. *Studying Horror Cinema*. Liverpool University, 2019.

Waddell, Calum. *The Style of Sleaze: The American Exploitation Film, 1959–1977*. Edinburgh University Press, 2018.

Waller A. Gregory. *American Horrors: Essays on the Modern American Horror Film*. Champaign: University of Illinois Press, 1987.

Wildwood, Gretchen: *Ancient Mesopotamian Civilization*. New York: Rosen Central, 2010.

Winter, Douglas E. *Faces of Fear: Encounters with the Creators of Modern Horror*. New York: Tor, 1990.

Wood, Robin. *Robin Wood on the Horror Film: Collected Essays and Reviews*. Detroit: Wayne State University Press, 2018.

Wood, Robin. *Hitchcock's Films Revisited*. New York: Columbia University Press, 2002.

Wood, Robin, and Andrew Britton, eds. *American Nightmare: Essays in the Horror Film*. Festival of Festivals, 1979.

Zinoman, Jason. *Shock Value: How a Few Eccentric Outsiders Gave Us Nightmares, Conquered Hollywood, and Invented Modern Horror*. New York: Penguin Books, 2011.

Newspapers

Baltimore Sun
Boston Globe
Boston Phoenix
The Bridgeport Post
Central New Jersey Home News
Chicago Sun-Times
Chicago Tribune
Cincinnati Enquirer
Cincinnati Post
Fort Lauderdale News
Fort Worth Star
The Fresno Bee
Green Bay Press-Gazette
The Guardian
Hartford Courant
Irish Times
Ithaca Journal
Lancaster New Era
Los Angeles Times
Lowell Sun
Miami Herald
Minneapolis Star
The Morning Call
Newsday
New York Daily News
New York Post
New York Times
Orlando Sentinel
Philadelphia Daily News
Pittsburgh Post Courier
Pittsburgh Press
Reno Gazette
San Francisco Examiner
Santa Maria Times
Tampa Bay Times
The Tennessean
Virginia News Pilots
Washington Post

Periodicals

Action
The American Conservative
Audience
Castle of Frankenstein
Catholic Advance
Cineaste
Cinefantastique
Cinema
Commonweal
Dark Side
Deep Red
Empire
Entertainment Weekly
Esquire

Fangoria
Film Comment
Film Quarterly
Filmmakers Newsletter
Film Score Monthly
Georgetown Voice
Hollywood Reporter
Journal of Medical Ethics
Life
National Catholic Register
New Republic
New York
New Yorker
Newsweek

People
Photon
Psychotronic Video
Rolling Stone
Rue Morgue
Saturday Review World
Sight and Sound
Skeptical Inquirer
Strange Magazine
Time
Variety
The Velvet Light Trap
Video Watchdog
The World

Websites
Bloodynews.com
Bright Lights Film Journal
Louder.com
Quillette
RockandRoll.com

ScoreMagacine.com
Sensus Fidelum
Slant
WTOP News

Documentaries and Films
A Decade Under the Influence
Biography, Lifetime
Dominion: Prequel to the
    Exorcist
The Exorcist
The Exorcist II: Heretic
The Exorcist III: Legion

The Exorcist: The Beginning
The Fear of God: 25 Years of
    The Exorcist
Friedkin Uncut
Intimate Portrait, A&E
Leap of Faith: William Friedkin on
    The Exorcist

Carlos Acevedo is the author of *Sporting Blood: Tales From the Dark Side of Boxing, The Duke: The Life and Lies of Tommy Morrison*, and the forthcoming *American Hellfire: Cults, Killings, Possessions, and Hoaxes of the Satanic Age*, all from Hamilcar Publications. He lives in Brooklyn.

The Devil Inside is set in 10-point Sabon, which was designed by the German-born typographer and designer Jan Tschichold (1902–1974) in the period 1964–1967. It was released jointly by the Linotype, Monotype, and Stempel type foundries in 1967. Copyeditor for this project was Debra Nichols. The book was designed by Brad Norr Design, Minneapolis, Minnesota, and typeset by New Best-set Typesetters Ltd.

Printed in the USA
CPSIA information can be obtained
at www.ICGtesting.com
JSHW020925221123
52461JS00001B/2

9 781949 590654